Teaching and Developing Writing Skills

Craig Thaine

Consultant and editor: Scott Thornbury

CAMBRIDGE
UNIVERSITY PRESS & ASSESSMENT

Shaftesbury Road, Cambridge CB2 8EA, United Kingdom

One Liberty Plaza, 20th Floor, New York, NY 10006, USA

477 Williamstown Road, Port Melbourne, VIC 3207, Australia

314–321, 3rd Floor, Plot 3, Splendor Forum, Jasola District Centre, New Delhi – 110025, India

103 Penang Road, #05–06/07, Visioncrest Commercial, Singapore 238467

Cambridge University Press & Assessment is a department of the University of Cambridge.

We share the University's mission to contribute to society through the pursuit of education, learning and research at the highest international levels of excellence.

www.cambridge.org
Information on this title: www.cambridge.org/9781009224468

First published 2023
20 19 18 17 16 15 14 13 12 11 10 9 8 7 6 5 4 3 2 1

Printed in Great Britain by CPI Group (UK) Ltd, Croydon CR0 4YY

A catalogue record for this publication is available from the British Library

ISBN   978-1-009-22446-8 Paperback
ISBN   978-1-009-22448-2 eBook

Teaching and Developing Writing Skills

Cambridge Handbooks for Language Teachers

This series, now with over 50 titles, offers practical ideas, techniques and activities for the teaching of English and other languages, providing inspiration for both teachers and trainers.

Recent titles in this series:

Teach Business English
SYLVIE DONNA

Teaching English Spelling
A practical guide
RUTH SHEMESH and SHEILA WALLER

Using Folktales
ERIC K. TAYLOR

Learner English (Second edition)
A teacher's guide to interference and other problems
EDITED BY MICHAEL SWAN and BERNARD SMITH

Planning Lessons and Courses
Designing sequences of work for the language classroom
TESSA WOODWARD

Teaching Large Multilevel Classes
NATALIE HESS

Using the Board in the Language Classroom
JEANNINE DOBBS

Writing Simple Poems
Pattern poetry for language acquisition
VICKI L. HOLMES and MARGARET R. MOULTON

Laughing Matters
Humour in the language classroom
PÉTER MEDGYES

Stories
Narrative activities in the language classroom
RUTH WAJNRYB

Using Authentic Video in the Language Classroom
JANE SHERMAN

Extensive Reading Activities for Teaching Language
EDITED BY JULIAN BAMFORD and RICHARD R. DAY

Language Activities for Teenagers
EDITED BY SETH LINDSTROMBERG

Pronunciation Practice Activities
A resource book for teaching English pronunciation
MARTIN HEWINGS

Drama Techniques (Third edition)
A resource book of communication activities for language teachers
ALAN MALEY and ALAN DUFF

Five-Minute Activities for Business English
PAUL EMMERSON and NICK HAMILTON

Games for Language Learning (Third edition)
ANDREW WRIGHT, DAVID BETTERIDGE and MICHAEL BUCKBY

Dictionary Activities
CINDY LEANEY

Dialogue Activities
Exploring spoken interaction in the language class
NICK BILBROUGH

Five-Minute Activities for Young Learners
PENNY MCKAY and JENNI GUSE

The Internet and the Language Classroom (Second edition)
A practical guide for teachers
GAVIN DUDENEY

Working with Images
A resource book for the language classroom
BEN GOLDSTEIN

Grammar Practice Activities (Second edition)
A practical guide for teachers
PENNY UR

Intercultural Language Activities
JOHN CORBETT

Learning One-to-One
INGRID WISNIEWSKA

Communicative Activities for EAP
JENNI GUSE

Memory Activities for Language Learning
NICK BILBROUGH

Vocabulary Activities
PENNY UR

Classroom Management Techniques
JIM SCRIVENER

CLIL Activities
A resource for subject and language teachers
LIZ DALE and ROSIE TANNER

Language Learning with Technology
Ideas for integrating technology in the classroom
GRAHAM STANLEY

Translation and Own-language Activities
PHILIP KERR

Language Learning with Digital Video
BEN GOLDSTEIN and PAUL DRIVER

Discussions and More
Oral fluency practice in the classroom
PENNY UR

Interaction Online
Creative activities for blended learning
LINDSAY CLANDFIELD and JILL HADFIELD

Activities for Very Young Learners
HERBERT PUCHTA and KAREN ELLIOTT

Teaching and Developing Reading Skills
PETER WATKINS

Lexical Grammar
Activities for teaching chunks and exploring patterns
LEO SELIVAN

Off the Page
Activities to bring lessons alive and enhance learning
CRAIG THAINE

Teaching in Challenging Circumstances
CHRIS SOWTON

Contents

Thanks

A book might have one author, but it is very much a team effort. I would like to thank the following people who have inspired and helped me in writing *Teaching and Developing Writing Skills*.

Karen Momber for her encouragement, patience and on-going support;
Scott Thornbury for his constructive expertise, and his very good ideas (*ngā mihi nui*);
Greg Sibley for his insight and commitment to shaping the text and making it better;
Jo Timerick for her enthusiastic and supportive management of everything;
Meria Dan for efficiently looking after the production of the book.

Many thanks are also due to the those behind the scenes for an enormous amount of work that ranges from such tasks as designing the book, compiling the index through to getting the final product where it needs to be:
Maxwell Anley, Ellen Bailey-Carson, Heidi Burrows, Priyanka Chavan, Kunal Das, Naveena Dayala, Moumita Giri, Darren Longley, Aradhna Mishra, Alexander Uglow, Lorrel Walker, Glen Warren, Rosie Wood, Jordan Worland, Nikki Youngman and Mohd Zeeshan.

Finally, a long-delayed thanks to Martin Parrott, who first sparked my interest in writing skills when he was my diploma tutor, many pages ago.

Acknowledgements

The authors and publishers acknowledge the following sources of copyright material and are grateful for the permissions granted. While every effort has been made, it has not always been possible to identify the sources of all the material used, or to trace all copyright holders. If any omissions are brought to our notice, we will be happy to include the appropriate acknowledgements on reprinting and in the next update to the digital edition, as applicable.

Keys: CH = Chapter, Intro = Introduction

Text

CH6: Graph taken from NZ On Air/Glasshouse Consulting, 'Where Are The Audiences?' 2021. Copyright © 2021 NZ On Air/Glasshouse Consulting. All rights reserved. Reproduced with kind permission.

Photography

All the photographs are sourced from Getty Images.

Intro: Halfpoint Images/Moment; **CH1:** Una Berzina/EyeEm; SDI Productions/E+; Oscar Wong/Moment; Henrik Sorensen/DigitalVision; monkeybusinessimages/iStock/Getty Images Plus; Tara Moore/Stone; Pattanasit Sangsuk/EyeEm; Westend61; **CH5:** LazingBee/iStock/Getty Images Plus.

Cover photography by Westend61/Getty Images.

Illustration

QBS Learning

Typesetting

QBS Learning

Introduction

Wanting and needing to write

It seems we human beings have always had the desire to communicate through visual markings. Our early ancestors left behind handprints, shapes and figures scratched or painted on cave walls, and other – sometimes intricate – markings on objects. A lot of these visual marks reveal a desire to record, to express, to communicate – in fact, exactly what propelled the development of what we now know as 'writing'. Sophisticated formal writing systems such as Egyptian hieroglyphs were developed much later, but can still be traced back thousands of years. It was not until relatively recently, however, after the onset of industrialisation around the start of the nineteenth century, that countries began to offer a basic free education resulting in widespread literacy.

Now, most people know how to write in their first language, but they tend to do so only when they need to, for example, when writing a CV with a covering letter in order to apply for a job, or sending an email to a business to complain about late delivery of an item they have bought online. However, for some people, writing is an important or main focus of their work and for many it is a means of expressing themselves, for example, on social media. There are also a few people who write merely for their own pleasure and as a creative endeavour usually associated with a range of literary forms.

It could be argued that, these days, we write more than we ever did because it has become easier to do so. Before the advent of Information Technology (IT), the mechanics of writing were managed by means of pen and paper or typewriters. Since then, IT has had a significant impact on first and second language writing. Computers and word processing software packages have facilitated the process of writing texts and have had significant impact on both first and second language writing. The internet and a range of online platforms have enhanced our ability to communicate with each other in writing with people all around the world.

These improvements in the mechanics of writing coupled with changes to the way in which we communicate using written language mean that writing has become of greater interest in English as a second language classrooms than it used to be. Allied with this has been the growth of English for Specific Purposes (ESP) in both academic and work settings where writing is either a core mode of transmission of knowledge or an important mode of communication. While the ability to *speak* a second language is likely to remain a dominant need for learners, the ability to *write* effectively in a second language is becoming increasingly important.

Writing in English language classrooms

Up until the latter part of the twentieth century, most writing that learners did in English language classrooms was associated with reinforcement of language learnt to develop overall competence in English (Richards, 2015). This included activities such as copying examples of language that had been taught orally, doing gap fill or sentence completion written practice, or doing dictations and writing translations between the learners' first language and English. A lot of this writing involved individual sentences or the combining of simple sentences into complex ones.

This kind of writing is still prevalent in English language classrooms today. It is now categorised as 'writing-to-learn' as opposed to 'learning-to-write' (Hirvela et al., 2018). Teachers sometimes conflate these two, but it is useful to make a distinction. Writing-to-learn includes activities such as gap fill, sentence completion and sentence transformation, all of which aim to consolidate and reinforce previously taught language. By contrast, learning-to-write places greater emphasis on learners writing texts. Writing-to-learn and learning-to-write both have a role to play in developing learners' overall competence in English. A critical question that teachers should ask themselves when planning lessons is: which of the two am I aiming to do?

Confusion between these different ways of characterising writing can result from concerns about learners' accuracy in English. Writing-to-learn is likely to place an emphasis on the accurate use of language in practice activities. Hirvela et al. (2018) point out that one way of viewing texts is as decontextualised objects made up of an 'orderly arrangement of words, clauses and sentences' (p.48). If writers follow grammatical rules, they will be able to give full expression to any meaning they wish to convey.

In other words, a text becomes a demonstration of a writer's accurate control of language. However, this view of text (or learning-to-write) is a very limited one and tends to ignore the fact that a piece of writing is also a communicative act. A text includes information and ideas that the writer wishes to communicate with a reader or readers. The ideas and information need to be as carefully arranged as the language so they are easy to understand. Furthermore, a text is not written in isolation and the context in which it is written and read needs to be taken into account. Clearly, language, grammar not least, has a role to play in the writing of a text. As Frodesen notes 'grammar serves as a resource for effective communication' in writing (2014: p.239). Conversely, in a writing-to-learn lesson, accurate grammar is an end in itself.

Texts and their organisation

In a landmark book, Byrne notes that writing can be used to reinforce previously learnt language but that it can also 'become a goal in itself' (1979: p.7). From the 1980s onwards, teachers and researchers began to view learning-to-write as the creation of texts (Richards, 2015). A text is perceived as an object, the end product of learner writing. This means the object can be studied in order to determine how different elements in the text might be arranged in such a way that the text as a whole is coherent (Hyland, 2016). Teachers began providing learners with example texts together with tasks that analysed text organisation and the kind of language used in the text. The aim was to offer learners scaffolding that would allow them to write similar texts of their own. Initially, learners could work with teachers to jointly construct a new text before then moving on to write their text independently. Below is a summary of some core approaches to analysing the organisation of written texts.

Paragraph building

As teachers and researchers began to understand the limits of a sentence-level focus on writing, they started to consider longer stretches of language. This was particularly the case in English for Academic Purposes (EAP) programmes, and there was an increasing awareness of the way in which paragraphs were constructed to create a unified whole. This involves identifying the topic sentence of a paragraph and the way other sentences develop and enlarge on the main idea in a topic sentence to build a well-constructed paragraph (Reid, 1994).

This approach has the benefit of focusing on longer stretches of language and helping learners to consider ways of organising their ideas. However, it does not always encourage them to see a text as a whole, and the placement of the topic sentence within a paragraph sometimes seems arbitrary to learners. Despite this, many teachers and English language writing programmes see a focus on paragraph building as a useful support mechanism for lower-level learners who are beginning to develop English language writing skills.

Text functions

Initially, paragraph building was usually focused on in tandem with the function of a written text (Reid, 1993). As Hyland notes, the approach 'focuses on broad text types and how language is used to get certain things done through writing, such as describing, narrating or reporting' (2019: p.4). This view of core macro functions has subsequently expanded. Written texts can also comment, explain, instruct, demonstrate, argue and persuade (Council of Europe, 2001). It is also possible to categorise written texts according to other micro functions they perform, for example, to compare and contrast, to advise, to warn and to request (Hyland, 2019).

A functional (or rhetorical) analysis views the text as a whole and perceives it as being made up of a series of paragraphs or broader structural elements such as Introduction-Body-Conclusion (Hyland, 2019). The analysis can also focus on specific language items related to the functional purpose of the piece of writing. For example, the analysis of a report that compares and contrasts two sets of data might highlight words and phrases such as *a key difference, the main similarity, while, whereas, by contrast.*

A key strength of a functional analysis of a text is the focus on the communicative intent of a piece of writing. It asks the question: what is this text trying to do? The focus on different structural elements and core language can be very supportive and useful for many learners, particularly those on EAP courses and those following courses that lead to some kind of examination that includes the writing of an essay (for example, IELTS and TOEFL). It's hardly surprising, therefore, that functional analysis of tests evolved largely in these learning contexts.

However, the kinds of texts focused on in these contexts tend to be aimed at a limited audience because the most likely readers are university tutors, examiners or students studying in the same context. As a result, an exclusively functional analysis does not always take into account the broader social context in which texts are written. For example, why is the writer writing the text and who do they wish to communicate with?

Discourse patterns

Another way of analysing longer stretches of text is by determining different patterns that exist in extended written discourse. McCarthy (1991) highlights three core discourse patterns:

1 Problem–solution – the writer describes some kind of problem and then goes on to suggest and possibly evaluate a solution to the problem. This pattern is frequently used in business reports, but is also central to crime fiction.

2   General–particular – the writer begins by making a general statement about a topic and then goes on to provide more specific details. This pattern is often adopted in advertisements that begin with a general (and often superlative) claim about a product then add details to support the initial claim. It can also be found in scientific academic writing.

3   Claim–counterclaim – the writer provides one point of view but then outlines a contrasting point of view. This pattern is frequently adopted in discursive essays that aim to provide a balanced argument on the topic of an essay, but it might also be used in postings to online forums.

These text patterns, McCarthy (1991) notes, can be embedded within one another. For example, in outlining a problem, a writer might provide some initial general information and follow this with specific details. Unlike text functions, discourse patterns are not always contained within the structural boundaries of paragraph or sentence. A problem and its solution can be described in one paragraph in one text whereas, in another, the problem might be outlined across a number of paragraphs.

Most writers who have English as their first language (L1) do not consciously employ discourse patterning when they write. McCarthy (1991) suggests these patterns are culturally based. This means that English L1 readers subconsciously expect this kind of patterning in the texts they read. When it is absent or awkwardly managed, they find the text lacks coherence and is difficult to understand. As Hyland points out, it is likely that learners will 'have certain preconceptions about writing, or schema, which they have learnt in their own cultures and communities and which may influence how they write in English' (2016: p.53).

This is associated with the notion of contrastive rhetoric (Connor, 1996) which aims to link written language to specific cultures. However, critics point out that this kind of comparison can become overgeneralised, and even 'essentializing', and does not take into account diversity at the local level. Despite this, an awareness of English language discourse patterns may be a useful tool if a teacher notices that a learner has problems associated with writing coherent texts in English.

Genres

Analysing a text as a genre is both a straightforward and a complex process. On one hand, genre can simply be defined as typical use of a written language with easily identifiable features (Hyland, 2016). For example, identifying what is an advertisement, a social media post or an email invitation is not difficult. However, understanding why it is easy for us to identify different genres is more complex.

Genre analysis involves taking into account writers and the many different contexts they are writing in. Writers write text in order to achieve something, for example, a product enquiry email to a company aims to get information, or a social media post about the first home someone has bought aims to let friends and family know the good news. In doing so, writers deploy rhetorical and discourse patterns that have become conventionalised within the cultural context, and they use these formal tools (often unconsciously) in order to get things done (Hyland, 2019). (Note how this differs slightly from text functions discussed above where it is the language of the text that is doing something and not the writer.)

This emphasis on the writer's intention to communicate means we need to consider the broader context of the texts they are writing. A key consideration is the audience that the writer is writing for. This is likely to determine the kind of language choices the writer will make. For example, the person sharing news about the purchase of a new home on social media might be able to begin with the sentence *I've finally bought it!* rather than *I've finally bought my first home!* The use of the pronoun in the first example assumes that the audience of friends and family know that the writer has been looking for a house for a long time, and they will, therefore, immediately understand that *it* refers to the new house.

An awareness of audience also encourages a writer to think about what information to include or not include in a text. For example, a marine biologist may want to report on an endangered marine environment. First, she might write some kind of briefing paper for colleagues at the research institute she works for, and then she may want to write a blog post for the general public to raise awareness of the dangers facing the marine environment. In writing the briefing paper, she can assume a level of knowledge and expertise from her colleagues, and key ideas and concepts will not need to be spelt out. However, her blog post will need to outline core concepts and perhaps find a way of making technical information comprehensible to a reader who is not a subject matter expert.

The social interaction that is implicit in our understanding of genre shows that different genres are like discourse patterns and are embedded in language culture. Subconsciously, L1 writers of English operating within the English language culture understand what different genres can achieve and are able to deploy the different steps or stages in order to achieve their goal (Hyland, 2019: p.19). For example, if someone writes a thank you text or email for a dinner, they are likely to begin by thanking the host, then commenting on the food and/or the pleasant evening, and then signing off probably promising to catch up soon. In some other cultures, this may seem over-elaborated and a simple 'thank you' may be sufficient.

Genre analysis examines the different language choices made by writers in relation to the context, the content and the audience. These choices might involve the style of the language (formal vs. neutral vs. informal) and the register (legal, scientific, academic, personal). It is also important to acknowledge that while some genres seem fixed, they have the potential to change in relation to contextual factors and the varying needs of writers (Paltridge, 2001: p.3). New genres can also develop quite quickly. The growth in social media platforms since the beginning of this century has seen a range of associated genres emerge.

Genre analysis is likely to give learners a very comprehensive view of a text. Its strength is the emphasis it places on the context for the piece of writing and the idea of writing for an audience. Hyland (2019) notes one potential drawback of genre analysis is that it sometimes assumes learners already have a degree of rhetorical understanding of English language texts. It also involves using a certain amount of metalinguistic terminology that some learners can find off-putting or difficult to understand.

Which text organisation?

The approaches to analysing written text that are discussed above are complementary. Teachers are likely to find most if not all of the core approaches to the analysis of model texts in teaching and learning materials they are using. They may well realise that the same text can be analysed using more than one approach, but wonder which is the most effective or useful approach to use. Note how this social media posting can be analysed using any of the approaches discussed:

Hey guys. We're really excited to announce the arrival of our baby daughter, Zoe! She arrived at 6.28 this morning and weighs 3.2kg. And you'll be pleased to know both mother and daughter are doing very well - very exciting. Charlie & Kate.

- Paragraph building – the first complete sentence is the topic sentence, and the remaining sentences develop this key piece of information.
- Text function – the text aims to announce and inform readers of important news as indicated by the verb *announce* and the phrase *you'll be pleased to know.*
- Discourse pattern: the text follows a general → a particular pattern (baby's arrival → time, baby's weight, health of baby and mother).
- Genre – focuses on information expected in a birth announcement, the text is supported by a picture, includes an informal greeting using *guys* which, with the ellipsis of *it's* in the final sentence ([*it's*] *very exciting*), suggests it is aimed at friends and family, and uses an exclamation mark and along with *excited* and *exciting* to convey emotion to the reader.

As noted above, genre analysis is broad in its focus and the example above indicates the way in which this approach provides teachers and learners with more to focus on. However, the full extent of genre analysis may not be suitable for some learner groups or writing lessons. For example, a teacher who is teaching an IELTS preparation class and focusing on persuasion essays might choose to limit the analysis to the function of model texts and highlight language of concession as a means of persuading the reader.

As a teacher, your choice of analysis model might also depend on your learners' needs. If you are teaching a business English course and focusing on reports, you might find that your learners' writing lacks coherence. The key issue in their reports might be signalled indirectly and responses to the issue might not be clearly indicated. The reports may seem to present a circular and inconclusive argument. In order to address these coherence issues, a problem–solution discourse patterning analysis of some example reports might be the most appropriate way of addressing your learners' needs.

In effect, it helps if teachers and learners see these different ways of organising and analysing texts as useful tools rather than a set of prescriptive rules about writing. It also pays to note Hedge's (2000: p.322) acknowledgement of the fact that text organisation is only 'relatively stable and predictable', and L1 writers of English are often flexible about the way they organise their writing.

The language in texts

Two key factors have a bearing on the difference between spoken and written English: time and distance. Two speakers are normally involved in synchronous communication and usually share the same physical space unless they are speaking online. This means they are able to refer to the space around them and perhaps point to things, and they are able to use paralinguistic features such as gesture to support their language (to some extent at least, also possible online via a video link). Conversely, writers are usually involved in asynchronous communication (unless it is online chat) and only rarely share the same physical space as their intended reader. Therefore, there is usually a 'message-in-a-bottle' element to written text.

If we compare examples of spoken and written language on the page, what differences are apparent? In spoken language, there is likely to be more ellipsis. For example, pronouns might be omitted, auxiliary verbs can also be omitted from questions, and determiners might be considered unnecessary before a noun (Carter & McCarthy, 2006). (However, ellipsis can be used in written language as a means of conveying ideas in an economical way – see below.)

Speakers are more likely to refer to the physical context using deictic devices such as determiners (*this, that, these, those*) and adverbs (*here, now, there, then*), often supporting their speech with gesture, eye contact and body language. There is also likely to be greater use of vague language – phrases such as *thing, or so, sort of* (Carter & McCarthy, 2006). If there is a breakdown in communication, a speaker can go back and reformulate their message to make it clear. Spoken language also involves more repetition and rephrasing, and speakers typically create extended utterances by linking a series of clausal units together, using coordinating conjunctions (*and, but, so*) (Crystal, 1995).

By contrast, written language needs to be more explicit because, with the exception of online chatting and texting, there is little opportunity to amend the message once the text is written and sent out or published. As a result, pronouns are used more consistently, and verb phrase elements are given in full. There is more likely to be more specification of nouns, for example, compare the likely spoken exponent in 1 with the written phrase in 2:

1   ...*these new trousers.*

2   ...*the new trousers that I bought last week.*

Likewise, writers are less likely to use vague language; again, for example, compare the spoken and written instructions:

1   *Pull that thing there – like this.*

2   *Pull down the lever on the left-hand side of the machine.*

There is a greater emphasis on sentence-level grammar in written language as opposed to the utterance-level focus of spoken grammar. Time also has a role to play here: writers often have more time to craft their text and the opportunity to come up with compact and efficient ways of expressing themselves that are more complex (Crystal, 1995), for example, with the use of noun phrases. In written language, there are more examples of subordination and sentences can include more than one instance of this (Crystal, 1995). Writers might also deploy passive voice in tandem with active voice as a way of managing the way information unfolds in a written text.

Sentence-level grammar

In the mid twentieth century, the predominant sentence-level view of written language in English language teaching meant there was a strong focus on accurate grammar within the sentence. Word and phrase order was important as was the correct use of verb phrases within the sentence. There was also a strong emphasis on combining clauses to make sentences more complex.

One area of phrase grammar that has been given greater prominence with the growth of EAP writing skills is a focus on the noun phrase. Most general English teaching materials place a strong emphasis on verb phrases and learning a range of verb forms. Noun phrase grammar tends to focus on the use of determiners before the noun. However, academic writing has a higher frequency of complex noun phrases that allow writers to pack information more densely into to subject of a sentence and express themselves more efficiently (Carter & McCarthy, 2006). For example, compare the following:

- *Financial controls, which are becoming more stringent, are an issue that's hotly debated . . .*
- *The hotly debated question of more stringent financial controls is . . .*

In the first example, information is strung out across the utterance by means of a relative clause. This is more typical of spoken language. In the second example, the complex noun phrase with the head noun *question* manages to integrate all information into the one phrase.

Cohesion

When teachers and learners first began analysing longer stretches of written discourse, it became necessary to extend the language focus to connections between sentences and paragraphs to ensure texts were cohesive. The following grammatical cohesive devices are now commonly taught in writing lessons:

- Reference – when pronouns refer back to people, things or ideas previously mentioned in the text. For example, the pronoun *this* at the beginning of a paragraph could be referring back to everything outlined in the previous paragraph.
- Substitution – when a substitute word replaces a word or clause previously mentioned in the text. For example, when the pronoun *one(s)* is used to refer back to a noun.
- Ellipsis – when words or phrases are omitted because the writer believes that what has been left out can be retrieved from the preceding text. For example, *The children sat in front, the parents behind and the in-laws on either side.* It is not necessary to repeat the verb *sat* (Carter & McCarthy, 2006).

Cohesive links in written texts can also be achieved by means of lexis. Words that are semantically linked across a text create lexical chains that help hold the text together. For example, in an essay on urban transport, a writer is likely to use a variety of words and phrases such as: *vehicles, traffic, cars and bikes, modes of transport* (Carter & McCarthy, 2006). This also means the writing has good lexical range.

Linking adjuncts are a further way of making texts cohesive. These can be individual words such as *furthermore*, or they can be phrases such as *on the other hand*. Linking adjuncts can be categorised according to the kind of meaning relationship that exists between one part of a text and another, for example: addition, result, contrast, time, concession, summary and listing (Carter & McCarthy, 2006). For example, *consequently* signals the result of previously discussed ideas, and *in spite of that* indicates that the writer is about to concede part of an argument they mostly oppose.

Fixed expressions

Textual analysis of written language has also focused on fixed expressions that writers use (Selivan, 2018). For example, in an academic essay, a phrase such as *it is generally agreed* can be used to hedge (Carter & McCarthy, 2006). In other words, the writer puts forward an idea without claiming ownership of it. In less formal written texts such as personal email messages, a writer responding to a friend might begin with a typical expression such as *lovely to hear from you*. These chunks of language are formulaic in nature and can often be ascribed to specific genres.

IT and language

The advent of IT and its associated e-genres has resulted in changes to written language, which has seen the emergence of new conventions. The clearest example is the use of abbreviations in text messages, such as *LOL*. However, as Crystal notes (2011), there is an increased use of ellipsis in some e-genres because there are constraints on the amount of language you can use, for example, the maximum 280 characters in any one tweet. English language learners often struggle to know what can be left out and abbreviated, and they also need to understand English language conventions associated e-genres.

The process of writing

Knowledge of texts and language alone do not always enable learners to write. Either in their first language or in English, they see the idea of having to write something as a series of problems that have to be solved. Learners may not know how to get started with a piece of writing or they may not know how to improve a first draft. In order to help them, teachers may often need to suggest strategies that allow learners to resolve different challenges that arise in the process of writing a text.

Since Flower and Hayes (1981) proposed an influential model of the process of writing, researchers and teachers have investigated and refined the description of the cognitive processes that writers might carry out when producing a text. Hyland (2019: p.11) provides the following simplified version of different steps in the writing process:

It is important to note that the model is recursive and not linear. For example, having responded to some kind of feedback, the writer may go back in the cycle and draft something new rather than merely revise what they have written. It is also useful to bear in mind that during the *drafting*, *responding*, *revising* and *editing* stages of the process, both the content of the text and the language used to express that content can be focused on.

As part of a language lesson, which might include work outside of class time, in the *prewriting* stage, learners might think about what they are going to write, take notes and perhaps plan the organisation of the text. They may also talk to their peers and perhaps do some kind of background reading or research on the topic of the text. In the *drafting* stage, learners write one or more drafts of their text. A period of time may elapse between writing different drafts. The *responding* stage involves seeking and responding to feedback from the teacher or from peers. On the basis of the feedback, learners then *revise* their text. The revision is likely to involve changes both to the content and organisation of the text. Dealing with language issues is more likely to occur at the *editing* stage. Finally, *publishing* involves making the text available to readers, for example, posting something online or perhaps submitting an assignment for assessment.

Many learners may already carry out some or all of these activities when they write in their first language. However, when asked to write in a second language, learners can become overly focused on language demands and may continue to perceive the aims of activities as more 'writing-to-learn'. As a result, they forget to deploy useful process strategies. In highlighting and developing these different strategies to learners, the aim is that they become automatic skills that are deployed when writing a text.

At times, teachers voice concern over the length of time required to work through the writing process described above. If learners are working on a longer piece of writing, it may take two or three days (with some of the work done as homework) for them to work through the different steps in the writing process. However, teachers may also choose to focus on one specific strategy in a writing lesson in order to deal with a specific need. For example, their learners might be overly focused on editing language rather than revising content, so revision strategies might be emphasised in a lesson.

Teachers also note that there is little time for learners to work though the writing process in a class that is preparing them for some kind of written examination. The argument is that time pressure means learners are unable to employ process writing strategies. However, this need not be the case. Learners can be taught to use key strategies efficiently in an examination context. For example, it can be suggested that they use a short period of time for prewriting in order to make notes on their ideas for the text, and then they can be encouraged to revise and edit their work in order to create a final draft.

The process of writing and Information Technology

IT and digital tools provide writers in general, as well as English language learners, with a great degree of support. Word processing programmes make it easy to save drafts of a text, make cuts and additions and move text around. They facilitate collaboration with other writers and editors with tools for commenting that are useful when giving feedback. These programmes also allow the writer to format a final draft so it is clearly laid out on a page.

As IT has developed and Artificial Intelligence (AI) has become more sophisticated, the notion of text authorship has come into question. It is now possible for a computer to produce a text or parts of a text in English with very little input from the apparent 'writer'. These tools and services only require a credit card and a few key words to generate a final product in no time at all. This is obviously problematic if the text concerned is being formally assessed in an academic context. There are software programmes that can detect some degree of plagiarism of this nature, but they are not keeping pace with the level of sophistication now offered by AI (Davies, 2022). Chandrasoma,

Thompson and Pennycook (2004) have suggested that, in response to the challenge that these digital tools present, we need to re-evaluate what constitutes plagiarism and consider the idea of a continuum of transgressive and nontransgressive intertextuality.

Product or process?

When process writing became popular in English language teaching in the 1990s, it was often perceived as a reaction against text-based approaches that viewed writing as the creation of a prespecified product. The broader aim of process writing was to make learners better writers by focusing on the creative processes of writing, and in doing so, their written texts would improve. This became a hotly debated dichotomy (Hyland, 2019). On one side, are those who see study and practice of the generic features of a text as being the core of effective writing. On the other side, are those who see successful writing resulting from the writer's deployment of particular cognitive skills.

Hyland (2019) suggests that the two views of writing are complementary. Rather than adhering strictly to one orientation or the other, it is perhaps more beneficial if teachers prioritise learners' needs. For example, if learners are having problems getting started with their writing, it helps to focus on prewriting strategies that encourage them to generate and organise ideas for a text before beginning a first draft. Conversely, if learners write personal social media postings that are too formal, it makes sense to focus on the genre, the audience and examples of less formal language exemplified in some model texts. It is also possible to use process and product approaches in tandem. A learner writes a first draft of a discussion essay, and then receives feedback that their writing does not state a clear opinion or argument. As a result, the teacher could provide model texts (products) and highlight examples of persuasive language before the learner moves on to revise or redraft their essay (process).

Expressive writing

Allied to process writing is an approach that sees writing as a way for learners to express their thoughts and feelings and be creative with written language. This is known as 'expressive', 'creative' or 'free' writing; in this book, the term 'expressive writing' will be used. The focus is on the activity of writing and the centrality of the writer.

By providing learners with opportunities to express themselves in writing, it is hoped that learners will find a written 'voice' that is unique to them. This is deemed more important than attempting to write a finished product. It means that teachers do not provide model texts, nor do they focus on specific writing strategies in an explicit way (Hyland, 2016: p.12). The teacher's role in expressive writing is to give opportunities for learners to write freely, perhaps providing stimuli at the prewriting stage.

While it can be argued that very few English language learners wish to maintain a blog, write fiction or necessarily develop a 'voice', there are some who find it easier to express themselves in writing. The act of engaging in written communication (even if there is no intention to write for an audience) may be a way for these learners to acquire language. This is another dimension of writing-to-learn. In the same way that learners can acquire language when engaging in communicative speaking activities, the same can be said for writing. IT has greatly facilitated the opportunity for this kind of freer writing to be done collaboratively in real time.

Writing in English language programmes

In many general English language programmes, speaking is often seen as the main productive language skill to develop. This is largely as a result of learners' needs and wishes as well as the kind of resources used in these programmes that aim to have a strong communicative focus and are weighted heavily in favour of speaking activities. By contrast, the development of writing skills is often seen as being of secondary importance. In some cases, the only writing that learners do is writing-to-learn language practice. However, IT tools and, in particular, the growth of social media has meant that writing is now a more common mode of expression and communication. This suggests that English language programmes should place greater emphasis on developing learners' writing skills. Interestingly, some learners do not perceive 'doing Facebook' as being writing.

A focus on writing skills in a general English language programme may comprise up to 25 per cent of the syllabus. At lower levels (below B1), learners are likely to engage in straightforward, everyday genres, for example, writing a personal profile or writing a text message to invite someone to dinner. At B1+ level and above, some learners begin to engage with more formal genres such as reports and essays because they have potential future needs as learners linked to doing an English language exam with a writing paper, or simply because the resources the teacher is using includes a focus on these genres. However, on many general English programmes, there may be very little writing skills development. For example, if learners are studying English specifically to use when travelling, writing activities might be limited to online form filling and email requests for travel and accommodation information.

Learners who are preparing for an examination that includes a writing paper (for example, B2 First, IELTS or Linguaskill) will need to spend more time focusing on developing their writing skills. Clearly, learners on these courses need to become familiar with the different genres used in the examination. However, there is a tension between this narrow focus on examination needs and developing learners' writing skills more broadly. Many teachers argue that overall competence in writing is more likely to lead to a good examination result.

On ESP programmes, in particular, EAP and what is commonly known as business English, writing is usually given more emphasis than in general English programmes. The writing needs of EAP learners are often significant because a large part of their activity when they move on to university programmes will involve writing. Furthermore, these learners are expected to write about complex ideas in a sophisticated way while following very specific conventions associated with genres used in their particular discipline. Likewise, business English can involve as much writing as speaking. In the business world, a significant amount of communication – both internally in the workplace and externally – is mediated through writing. Again, there are strict conventions for writing in this context.

As is the case in any English language programme, the key determiner of the scope and extent of the writing strand of the syllabus should be the learners' needs. Teachers need to understand this not only in terms of general writing needs *per se* but in terms of specific needs in relation to genres, language and strategy deficit. Given the different ways that researchers and teachers have explored a range of approaches to developing writing skills in the past 40 years or so, there is now a good range of options that allow teachers to identify learners' different needs and formulate a writing programme that addresses them.

Writing lesson methodology

Genre-based approach

A genre-based approach to text analysis comes with clearly articulated methodology in the form of a teaching–learning cycle (Hyland, 2019: p.20):

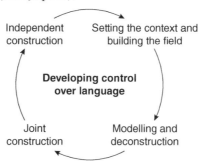

The broad aim of this approach is to offer learners support. There is a large degree of teacher mediated activity in the initial 'setting the context and building the field stage' when the context of the genre is established, and the teacher helps learners generate knowledge and content to be included in the text. After analysing example models of the genre in the next stage, the learners go on to practise writing their own examples. This can be done in pairs as 'joint construction' and with support from the teacher. Learners should then be equipped to write their own text independently. Throughout the process, learners develop their knowledge of language associated with the genre. It is likely that the different stages of the cycle would span a series of lessons.

Hyland's model of a genre-based approach offers learners good support in the initial stages of the cycle and provides a clear context for the writing. The analysis of model texts is also helpful. However, the model can present challenges in certain teaching and learning contexts. The length of time it takes to work through the cycle may be difficult to manage on courses where the development of writing skills is not the primary focus of the programme. The initial stage of setting the context could be problematic if learners have very limited knowledge of the genre they are focusing on. As noted above, writing genres are underpinned by cultural conventions and if these are unfamiliar to learners, attempting to set the context before they have seen and analysed a model may prove to be a frustrating task. Furthermore, some teachers and learners may see a genre approach as overly prescriptive and thereby stifling creativity.

There are also classroom management issues associated with the Hyland model. In the 'joint construction' stage, it may not be possible for learners to work collaboratively. For example, if the genre they are writing is an opinion-based essay and learners have very different opinions about the proposition of the essay, collaboration will be a challenge. The joint construction phase implies a high degree of teacher support and intervention with individual learners because they need to spend time working together, negotiating the content and language of the text under consideration. In large classes, this becomes very difficult to manage in class time. While it can be argued some of this intervention can be managed online outside class time, this adds considerably to a teacher's workload.

There are two simplified alternatives to the genre-based approach: *text based* and *task based*. These may provide teachers with more flexibility.

Text-based approach

Suggested by Hedge (2000), this approach introduces a model, or example text early in a writing lesson. The steps in the procedure are set out in the table below.

Stage	Notes
Text analysis	• Lead in to activate knowledge on the topic of the lesson and/or the model text; may also include activating knowledge of genre. • Reading comprehension activities so learners understand the content of the model text. • Analysis of one or two key language features of the model text (generic, functional, grammatical or lexical); can be teacher-fronted or by means of learner-centred tasks.
Scaffolded practice	• Learners practise language features highlighted at the analysis stage; activities can range from controlled to freer.
Independent writing	• Learners work alone or collaboratively (depending on the nature of the text) to write drafts of the text.

This approach is similar to a Presentation–Practice–Production mode of focusing on grammar and vocabulary. Some teachers and learners may find this overly schematic and/or prescriptive. However, it does provide support for learners who are engaging with a genre for the first time. It also replicates the writing behaviour of fluent speakers of English as, more often than not when required to produce some writing in a genre they have not engaged with before, they will use models to help them create their own text.

In contrast to the genre-based approach, text-based methodology targets specific features of the genre to highlight during the course of the lesson. While this may occur in a genre-based approach, the methodological description is very open-ended and suggests a focus on a broad range of genre features. This breadth of focus may overwhelm some learners and result in a time-management problem in some teaching and learning contexts. A text-based approach gives teachers more flexibility in terms of time management and it also allows teachers to tailor the analysis in line with learners' specific needs.

Task-based approach

This approach is taken from task-based methodology as outlined by Willis & Willis (2007). It requires learners to write a text before they have read or analysed any models and employs the following procedure:

Stage	Notes
Task	• Lead in to activate knowledge on the topic of the task/text. • Learners read task instructions – the task may involve only writing or writing a text may be one of the activities that learners carry out as part of the task. • Optional reading: learners read background information associated with the task or text content; NB this reading should not include a model of the kind of text they will write. • Learners write text individually or collaboratively.
Model text	• Learners read an example(s) of the kind of text they have just written and compare them to their texts. • Learners identify language features in the model text that can improve their texts, or the teacher directs them to specific language features.
Redrafting	• Learners redraft or revise their texts and share with other learners in the group.

The writing of a text can be a task in and of itself, or it can be one component of a broader task-based activity (Willis & Willis, 2007). For example, learners might engage with a problem-solving task that focuses on water shortages in their local area. The task as a whole could involve reading and listening as well as a variety of speaking activities. One outcome of the task could be a written proposal that outlines a strategy for dealing with the problem.

A task-based approach to writing acknowledges that learners may already have knowledge of the genre they are writing, and the first version of the text that they write can act as a diagnostic tool for the teachers to help them understand the extent of their learners' knowledge and ability to write a specific genre. However, trying this approach with a group of learners who have little knowledge of the genre could be too great a challenge and result in frustration.

One strength of this approach is that the task-driven nature of the activity emphasises meaning and connects the writing to the real world and all the contextual factors associated with it. Providing the model text acts as the 'focus on form' stage of a more generic task-based lesson. It can be left very open, and learners are free to determine their own needs in terms of focusing on aspects of the genre they feel are missing from their first draft. Alternatively, teachers can direct learners' attention towards certain language features in the model because they have previously identified learner needs associated with this area of language (Willis & Willis, 2007).

In both the text-based and task-based approach, it is worth noting the key role that reading has to play in eventually writing the text. Learners read a model text in order to understand how it is organised and to find examples of relevant language features. Learners also might read other texts in order to gather information that can be used as content in their writing. For example, if a learner has to write an essay on the topic of appropriate punishment for minor youth crimes, she may want to read articles to find examples of the kinds of punishment that have been imposed in her own and other countries. In academic writing, this kind of background reading forms a core part of the process of writing an essay or report.

Expressive writing approach

It is unlikely for a teacher to have an entire class of learners who wish to engage in expressive writing activities (unless a class has been formed for this express purpose). This means that many learner groups will be reluctant to spend long periods of time in class writing texts where they are free to express their creativity or ideas. However, there are some teachers who carry out activities in class that focus on some form of expressive writing. They see this as an opportunity to develop learners' fluency in writing as well as a chance to develop creative thinking skills. For example, a teacher can play a piece of music and ask learners to write some kind of response to it, perhaps how it makes them feel or what visual images it creates, or whether they associate it with some kind of past event in their lives.

The aim in this kind of activity is to point learners towards different stimuli that can help them get started with their writing. Learners might read a poem or the headline of a news item, or look at a painting or photograph, or they could react to a personal experience. The teacher could then suggest that learners continue to use these stimuli to maintain some kind of diary or journal. Teachers may wish to set up some kind of framework that facilitates this kind of writing and provide learners with suggestions on how to maintain their diary or journal. For example, Nelson (1991) encourages learners to select topics that interest them individually and as a group, and to write freely taking advantage of peer support. Whether the learner chooses to share their writing with their peers and/or the teacher should be at the discretion of the learner.

Expressive writing points to larger writing projects that learners can engage in. This might involve creating and publishing a class blog or wiki or online forum. Learner groups who enjoy fiction could attempt creating a group novella in a fictional genre they all enjoy. Another possibility is to set up some kind of online interaction with a group of learners in another country. Projects of this nature usually require attentive management on the teacher's behalf. However, when they are successful and learners engage with the project, they are very motivating and rewarding, and they provide opportunities for meaningful written communication.

Writing process strategies

None of the models above state explicitly where writing process strategies can be deployed. In effect, these strategies underpin all methodological models. Teachers have flexibility in how they map process writing strategies on to these models. In a genre-based approach, the initial setting of the context stage is an opportunity to focus on prewriting strategies while the joint construction stage is likely to include some kind of focus on drafting, responding and revising.

In a text-based approach, there is a greater emphasis on prewriting strategies in the text analysis stage of a writing lesson. Teachers may also encourage learners to use other prewriting strategies such as generating ideas and planning their writing (Hedge, 2000) before they begin independent writing. One or more of the remaining process strategies might then be emphasised during the rest of the independent writing stage. In a task-based approach, prewriting and drafting strategies can be focused on when learners write the first version of the text. The remaining strategies can be incorporated into the lesson after the model text has been introduced. In summary, there are a lot of methodological choices that teachers can make when they teach writing in English language classrooms. As Hyland notes, 'L2 writing classrooms are often a mixture of more than one approach and ... teachers frequently combine these in imaginative and effective ways' (2019: p.22).

Managing writing lessons

The interaction of writing lessons tends to be very learner-centred, particularly after initial teacher-fronted stages that set the context, provide input and build the field. Learners can engage in activities and tasks either working alone or together in pairs or small groups. This provides the teacher with good opportunities to move around the classroom, monitor learners' progress and, if appropriate, engage with them on a one-to-one or small-group basis, thereby responding to learners' individual needs. It should also be obvious, therefore, that not all learner-centred interaction during a writing lesson involves writing. Learners often talk about ideas they might include in their writing, and then perhaps jointly plan the organisation. If they write together, there will be oral negotiation of the content of the text and, having completed drafts and shared their writing with other learners, there may also be oral feedback to each other. As such, writing lessons can often involve a lot of speaking practice for learners. This is something learners may not be aware of, and it can therefore be useful to explain this at the outset.

Time is an essential classroom management issue in writing lessons. Often there are very good reasons for getting learners to write in class, for example, when they need to practise timed essays in preparation for sitting the writing component of an English language examination. Also, when the writing activity involves some kind of collaboration, it often needs to be carried out during the course of a lesson. However, when this is not the case, and writing is not a core component of the syllabus, learners can feel a degree of resentment spending large periods of class time writing, particularly if they are writing on their own.

It's important, therefore, to set very clear time limits for writing activities. Another strategy is to carry out prewriting and analysis tasks during the course of the lesson and ask learners to write a draft as part of their independent study outside the class. However, there may be some learners who are unable or reluctant to do this kind of homework task, which, in turn, can create a new set of problems. If a subsequent lesson is based around the assumption that all learners have completed a first draft, the teacher will need a contingency plan of some kind for those learners who have not written their draft.

Whether a class uses a digital device to carry out writing tasks will largely depend on the resources of the institution they are working for and what devices the learners themselves are able to bring to class. Word processing programmes usually come with their own language checking features, which can be helpful for learners to complete a writing task. There is a strong argument that if fluent speakers of English have access to these tools, so should learners. However, some teachers feel that the degree of support offered by word processing programmes does not provide learners with an appropriate level of challenge in terms of developing their overall language competence. Clearly, learners who are preparing for a paper-based written examination need to practise writing, and possibly handwriting, without the support of digital tools. In effect, the use of IT is something all teachers need to consider in a principled way in light not only of their learners' writing needs but also taking into consideration their broader English language learning needs.

Feedback on writing

Learners can receive feedback on their writing from teachers and their peers. This can occur at different stages in the writing process. Developmental feedback can occur during the responding, revising and editing stages of the process model described above. After publishing (in some teaching and learning contexts, this might just mean handing in a final draft of the text), feedback is more likely to be summative in nature.

Feedback can involve either praise, criticism or suggestions for improvement and can comprise some or all of the following:

- Response to the content – the reader responds to the ideas in the text.
- Evaluation of the content – the reader decides whether ideas are fully developed.
- Organisation and coherence – the reader decides whether the ideas in the text are organised clearly.
- Language appropriateness – the reader decides if the style and register are appropriate to the genre and whether there is a suitable level of complexity in the writing, for example, in academic writing.
- Language accuracy – the reader decides if grammar and vocabulary are used correctly.

Many teachers and learners are overly focused on feedback on language accuracy. Hyland and Hyland (2019) note that error correction was firmly embedded in the idea of feedback on writing until the 1990s when teachers began to respond to different elements of learner writing. Another possibility is that a focus on accuracy is linked to learners' overall English language acquisition and writing is seen as a tool for determining and responding to learners' broader language needs. In order to reinforce the notion of writing being a communicative act, it helps if teachers and learners aim to balance feedback on language with feedback on the content of learners' writing.

Peer feedback on writing is seen as a way for learners to support each other in the development of their writing skills. As Hyland & Hyland (2019) have observed, when learners discuss their responses to each other's writing, there is the potential for them to broaden the content of their writing and develop critical thinking skills at the same time. Peer feedback also has the potential to be perceived as less judgmental than that of the teacher. However, studies indicate that learners tend to prefer teacher feedback to that received from their classmates (Hyland & Hyland, 2019).

Traditionally, feedback on learner writing has either been provided as learners write in class, or after they have submitted a piece of writing for evaluation. Teachers often develop a system of symbols that provide prompts for improving writing, for example, the letters 'WO' might suggest there is a problem with the word order and the abbreviation 'para.' might suggest the learners needs to reconsider the organisation of part of the text (Hedge, 2000). Depending on the IT resources within an institution, it is now possible for a teacher to provide learners with feedback as they write in the same way that teachers can give feedback on oral language while learners carry out a speaking activity.

Whether their feedback is developmental or summative, synchronous or asynchronous, there are some key questions teachers should consider when giving feedback on learner writing:

- What kind of feedback should I give?
- How much feedback should I provide?
- How explicit do my comments/suggestions need to be?
- What is the correct balance between praise, criticism and suggestions for improvement?

Again, IT has made changes to the nature of feedback on writing. Software programmes are able to evaluate learners' written work and provide a grade. Some formal tests with a writing component (for example, Linguaskill) are offered online and questions are automarked. This means test takers receive results within 12 hours.

How to use this book

Each chapter of the book begins with a brief overview of the focus of that chapter. This is followed by a range of activities that can be used in the classroom. The first seven chapters focus on a specific communicative purpose of written communication. For example, Chapter 1 focuses on genres where learners need to write about themselves while Chapter 4 includes genres that are instrumental to getting things done on a daily basis. Chapters 6 and 7 deal with written communication in two specific contexts: academic and workplace settings respectively.

Chapter 8 differs in that it shifts the focus from student to teacher, and outlines a series of activities for professional development associated with the teaching of writing skills. The activities blend action–research and enquiry with ideas for engaging with learners in an alternative and in-depth way. The first seven activities in Chapter 8 are linked to each topic of the first seven chapters of the book.

Activities

The varied set of activities for each chapter incorporates a range of levels and interaction patterns. All of the following are focused on:

- vocabulary, grammar and discourse
- the mechanics of writing (spelling, punctuation, etc.)
- text organisation
- specific genre features
- stages in the writing process
- evaluation and feedback on learner writing

The book aims to offer a flexible approach for teachers allowing them to dip into any chapter which is relevant to a particular juncture in their teaching. It is not necessary to read or use the materials in sequence. The activities can be integrated with the teaching and learning materials that teachers are using to help develop and practise learners' writing skills.

Each activity is set out for the maximum ease of use and includes: an outline of what the activity entails; a suggested level; an estimated time to complete (this is indicative and will inevitably vary in terms of the level of the group and the size of the class); a clear aim; and a description of any preparation you might need to do along with a step-by-step description of the procedure. The preparation notes often also indicate any example materials that are included, but often also suggest how they can be adapted or how alternative materials can be created.

This is followed by a *Think further* section which indicates a key writing skill or learning point to highlight to learners. Then there are notes on ways in which the activity and example materials can be adapted, for example, if the learner group needs more support or would benefit from an increased level of challenge. Finally, a rationale outlines the way in which the activity can benefit learners and aid the development of their writing skills. The rationale also provides a reason for some of the methodological choices made in the procedure of the activity. The example materials that are provided are photocopiable resources that can be used in class.

References

Byrne, D. (1979) *Teaching Writing Skills*. Harlow, Longman.

Carter, R. & McCarthy, M. (2006) *Cambridge Grammar of English*. Cambridge, Cambridge University Press.

Chandrasoma, R., Thompson, C. & Pennycook, A. (2004) Beyond Plagiarism: Transgressive and Nontransgressive Intertextuality. *Journal of Language Identity & Education*. 3/3, 171-193.

Connor, U. (1996) *Contrastive Rhetoric*. Cambridge, Cambridge University Press.

Council of Europe (2001) *Common European Framework of Reference for Languages: Learning, teaching, assessment*. Cambridge, Cambridge University Press.

Crystal, D. (1995) *The Cambridge Encyclopedia of Language (Third Edition)*. Cambridge, Cambridge University Press.

Crystal, D. (2011) *Internet Linguistics*. Abingdon/New York, Routledge.

Davies, W. (2022) How many words does it take to make a mistake? *London Review of Books*. 44/4, 3-8.

Flower, L. & Hayes, J. (1981) A cognitive process theory of writing. *College Composition and Communication*. 32: 365-87.

Frodesen, J. (2014) Grammar in Second Language Writing. In: Celce-Murcia, M., Brinton, D. M. & Snow, M.A. (eds.) *Teaching English as a Second or Foreign Language (Fourth Edition)*. Boston, National Geographic Learning.

Hedge, T. (2000) *Teaching and Learning in the Language Classroom*. Oxford, Oxford University Press.

Hirvela, A., Hyland, K. & Manchón, R. M. (2018) Dimensions in L2 writing theory and research: Learning to write and writing to learn. In: Manchón, R. M. & Matsuda, P. K. (eds.) *Handbook of Second and Foreign Language Writing*. Boston/Berlin, Walter de Guyter Inc., pp.45–63.

Hyland, K. (2016) *Teaching and Researching Writing (Third Edition)*. Abingdon/New York, Routledge.

Hyland, K. (2019) *Second Language Writing (Second Edition)*. Cambridge, Cambridge University Press.

Hyland, K. & Hyland, F. (2019) Contexts and Issues in Feedback on L2 Writing. In Hyland, K. & Hyland, F. (eds.) *Feedback in Second Language Writing: Contexts and Issues Second Edition*. Cambridge, Cambridge University Press.

McCarthy, M. (1991) *Discourse Analysis for Language Teachers*. Cambridge, Cambridge UniversityPress.

Nelson, M. W. (1991) *At the point of need: Teaching basic and ESL writers*. Portsmouth, NH, Heinemann Educational Books.

Paltridge, B. (2001) *Genre and the Language Learning Classroom*. Ann Arbor, The University of Michigan Press.

Reid, J. M. (1993) *Teaching ESOL Writing*. New Jersey, Prentice Hall Regents.

Reid, J.M. (1994) *The Process of Paragraph Writing (Second Edition)*. New Jersey, Prentice Hall Regents.

Richards, J. C. (2015) *Key Issues in Language Teaching*. Cambridge, Cambridge University Press.

Selivan, L. (2018) *Lexical Grammar: Activities for teaching chunks and exploring patterns*. Cambridge, Cambridge University Press.

Willis, D. & Willis, J. (2007) *Doing Task-based Teaching*. Oxford, Oxford University Press.

1   Writing about yourself and other people

Fifty or so years ago, common genres in which people might have written about themselves or other people included personal letters, job applications or, in some cases, personal diaries. Now, online communication, and in particular writing associated with social media, has given rise to more varied ways that we write about ourselves and other people. People are encouraged to write online profiles for themselves as well as social media postings that talk about their activities and those of their friends and family.

Functions, genres and patterns

Despite this shift in focus, the underlying function of writing about yourself and other people has not really changed. While there are now new genres that focus on personal information, they mostly aim to either describe a person and/or narrate events in their lives. While the text may tell a personal story to the reader, for the writer, a narrative may be an attempt to bring coherence to and make sense of their lives to date (Page, 2012). It could be argued that there is an implicit persuasive function that underpins a personal profile (i.e. let my description convince you what a good person I am or my friend or relation is), but the primary functional aim is to describe and create a clear picture of a person's background, characteristics and qualities.

Personal profiles are a form of biography, which is a genre with a long, historical tradition. Most users of English are unlikely to write full-length books about themselves or another person. Rather, they are more likely to write some kind of personal profile, and they are now more likely to do this online. There has been a proliferation of new online genres in which people introduce themselves and write about their lives. Some have very specific conventions, for example, the writer may be limited in the number of words or characters they can use. The language choices of writers of these genres may differ significantly from a more traditional view of written language. The lexical choices may be very informal and more associated with spoken language, and there is often use of abbreviations and non-alphanumeric characters. Another feature of these genres is that they are often supported by visuals, particularly emojis and sometimes photographs.

A key influence on the genre structure of many of these online profiles is the fact that writers usually have quite a clear sense of the audience they are writing for and the expectations of the readers. As such, an online description of a family wedding is likely to be aimed at friends and family of the married couple and will probably make assumptions about the reader knowing the people at the wedding, for example, *Best-dressed guest? Our favourite aunty, of course, no prizes for guessing!* Lomborg (2011) notes social media genres are often determined by a format offered by the digital platform, so there might be a set of limited fields where users are invited to input information about themselves and perhaps upload a photograph of themselves. Despite such prescriptive formats, social media genres are to some degree unstable because users communicate with each other directly, and the content and language used in the text is not mediated or edited in any way unless it contains what has been deemed to be inappropriate content.

While online profiles of people can be informal and flexible in nature, the potential for them to be read by a wide range of people means a degree of care should be taken in the way they are written. For example, a Twitter profile may be read by a prospective employer and thereby influence a decision on whether to offer a job or not. Likewise, what someone writes about a family member, even if intended to be read only by other family members, could be accessed by a much wider audience. Online personal profiles tend to vary in terms of their level of self-disclosure, and in the case of virtual worlds in online games and imaginary communities, an online profile may be entirely invented or a mix of reality and fiction (Page, 2012). While learners are likely to be aware of this dynamic in their first language, they will probably need to develop critical awareness of their online English language identity and that of the people they interact with.

The most common discourse pattern found in a lot of descriptive writing is a general–particular pattern. For example, a complete description of a person might begin with a broad statement about the person's appearance and personality. It might then move on to provide details of the person's face and physique and then describe their character. General–particular patterning can also be embedded within the description itself. A general statement about a person's easy-going personality might be followed by specific details such as stating that the person laughs a lot and never seems to worry about problems.

Language

A core feature of texts about people is descriptive language. Writers need to be able to draw on a good range of lexis, particularly adjectival phrases, in order to provide an accurate description of themselves or other people. Sometimes profiles can involve comparing one person with another, which will involve comparative language. Profiles of people will often include some kind of background information. This means learners will need to be able to use narrative tenses effectively together with time expressions as cohesive devices. Describing someone's background may also involve outlining reasons for decisions taken in the past, so reason–result cohesive linking words and expressions can often also be found in profiles of people. If a text about another person is supported by a visual, it is likely to include referring language such as: *here we are . . . , this photo was taken . . . , that's my brother next to . . . , as you can see . . . .*

In the classroom

As well as real-world genres, profiles of people have a role to play in English language classrooms. At the beginning of a course, learners will sometimes write profiles of themselves or their classmates as part of the process of establishing group dynamics. It is a way for learners to get to know each other and establish good interpersonal relationships in the classroom. Class blogs and/or learning management systems (LMS) have greatly facilitated this process. The writing of profiles of people can sometimes occur in rubrics for the written component of examinations, for example, *Write an article about a family member you admire.* As a result, learners may need practice writing profiles of people because they may occur in the examination.

References

Lomborg, S. (2011) Social media as communicative genres. *MedieKultur Journal of media communication research.* 27(51) August 2011.

Page, R. E. (2102) *Stories and Social Media: Identities and Interaction.* New York and Abingdon, Routledge.

1.1 Information improvement

Outline	Students have a competition to correct spelling errors and punctuate personal information, before writing one of their own.
Level	Beginner to Pre-intermediate (A1–B1)
Time	20 minutes
Aim	To practise spelling and pronunciation in the context of personal information.
Preparation	You will need to make available for each group or pair, a sentence with punctuation and spelling errors (see *Example*).

Procedure

1 Put students in small groups or pairs and then hand out the text face down, or have it ready to display.

2 The text is revealed, and students have a race to find and correct four spelling errors. Groups put their hands up as they finish.

3 Check the answers. The first group to correct all four words correctly is the winner.

4 Now students have a competition to punctuate the text adding capital letters, full stops and apostrophes – give examples of these if necessary.

5 The first group to finish and add punctuation correctly is the winner.

6 Ask students to write their own personal profile and get them to check each other's spelling and punctuation in pairs.

Example

hallo my names anna molina im from madrid in span im in a class with my teachir kate in room sevn

Key

Spelling mistakes: hallo, span, teachir, sevn
Punctuation: Hello. My name's Anna Molina. I'm from Madrid in Spain. I'm in a class with my teacher Kate in room seven.
Also possible: Hello, my name's . . .

Think further

Ask students to think of situations when they will maybe need to write by hand in English, for example, completing a form to check into a hotel. Also, suggest learners make a note of words they have problems spelling – they could put these words in a notebook, online or in their phone.

Notes

You can create your own text based on local information and including typical spelling problems your learners have.

Rationale

While word processing programmes help students with spelling and punctuation, there are some situations in which personal information needs to be completed by hand. This activity aims to indicate to students at lower levels the importance of these key writing skills.

1.2 Simple selfies

Outline	Students read example selfie captions and practise typical expressions before writing and posting their own selfies.
Level	Beginner (A1) and above
Time	30 minutes
Aim	To model and practise captions for selfies to be posted online.
Preparation	You will need to make available to each student a worksheet such as the one below. You could create a worksheet with selfies about you and your life – students may find this more motivating. Ask students to bring their mobile phones to class.

Procedure

1 Students complete ex. 1–3 on the worksheet.

2 Put students into pairs (or threes). They take a selfie of themselves and collaboratively write a caption with two sentences.

3 Put pairs together to read and compare each other's captions.

4 Students can publish the selfies on their own social media platforms. Or, if you have a class learning management system or blog, the selfies can be published there.

Key

ex. 1   1–d, 2–c, 3–a, 4–b

ex. 2   a   Here I am with my friend Maria.
      b   I love my new bicycle.
      c   Here we are at the concert in the park.
      d   This is us in our tango class.

ex. 3   a–iii, b–iv, c–i, d–ii

Think further

Elicit from students, expressions from the examples on the worksheet that can be used with lots of different selfies, e.g. *here I am, here we are, this is me, this is us, I/we love/enjoy/hate.*

Notes

If you want to use the worksheet with higher levels, you could rewrite the captions, e.g. for photo 1: *Here I am first thing in the morning wondering what my day's going to be!* You could then move straight from examples to getting students to write their own captions.

Rationale

Simple selfie captions are a way for very low level learners to have the opportunity to write an authentic text. Given that the selfies with captions can be posted online, students have a very real sense of audience for their writing. The activities in the worksheet aim to highlight expressions and ways of structuring the captions. *Think further* aims to generalise this language so students can use it for other selfies.

◥ *Worksheet 1.2*

1 Match pictures 1–4 with sentences a–d.

a I love this takeaway food from the restaurant next door. It's so good.
b Here we are on holiday in Switzerland. It's really cold.
c Here I am with my son. We're playing basketball together.
d This is me in the morning. I'm thinking about my day.

2 Put the phrases together to make sentences.

a with my	here I am	friend Maria
b bicycle	my new	I love
c in the park	here we are	at the concert
d this is us	tango class	in our

3 Add e) sentences (i–iv) to the sentences in ex. 2.

i I love this music.
ii It's a difficult dance!
iii We're having coffee and cake.
iv It's easy to ride.

From *Teaching and Developing Writing Skills* © Cambridge University Press 2023   PHOTOCOPIABLE

1.3 Write a lie

Outline	Students write a paragraph about themselves, including one 'lie', then try to guess each other's piece of false information.
Level	Elementary (A2) and above
Time	20 minutes
Aim	To provide freer practice writing personal information; to help students get to know each other and foster positive group dynamics.
Preparation	Write a paragraph of at least four connected sentences about yourself that includes one piece of false information.

Procedure

1 Show students the paragraph you have written and tell them one piece of information is not true.

2 Students read the paragraph and ask you four 'wh-' questions about the information to try and work out / guess the lie. If they don't guess, tell them.

3 Students then write their own paragraph of at least four connected sentences about themselves and include one lie.

4 In pairs, students swap their paragraphs and ask each other four questions to try and work out the lie.

5 Do feedback with the group – find out who guessed correctly and what interesting true information students found out about each other.

Think further

Ask students if they believe everything people write about themselves online. Ask if they know anyone who has written something that is not one hundred per cent accurate about themselves. Ask why they think people do this sometimes.

Notes

This activity is best used early in a course, but it could be used mid-course with a group where students always sit in the same place and work with the same people. The example paragraph you provide about yourself should be graded according to the level of the learners.

Rationale

Although this activity is often done as speaking practise, it can be equally engaging as a written exercise. In fact, asking students to write a paragraph not only gives them a chance to practise writing skills, but also gives them more thinking time to think of a plausible lie.

1.4 The follow up

Outline Students match personal information questions to follow up questions, then write their own follow up questions as preparation for an interview, and as a basis for a profile.
Level Pre-intermediate (B1) and above
Time 50 minutes if profiles are written in class (30 minutes if done as homework)
Aim To model the strategy of asking follow up questions in a personal information interview; to provide freer written practice of question forms; to practise writing a personal profile.
Preparation Make available for students a set of information and follow up questions (see *Example*).

Procedure

1   Ask students to read the questions about personal information (see *Example*, questions 1 to 8). Point out that asking just one question about each topic may not produce much information.

2   Students then match the first set of questions with a set of follow up questions (see *Example*, questions a-h).

3   Check answers with the class and then ask students to cover the follow up questions.

4   In pairs, students write new follow up questions for the first set of information questions.

5   Put students into new pairs to interview each other using the original questions and their new follow up questions. They should make written notes.

6   Finally, students work alone and use the information from the interviews to write profiles of the student they have just interviewed.

Example

1   How old are you?
2   How many people are there in your family?
3   What do you do?
4   What do you like doing in your free time?
5   Why are you learning English?
6   What's your favourite food?
7   What kind of music do you like?
8   Where would you like to go for your next holiday?

a   Where do you work/study?
b   How often do you eat it?
c   How well do you want to speak it?
d   *No follow up question*
e   What do you want to do there?
f   Who's your favourite singer or musician?
g   When did you start doing that?
h   Do they all live in (*city/country name*)?

Key
1–d, 2–h, 3–a, 4–g, 5–c, 6–b, 7–f, 8–e

Think further
Establish that it often helps to ask a follow up question so that students get more information from the person they are talking to. It also shows interest and encourages the person to say more.

Notes

The example questions are aimed at lower levels. At higher levels, you can write questions that are more complex in terms of content and grammar. At all levels, you could tailor the questions to suit the needs and interests of the learner group.

Rationale

The writing of class profiles can be a useful 'getting to know you' activity at the beginning of a course. The profiles can be put up around a classroom or posted in a learning management system or class blog. This activity aims to help students to collect more detailed information about their interviewee that enables them to write a more comprehensive and interesting profile.

1.5 Questioning the event

Outline	Students interview you about a recent event in your life via written questions, and then they write a report about the event.
Level	Pre-intermediate (B1) and above
Time	40 minutes
Aim	To practise formulating written questions; to provide freer practice of writing a narrative.
Preparation	No preparation is necessary though you might want to provide blank slips of paper for students to write their questions on.

Procedure

1 Tell students about a recent event in your life (e.g. *For my last holiday I went to Vietnam*), but don't provide too many details.

2 Tell students they are going to write a report of this event. Explain they can get more information about what happened by writing questions for you to answer.

3 In groups, students decide on and write questions – set a time limit of one or two minutes. The questions are then delivered to you.

4 If the language in the question is incorrect, indicate where the problem is and send the question back for correction. Write answers to all correct questions as you receive them – this should be an ongoing, back and forward process, but set a time limit for it.

5 Once students have enough extra information, they write their report in groups. They decide on a coherent order for the information, make adjustments to grammar (e.g. changing the pronoun from first to third person) and add cohesive devices where appropriate.

6 Each group reads the reports of the other groups. Ask the whole group what differences there were in the reports.

Think further

Establish with students that the content of a text is often the result of the writer's interests and what they choose to focus on. The variations in each group's version of the narrative were the result of what information they chose to focus on in their questions.

Notes

If teaching online, communication between you and the students could be done by means of text messages rather than using the messaging facility of your online platform – this ensures that groups aren't privy to each other's information. With some groups, you may prefer to keep this activity fluency-focused. You can do this by not asking for corrections if the language in students' questions is incorrect. However, questions should still be returned if you cannot understand what students want to know.

Rationale

Students are usually keen to find out about their teacher and it is quite common to do this orally. Maintaining an on-going 'long conversation' between you and the students over the duration of a course is very motivating for students. This activity forms part of that 'conversation', but it moves it into written form. This is relevant given the amount of written communication involved in maintaining conversations across social media platforms.

Reference

This activity is adapted from 'Paper Interviews' (Meddings & Thornbury 2009).
Meddings, L. & Thornbury, S. (2009) *Teaching Unplugged*. Surrey, Delta.

1.6 All sorts of results

Outline	Students make notes of the results of the learning situations of different people, which they then develop into full sentences and finally into profiles.
Level	Pre-intermediate to Upper intermediate (B1–B2)
Time	30 minutes
Aim	To provide freer practice of result linkers used in character profiles.
Preparation	Write four sentences about four people in different learning situations (see *Example*).

Procedure

1   Put students in small groups and show them the sentences about the four people.

2   Students think of a result (or results) for each sentence and make notes without using any linking words, and without indicating which person they are connected to. Do an example on the board, e.g.
Mario started learning English when he was 60 years old. – he was the oldest student in the class

3   Students swap their result notes with another group.

4   In their groups, students try to guess which result goes with which person in the sentences.

5   Show the following result linkers: *therefore, so, as a result*. In their groups, students then use these linkers and work together to write mini-profiles. They copy the first sentence from step 1 and add a result.

6   The groups swap back their completed profiles and check whether they match the original ideas.

7   Individually, students then write their own examples about a past learning experience and its result(s).

Example

Mario started learning English when he was 60 years old.
Gabriella started going to dance classes when she was six years old.
Jim began playing the guitar when he was 14.
Zoe started studying law just after her thirtieth birthday.

Think further

Establish with students the different positions in the sentence of the linkers and the punctuation used. Remind them that it helps to make a record of this information about linkers when they make a note of them.

Notes

The situations in the example sentences are associated with learning. You can create your own examples on the same topic or use a different topic. You could do a similar activity at a higher level, but incorporate higher-level result linkers (e.g. *consequently*) as well as reason linkers (*because, since, as,* etc.).

Rationale

Compared to a more typical gap fill or matching task, this activity is more creative because it gets students to generate their own ideas. The second step in the activity gets students focused on result meaning rather than worrying about linkers. The group swap provides students with a sense of audience.

1.7 Guess who

Outline	In small groups, students write clues about the identity of a famous person which they read out for other groups to guess.
Level	Pre-intermediate (B1) and above
Time	35 minutes (20 minutes if the final writing is done as homework)
Aim	To model ways of including interesting content in personal profiles; to revise a range of tenses.
Preparation	You will need to make a set of prompts available to your students (see *Example*). This activity is more successful if students can use mobile phones in class, so remind them to bring them to the lesson.

Procedure

1 Do an example of the guessing game with the whole class using the clues in the example.
   a. Put students in small groups.
   b. Read a clue and students write down who they think the person is – they shouldn't call out. Move around and check their answers. If a group gets the correct answer, they win five points and retire from the game.
   c. Read the next clue and the remaining groups write another name in order to win four points.
   d. Continue in this way until all groups have guessed the person or you reveal the answer.

2 Show the clue prompts to students. Ask them to select a famous person and write clues using the prompts to help them. Point out they should begin with a difficult clue and make the final clues easier. They can use mobile phones to research information. Monitor and help.

3 Each group takes a turn to read out their clues and check the answers of other groups. Keep a record of scores to determine the winning group.

4 Students write a profile of the famous person that includes the interesting facts with other biographical information. This could be done as group work in class or individually at home.

Example
Clues
1 This female singer is allergic to cats. (5 points)
2 She has appeared in a show on Broadway. (4 points)
3 She doesn't like her first hit song anymore. (3 points)
4 She was born in Florida but grew up in New York. (2 points)
5 Her first album was called *Yours Truly*. (1 point)
Answer: Ariana Grande

Clue prompts

This male/female (*job title*) is/was . . .

She/He likes /doesn't like . . .

She/He has done/played/sung/acted in/written . . .

She/He was born in . . . grew up in . . .

Most people know/don't know that she/he . . .

In (*year*) she/he went/did/played/sang/acted in/wrote . . .

Think further

Ask students if a profile is more or less interesting if they use the less well-known information in the clues as well as typical biographical information. Elicit from them the idea that doing research and finding extra, unusual information can make profiles more interesting to read.

Notes

This activity can just be used as an end-of-week game without getting students to write the profile. You could adapt the prompts in such a way that they serve as revision of grammar points taught during the week. You can also specify the field and/or era of the famous people to be guessed, for example, famous film stars from the past ten years.

Rationale

The class time writing practice that students get in this activity might be limited to the writing of the clues. However, the key takeaway point is the value of doing some research online to make the content of a profile more interesting, using less well-known facts and figures. The competitive element is a way of boosting students' motivation.

1.8 Make it more interesting

Outline	Students improve a description of a daily routine by adding contextual information and having in mind a specific audience for the text.
Level	Pre-intermediate (B1) and above
Time	35 minutes
Aim	To demonstrate to students how awareness of context and audience can help improve the content of writing.
Preparation	You will need to make available to students a worksheet similar to the one below.

Procedure

1 Students read the example paragraph on the worksheet below that lacks detail and interest. They complete ex. 1–3. Check answers after each exercise or after students have completed the worksheet.

2 Divide the class into two groups, A and B. Group A rewrites the text as a social media post, and Group B rewrites the text as an email. Depending on the context and audience, they add information to make the paragraph more interesting.

3 Then pair each student from Group A with a student from Group B. Pairs swap their texts and note differences in information.

4 Ask students for any interesting examples of added information.

Key
ex. 1 a The daily routine of an English language student.
      b Not very – it just contains simple facts.
ex. 2 Both sentences a and b can be placed after the first sentence in the paragraph.
ex. 3 i–b, ii–a

Think further
Show students these two categories: *personal comment* and *description*. Ask learners which of these two they used most when adding information to the example paragraph. Check whether they could have used the other feature a little more.

Notes
An extension to this activity is to ask students to write about their own daily routine for a specific audience. They should aim to add information to make it interesting for the target reader.

Rationale

Sometimes students' writing has the appearance of a series of sentences containing only minimal, factual information. Introducing a specific context and the idea of audience should encourage them to add detail and a degree of colour to their writing. At the same time, it can nudge them towards using more complex written language and thereby encouraging them to extend their range.

◤ *Worksheet 1.8*

I get up at 7.00am and have breakfast. I go to my English school at 8.00am by bus. The lesson starts at 9.00am and finishes at 12.30pm. In the afternoon, I sometimes study in the school's Learning Centre, but sometimes I go out with my classmates for a coffee. I do some physical exercise when I get home and have dinner at 7.00pm.

1 Read the paragraph and answer the questions.
   a What does the paragraph describe?
   b How interesting is it to read?

2 Where could these sentences be added to the paragraph?
   a *People here have a large breakfast and I always feel so full after.*
   b *It's nice to have time for breakfast – I usually don't eat it because I have to get to work early.*

3 Match these two contexts with the sentences in ex. 2.
   i A student studying on an intensive English course in their home country and writing a social media post.
   ii A student studying in the UK writing an email to an English-speaking friend.

1.9 Coherent order

Outline	Students reorganise a profile of a person so the information is ordered to a general–particular discourse pattern, and then write their own profile.
Level	Intermediate (B1+) and above
Time	40 minutes if writing the profile in class (10 minutes if the profile is done as homework)
Aim	To demonstrate how a general–particular discourse pattern can be used to structure descriptive writing in a coherent way.
Preparation	You will need to make available to each student a profile for reorganisation (see *Example*) and if you wish to, an example answer.

Procedure

1   Ask students to read a description of a person (not coherently ordered) and decide whether it is similar to anyone they know.

2   Students then divide the text into paragraphs and decide on the main idea in each paragraph.

3   Check answers with the whole class.

4   Tell students the order of sentences within each paragraph can be improved and, in pairs, get them to reorder the sentences. Point out they may need to change nouns into pronouns or vice versa.

5   Check answers by showing the model answer.

6   Show the following text patterns and ask students how the information in each paragraph of the model answer is ordered:

general ➜ *particular*   *particular* ➜ *general*

7   Students then write a profile of a relative or close friend with clear paragraphing and general–particular information patterning.

Example

[1]My grandmother never felt comfortable at parties or any other kind of large social group. [2]She would often sit very quietly and just watch and then leave as soon as she could. [3]My grandmother was quite a shy woman who didn't speak a lot. [4]Her favourite social activity was getting together with family members for a meal that she cooked. [5]She was an only child and grew up in a small town where she didn't have many friends. [6]Also, her own mother was strict with her because she worried other people would have a negative impression of my grandmother. [7]I think her own shyness was the result of her childhood. [8]My great grandmother kept her daughter at home and didn't let her daughter join sports clubs or other social groups. [9]She loved reading us stories and was very clever at changing her voice for each character in the story. [10]And she used to make us clothes all the time and they were always beautifully made. [11]My grandmother was not like a traditional grandmother who laughed and played and had fun with her grandchildren. [12]However, she always paid us a lot of attention and when we went to visit her she always prepared our favourite foods. [13]She made all her grandchildren feel very special and we all felt very close to this shy, sensitive woman.

Key
Division of sentences into paragraphs and main ideas: 1–4 grandmother's shyness; 5–8 grandmother's childhood; 9–13 grandmother's behaviour with her grandchildren.

Model answer

My grandmother was quite a shy woman who didn't speak a lot. She never felt comfortable at parties or any other kind of large social group. She would often sit very quietly and just watch and then leave as soon as she could. Her favourite social activity was getting together with family members for a meal that she cooked.

I think her own shyness was the result of her childhood. She was an only child and grew up in a small town where she didn't have many friends. Also, her own mother was strict with her because she worried other people would have a negative impression of my grandmother. My great grandmother kept her daughter at home and didn't let her daughter join sports clubs or other social groups.

My grandmother was not like a traditional grandmother who laughed and played and had fun with her grandchildren. However, she always paid us a lot of attention and when we went to visit her, she always prepared our favourite foods. She loved reading us stories and was very clever at changing her voice for each character in the story. And she used to make us clothes all the time and they were always beautifully made. She made all her grandchildren feel very special and we all felt very close to this shy, sensitive woman.

Think further
Elicit from learners that ordering information in a logical way helps not only the writer, but also the reader. It makes their writing easier to read and understand.

Notes
In order to add a level of challenge for higher-level classes, the sentences in the example text could be mixed up further.

Rationale
Students often spend a lot of time thinking about correct use of language, but don't consider the value of thinking how they order information coherently within a text. A lot of descriptive writing adheres to general–particular discourse patterning.

1.10 Who's tweeting?

Outline	Students analyse example Twitter profiles, write their own and then guess the identity of other profiles.
Level	Intermediate (B1+) and above
Time	35 minutes
Aim	To analyse the structure of and practise writing a Twitter profile.
Preparation	You will need to make a worksheet such as the one below available for each student.

Procedure

1   Students read the Twitter profiles and decide which of the two people they would prefer to follow on Twitter.

2   Elicit from students the aim of these profiles, i.e. to show the kind of person you are and to make yourself appear as interesting as possible.

3   Students complete the reading comprehension task in ex. 1.

4   Students complete an language analysis task in ex. 2. When you check answers, elicit or point out that noun phrases are often used to talk about jobs, family, friends and interests and verb phrases for the attitude to life.

5   Students work alone and write a Twitter profile – they should try to make it as interesting as possible and observe the 160-character maximum rule.

6   Put students in groups of six to eight with a group leader. The leader collects the profiles and reads each one aloud (including their own) without saying who wrote it. The other group members guess who the profile is about.

Key
ex. 1 a, b, c, d, f
ex. 2 b, c

Think further
Elicit from students why noun phrases are more common in this kind of profile. Establish that the low character count means that information needs to be given as efficiently as possible. Noun phrases are often a useful way to do this.

Notes
The profiles in the worksheet are aimed at a higher level because the creative use of noun phrases requires a good level of competence. However, this activity could be adapted for lower levels by simplifying the language. The easiest way to do this is to use the verbs *like* and *love*. For example, the first profile would read *loves fitness, coffee and her two children Sasha & Joe*.

Rationale

Some online templates and digital media require writers to limit the number of words or characters they can use. The Twitter profiles are a clear example of this – users are allowed a maximum of 160 characters. Students need guidance on how they can do this – the kind of language they can use and what can be left out.

▶ Worksheet 1.10

@MarleneF
Pilot, fitness fanatic, coffee addict & devoted Mum to Sasha & Joe. Always laughing.

⊘ San Francisco ✎ mf.pt/04oSJ 🖩 Joined March 2016

@RyanWalsh
Nurse, best friend to everyone, part-time guitarist, lover of crime fiction. Life should be interesting.

⊘ Dublin ✎ rw.ne/11aCF 🖩 Joined June 2020

@KandaT
English language teacher, movie fan, grammar hater, pretty good cook.
Passionate about people.

⊘ Bangkok ✎ kt.elt/34gcP 🖩 Joined October 2022

@JorgeGomez
Adventurer, outdoor enthusiast; free solo rock climber; expert kayaker; environmentalist. Love the planet you live on.

⊘ Mexico City ✎ jg.avr/2fKE 🖩 Joined January 2019

1 What do the profiles about tell you about these people? Tick the relevant boxes.

a ❑ job   b ❑ family   c ❑ friends
d ❑ interests   e ❑ travel   f ❑ attitude to life

2 Tick the things that are true.
Twitter profiles use:

a ❑ complete sentences.   b ❑ words and phrases.
c ❑ mostly noun phrases.   d ❑ mostly verb phrases.

1.11 Rich description

Outline	Students write a paragraph of a physical description of someone they know, compare with an example text and then consider inappropriate lexical choices for descriptive language.
Level	Intermediate (B1+) and above
Time	60 minutes (40 minutes if students' first draft is done as homework)
Aim	To demonstrate to students the need to consider context carefully when making alternative lexical choices in their writing.
Preparation	You will need to make a worksheet such as the one below available for your students.

Procedure

1   Students write a physical description of someone they know, such as a family member or friend (see suggestion in *Notes*).

2   Students complete ex. 1 and 2 on the worksheet.

3   Check answers with the class.

4   Establish with students that the description words can be changed. Ask what they could use to help do this and elicit: dictionary, thesaurus.

5   Students then read another version of the description that uses inappropriate words (see ex. 3 on the worksheet). Ask if the changes improve the text and why or why not.

6   Elicit that the second version isn't an improvement. Establish that the new words came from a thesaurus, but are not appropriate because they don't collocate with the words they are adjacent too or they change the meaning slightly.

7   Point out to students that dictionaries are often preferable to a thesaurus because they explain meanings and give examples. For example, the Cambridge Online Dictionary states that 'pretty' is used to describe girls and women. This dictionary also has a thesaurus function that gives more context information. If possible, show some examples.

8   Students work in groups of three or four. They read the first draft of each other's paragraphs and make suggestions for alternative vocabulary choices, but check their meaning and use in a dictionary.

9   Students write their second draft as homework.

Key
ex. 1 only the face
ex. 2
My uncle is the [1]*best-looking* member of our family. His eyes are the first thing you notice about him. They are [2]*pale* blue, and when he looks directly at you, they seem to read your thoughts. Then you notice his face, which is [3]*well-shaped* with [4]*high* cheekbones and framed by [5]*fair* hair. And after that you notice his smile. His lips stretch back to show [6]*perfect* white teeth. But it is the [7]*warmth* of his smile that you feel most. The [8]*ice-cold* of his eyes changes and becomes like blue sky on a summer's day.

Think further
Establish with students the benefit of not merely listing new vocabulary that they make a record of. They should also write example phrases and sentences that show how new lexis is used.

Notes
It saves class time if students write the first draft for homework. However, this runs the risk of some students not having completed the homework task and, if so, you will need to group students carefully in step 8 of the activity, so each group has enough drafts to share around. An extra activity could be added after step 3 in which students read the text again and underline any useful phrases or expressions they could use in their second draft.

Rationale
While students at B1+ level and above often need to extend the range of vocabulary they can use, they need to start paying attention to variations in meaning (e.g. connotation) and use (in particular, collocation). It is important to highlight the point about alternative choices needing to be appropriate to the context of the writing and that not all synonyms can be swapped automatically.

▶ *Worksheet 1.11*

1 Read the description. Is the description about the person's face or their whole body?

My uncle is the [1]_____ member of our family. His eyes are the first thing you notice about him. They are [2]_____ blue, and when he looks directly at you, they seem to read your thoughts. Then you notice his face, which is [3]_____ with [4]_____ cheekbones and framed by [5]_____ hair. And after that you notice his smile. His lips stretch back to show [6]_____ white teeth. But it is the [7]_____ of his smile that you feel most. The [8]_____ of his eyes changes and becomes like blue sky on a summer's day.

2 Complete the description with the words and phrases from the box.

well-shaped	pale	ice-cold	perfect
warmth	best-looking	high	fair

3 Compare the description in ex. 1 with the description below. Which is better? Why?

My uncle is the [1]*prettiest* member of our family. His eyes are the first thing you notice about him. They are [2]*dull* blue, and when he looks directly at you, they seem to read your thoughts. Then you notice his face, which is [3]*well-built* with [4]*steep* cheekbones and framed by [5]*light* hair. And after that you notice his smile. His lips stretch back to show [6]*pure* white teeth. But it is the [7]*passion* of his smile that you feel most. The [8]*frost* of his eyes changes and becomes like blue sky on a summer's day.

From *Teaching and Developing Writing Skills* © Cambridge University Press 2023   PHOTOCOPIABLE

1.12 Experience evaluation

Outline	Students evaluate an article according to specific criteria, then write a first draft and evaluate another student's writing.
Level	Intermediate (B1+) and above
Time	60 minutes (25 minutes if step 5 is done as homework with follow up in a subsequent lesson)
Aim	To provide practice in evaluating writing for content and communicative purpose.
Preparation	You will need to make a worksheet such as the one below available for your students.

Procedure

1 Show students the following writing task instructions:
   Write an article for an online school magazine about a childhood experience where you felt free from your parents.

2 In pairs, students discuss what content they might include for this writing task. They can also discuss what grammar structures they think would be in the text and how it could be organised.

3 Give each pair of students the worksheet, and ask them to read and evaluate the article according to the criteria and note down their evaluation.

4 In small groups, students compare their evaluations. Then do whole class feedback, and point out any ideas in the Key if they are not mentioned by students.

5 Individually, students write a first draft for the writing task, then swap with a partner and give feedback according to the four criteria.

Key

Task achievement: The description of going camping is clear enough, but the idea of independence from the writer's parents is not developed enough.

Communicative achievement: The events of the story are clearly outlined, but there is little description of how the writer felt except to say 'cool, I loved it'. The writer could use a wider range of adjectives to describe their reaction. Also, the writer could describe how they felt about different events, for example, the morning swim, the breakfast. Given this is meant to be an article, the writer could be more neutral in terms of style.

Clear organisation: The content of each paragraph is clear, but the order of paragraphs 2 and 3 would be better reversed.

Cohesion: There is very little use of linking devices and the writer uses a lot of short sentences that could be joined with a conjunction, relative pronoun or linking word. At times, the writer needs to reiterate the full noun phrase 'my cousins' or 'my cousins and I'. A few sentences contain a subject but no verb.

Think further

Elicit from students that correct vocabulary and grammar were not included in the evaluation criteria. Point out to them that the vocabulary and grammar in the example is mostly correct, but this doesn't make it a successful and communicative piece of writing.

Notes

A possible variation for this activity is to get students to write their first draft before they evaluate the example text. If so, students could be encouraged to do self-evaluation before getting feedback from another student. This activity can be adapted to fit any topic or theme you are focusing on in a writing class. You would need to write or find an accompanying text for students to evaluate. Using anonymized pieces of writing from a previous class might be a possibility.

Rationale

When asked to evaluate each other's writing, students tend to focus on correct use of language and don't consider broader issues such as communicative effectiveness and text organisation. In this activity, evaluation of language accuracy is omitted (except for the focus on cohesion) in order to broaden students' evaluative focus. This, in turn, may help develop their self-evaluation skills.

▶ Worksheet 1.12

Camping and free

I went camping. It was my first time free from parents. It was with my cousins. They're all a bit older than me. It was cool. I loved it.

On the first night couldn't sleep. I excited and insects were biting. After midnight the wind was stronger. Half the tent blew down. It wasn't easy to put it up again. No parents to help. We laughed. It kind of crazy.

The tent was on the edge of a forest. There was a river. All four in the same tent. I thought they had been camping before. We struggled to get the tent up. They didn't know much more than me.

First day and sunrise. Woke up and it was a beautiful day. We for a swim in the river. We had breakfast. We went exploring in the woods. We found a swing on a tree. You could swing out and jump in the river. I enjoyed being away from my parents. It was cool. I loved it.

Evaluation

Task achievement

Communicative achievement

Clear organisation

Cohesion

1.13 Research in common

Outline	Students research two famous people and makes notes about key similarities and differences.
Level	Pre-intermediate (B1) and above
Time	30 minutes
Aim	To practise prewriting research skills.
Preparation	Prepare a list of names of famous people – enough so that each pair of students in your class has two names. It's more interesting if the names are from a wide range of fields so the pairs of famous people are unlikely, e.g. John F. Kennedy and Adele. Students should bring mobile devices to the lesson.

Procedure

1 Show students the instruction for writing:
   Write an article of between 150 and 200 words about two famous people. What similarities and differences are there between them?

2 In small groups, students discuss how they would approach this writing task. When you conduct feedback on their discussion, establish that they will need to do some kind of online research.

3 Put the following categories on the board:
   background, achievement, interests, personal qualities.

4 Put students in pairs and give each pair the names of two famous people – these should be randomly selected.

5 In their pairs, students research online about their two famous people. They should try to find out anything they have in common as well as the key differences between the two people.

6 Each pair reports back to class on what they have found out.

7 Students then write their article as homework comparing and contrasting their two famous people.

Think further

Establish from students that their research needed to be focused on key differences and things in common for the two people. Point out that this is more active than just copying what they read.

Notes

With a higher-level group, you could increase the level of challenge by getting students to select three famous people.

Rationale

Many general English writing tasks benefit from some degree of research. This does not need to be academic in nature, but it is a useful study skill to know how to focus research. Finding out commonalities between the famous people is a way to ensure students process and sift the information they are reading rather than merely copying chunks of text. This activity would be particularly relevant to a group of learners who are likely to transition from general English to an English for Academic Purposes (EAP) programme.

1.14 Helpful signposts

Outline	Students read a narrative about how a couple met adding appropriate time expressions before writing their own text.
Level	Intermediate (B1+) (or any level depending on text)
Time	50 minutes (25 minutes if the final writing step is done as homework)
Aim	To expand the range of time expressions that students can use in a narrative.
Preparation	Prepare a narrative without linkers with a relevant timeline (see *Example*).

Procedure

1 Students read a narrative text that doesn't include time linkers (see *Example*). Don't let students see the timeline at this stage. Ask students if they know of any couples who met in a similar way.

2 Elicit from students that the time of events isn't clear because there are very few time expressions.

3 Show the timeline for the story and students complete the text by adding time words and expressions where there is a ^, but without using specific dates. It's possible to join some sentences together.

4 Show students the model answer to compare with their version. Tell them many other variations are possible – check any queries.

5 Students write about how a couple they know got together – this can be done as homework.

Example

www.myblogabout.com

What would you like to order? My brother's long-distance love ended up on the menu.

This story is about my brother Mike and his wife Adriana. They met more than ten years ago. ^ Mike was living in Melbourne, where he had been born, and Adriana was living in Porto Alegre in Brazil. They met for the first time. ^ they were both on holiday in New Zealand

They were in Queenstown and went to do a bungy jump on the same day. It was Mike's turn to jump, but he got really scared and wanted to change his mind. Adriana was standing behind him and she could see how frightened he was. She took his hand, gave him a big smile and said, 'you can do it – it will be wonderful'. This gave Mike the courage he needed, and he jumped. And it was wonderful.

Adriana jumped ^. Mike waited for her and invited her out to dinner to thank her for helping him make the jump. ^ they spent two days together sightseeing in and around Queenstown. ^ they got on really well. This was the end of Mike's holiday, but it was only the beginning of Adriana's so they had to say goodbye to each other.

^ they kept in touch with each other by email and social media. However, they both kept thinking about the huge distance between Australia and Brazil and they realised there was little possibility they would meet again. ^ their communication stopped.

^ Adriana was feeling bored with her life in Porto Alegre. She had loved her holiday in New Zealand, so she decided to apply for a working holiday visa to spend a year there working and improving her English. She went to live in Wellington, the capital city, because she had got to know some people there ^ she had been on holiday.

^ Mike was also feeling bored with his job as a digital artist in Melbourne. He was just given small jobs to do and the pay was bad. He saw a job advertised at an interesting special effects company in Wellington so he applied for it and got it.

^ he went out for dinner with colleagues from work. ^ they were ready to order their food. The waitress appeared. It was Adriana. They couldn't believe they had met again. ^ all my family went to Wellington for their wedding. They now have two small children.

Timeline

2013	*2014*	*Jan 2015*	*May 2015*	*Nov 2015*
Mike & Adriana meet.	*They stopped communicating.*	*Adriana moves to Wellington.*	*Mike moves to Wellington.*	*They marry.*

Model answer

www.myblogabout.com

What would you like to order? My brother's long-distance love ended up on the menu.

This story is about my brother Mike and his wife Adriana. They met more than ten years ago. <u>Back then</u>, Mike was living in Melbourne, where he had been born, and Adriana was living in Porto Alegre in Brazil. They met for the first time <u>while</u> they were both on holiday in New Zealand

They were in Queenstown and went to do a bungy jump on the same day. It was Mike's turn to jump, but he got really scared and wanted to change his mind. Adriana was standing behind him and she could see how frightened he was. She took his hand, gave him a big smile and said, 'you can do it – it will be wonderful'. This gave Mike the courage he needed, and he jumped. And it was wonderful.

Adriana jumped <u>immediately afterwards</u>. Mike waited for her and invited her out to dinner to thank her for helping him make the jump. <u>Then</u> they spent two days together sightseeing in and around Queenstown. <u>During that time</u>, they got on really well. This was the end of Mike's holiday, but it was only the beginning of Adriana's so they had to say goodbye to each other.

<u>After that</u>, they kept in touch with each other by email and social media. However, they both kept thinking about the huge distance between Australia and Brazil and they realised there was little possibility they would meet again. <u>One year later</u>, their communication stopped.

<u>Two years later</u>, Adriana was feeling bored with her life in Porto Alegre. She had loved her holiday in New Zealand, so she decided to apply for a working holiday visa to spend a year there working and improving her English. She went to live in Wellington, the capital city, because she got to know some people there <u>when</u> she had been on holiday.

<u>In the meantime</u>, Mike was also feeling bored with his job as a digital artist in Melbourne. He was just given small jobs to do and the pay was bad. He saw a job advertised at an interesting special effects company in Wellington so he applied for it and got it.

<u>At the end of his first week of work</u>, he went out for dinner with colleagues from work. <u>When</u> they were ready to order their food, the waitress appeared. It was Adriana. They couldn't believe they had met again. <u>Six months later</u> all my family went to Wellington for their wedding. They now have two small children.

Think further

Elicit from students which time expressions they use frequently when writing a narrative, and then ask them which one(s) they should aim to use a little more in their writing.

Notes

This activity can be done with any level by creating a text that is appropriate for the students. It's more interesting if you can base the text on something that is true from your own family. If you use the example text and you feel your students need more support, you could supply some of the underlined words and expressions in the example answer on the board. The sample answer is obviously not the only way to add time expressions to this text but an example students can compare their own texts against.

Rationale

Students at most levels can usually use time expressions, but they often tend to overuse dates followed by *then* and *next*. This activity aims to increase their range.

2   Writing to people you know

When we write to people we know, we mostly use digital tools such as text messaging, email and social media. Although many of us still send physical cards for birthdays or other special events, few people now handwrite letters or holiday postcards – these are now perceived as old-fashioned modes of written communication. In a first language context, the people we know and write to might include family, friends and acquaintances. However, in a second language context, it is not usually the case that written communication with family takes place other than in a person's first language.

Functions, genres and patterns

Core rhetorical text functions can be found in written communication aimed at family, friends and acquaintances. For example, a post on social media about a person's exciting weekend will probably narrate events and describe experiences. However, interpersonal texts are more likely to involve a more specific micro function. Email and text messages may request, invite, suggest, offer, warn, give advice, etc. They often fulfil the same communicative purpose as spoken functional language and the expressions used are often very similar. For example, the invitation *Would you like to come to dinner on Friday night?* is appropriate in a conversation and as an invitation in a text message. However, it might be written using abbreviations and ellipsis, for example, *Wd u like 2 come 2 dinner Fri nite?* Crystal (2011) notes that writing with digital tools has resulted in a kind of blend of spoken and written language with its own characteristics.

Spoken language is usually negotiated across a series of turns between two (or more) speakers whereas written language is often one continuous text. We can see this illustrated in the following example – one spoken and one written text with the same communicative purpose:

Conversation
A: My parents are coming round tonight.
B: Nice.
A: Yeah, but I've got to clean my flat.
B: Not so nice.
A: Thing is – my vacuum cleaner is broken.
B: Oh dear.
A: Could I borrow yours?
B: How long will you need it for?
A: Just this afternoon.
B: Sure – that's fine.

Text message

My parents are coming tonight - got to clean up my flat. Just realised my vacuum cleaner is broken. Can I borrow yours? Only need it for the afternoon.

Biber and Conrad (2019) note that this kind of written communication does not necessarily take place in the same space and time. The lack of a shared physical and temporal context will sometimes require a degree of explicitness because there is often limited opportunity for the speech act to be negotiated and for misunderstanding to be repaired. In the example above, the writer outlines the situation, makes the request and signals the outcome of the request thereby taking into account all the information negotiated in the conversation. The production of written language is slower, and writers of electronic communication have the possibility of revising, editing and refining their message.

What is missing from the written text message above is the final reply. The recipient of the message could text back saying, for example, *No problem – get it now?* Texts and email messages are usually interactive in the way spoken language is, and a series of electronic exchanges between two people can seem like a spoken conversation (Biber & Conrad, 2019).

When looking at interpersonal texts from a genre perspective, a key consideration is the intended audience of the text. While the texts focused on in this chapter are aimed at people the writer knows, as suggested above, this can range from a close friend to someone who is no more than an acquaintance. With a friend, the writer can perhaps be more direct and less explicit because they can make assumptions about what their audience knows. Conversely, when the audience is an acquaintance who the writer does not know very well, they may need to craft their message more carefully.

There is a second consideration associated with the audience, particularly when making a written request. This concerns the degree of imposition the writer is making. If the request is the loan of a vacuum cleaner for an afternoon, there is probably little imposition. However, if the request is for a loan of a sum of money, the stakes are higher. The writer may choose their mode of communication more carefully, for example, an email rather than a text message. In addition, more considered and polite language is likely to be used, for example, *I was wondering if you could lend me $1,000 for a couple of months* rather than *Can you lend for $1,000 for a couple of months?*

A further genre marker associated with the relationship between the two writers is recognised by Biber and Conrad (2019). If the two people are communicating by email and they know each other very well, they usually do not bother with a salutation, or, if they do, it is likely to be just *hi*. If the communication builds into a back-and-forth chain of emails, salutations are almost never used, except in the first message. However, when the two correspondents do not know each other very well, they are more likely to use *Dear* + name. Whether they use a first name or a title + surname depends on the relationship between the two writers.

As in Chapter 1, many of the interpersonal modes of communication involve digital forms of communication, and these have their own genre conventions that may involve brevity of text, abbreviations and visual support, such as emojis. These genres often have specific formats and ready-made templates, and the writer merely needs to fill in the template with appropriate information. For example, there are numerous templates of invitations to weddings, birthday parties and such like. However, if someone wants to personalise these templates in some way, they will need to deploy their own writing skills.

A problem–solution discourse pattern is commonly found in interpersonal written communication. In the example request to borrow a vacuum cleaner above, the background concerns the parents' visit, the problem is the unclean apartment and the solution is the loan of the vacuum cleaner. Another discourse patten that can occur is general–particular. For example, an announcement often begins with a general piece of information (what the announcement is about) and then goes on to provide detail, as we can see in the following: *I've just sold my house for a million dollars!* (general) *It was only on the market for two weeks and 15 people turned up for the auction.* (particular).

Language

As indicated above, the functional nature of much of this interpersonal writing involves the use of functional exponents. Therefore, a writer needs to consider various ways of, for example, giving advice and choosing the most appropriate expressions for the intended audience of the written advice. This would also be the case when making a request involving a significant degree of imposition, as already mentioned. In order to add politeness, a writer is likely to use past tenses to make the request, e.g. *I was wondering if you could help me.* Cohesive devices, more specifically those that enumerate, can be used to structure the nature of a request or piece of written advice.

Some grammar points are linked to specific genres, for example, narrative tenses will be used when relating past events in a social media post, and the present perfect is used to make a newsworthy announcement. In a corpus study that compared personal email messages with emails between strangers and those written in the workplace, Biber and Conrad (2019) noted a greater frequency of activity verbs and time/place adverbs in personal email messages. They attributed this to the fact that the content of these messages typically focuses on everyday activities.

In the classroom

The kinds of texts focused on in this chapter are suitable for learners at lower levels. The function of many of the texts is likely to match spoken functional language that learners have studied. In some cases, it may be worth considering a writing activity that focuses on similar functional exponents as a means of consolidating spoken language. It is often possible to provide a classroom-based context for this language and to get students writing to each other or communicating as a class. IT resources can often facilitate this kind of communication between students. However, it is also useful to provide a range of contexts for interpersonal communication so that learners get practice addressing different audiences. A genre involving interpersonal written communication is sometimes included in English language exams at a lower level such as Cambridge B1 Preliminary.

References

Biber, D. & Conrad, S. (2019) *Register, Genre, and Style Second Edition.* Cambridge, Cambridge University Press.

Crystal, D. (2011) *Internet Linguistics: A Student Guide.* Abingdon, Routledge.

2.1 **Wrong prediction**

Outline	Students correct predictive text mistakes in text message invitations.
Level	Elementary (A2) and above
Time	20 minutes
Aim	To encourage checking of text messages; to practise accurate spelling.
Preparation	You will need to make a set of text messages with errors available for students (see *Example*). Ask students to bring their phones to class.

Procedure

1 Elicit what predictive text is and establish that it can create mistakes – show an example.

2 Individually, students read the text messages and correct them. Point out that abbreviations aren't mistakes. You could set a time limit or make it a race.

3 Check the answers with the class.

4 In pairs, students text an invitation to each other and include one predictive text mistake. They identify each other's mistake. (If any students don't have their phone with them, they can write the text message on a piece of paper.)

5 Do whole class feedback and share some of the example mistakes.

Example

1 **Liz** — Hi Jose I'm meet tongue Clara & Max for a coffee @ CocoCafé. Warm to join us?

2 **Dan** — We're all giving to the brand for a swim. Why not come too?

3 **Liz** — Wd u like to cinema for dinner tomorrow night at 7pm? My frowns Jian & Mei are coming too

4 **Leo** — Hi Mariel. Have to bit some new shoes. Want to come & help me chips?

Key
1 meet tongue – meeting; warm – want 2 giving – going; brand – beach 3 cinema – come; frowns – friends
4 bit – buy; chips – choose

Think further
Elicit from learners that predictive texts and spell checks don't correct all mistakes. Establish that it's a good idea to check texts and emails they send to other people – sometimes simple errors can make a message difficult to understand.

Notes

The example messages above would be suitable for an A2 and B1 class. If teaching a higher level, you could create messages with mistakes that involve lexis at a higher level. Make sure students are comfortable sharing their phone numbers with each other – let them decide who they want to pair up with for this activity. This activity can work well as a warm up task.

Rationale

While predictive texts and spell checks offer students a lot of support when they produce written language, they are not foolproof. Predictive text mistakes can sometimes be amusing – highlighting this can make this activity a light-hearted way of encouraging students to focus on language accuracy.

2.2 Opening and closing dictation

Outline	Students write email openings and closings for names that you dictate.
Level	Elementary to Pre-intermediate (A2–B1)
Time	10 minutes
Aim	To present and practise different email salutations and closings according to a writer's relationship to the recipient.
Preparation	Think of the full names of five or six people that your students will recognise and know how to spell.

Procedure

1   Show students the following ways of beginning email messages:

Dear + Mr/Mrs/Ms   Dear + Name   Hi/Hello

2   Elicit which you would use with: a friend (*Dear + Name, Hi/Hello*), a colleague (*Dear + Name* or *Hi/Hello* if you know them well), an acquaintance (*Dear + Name* or *Dear + Mr/Mrs/Ms* if you don't know them well).

3   Do the same with email closings: *Love* (good friends), *Best* (friends, colleagues, acquaintances), *Kind regards* (colleagues, acquaintances), *Sincerely* (formal acquaintances you don't know well at all).

4   Read out some example names, both the first name and surname. Also say one of the categories with name, e.g. *friend, acquaintance, your boss,* etc. Students write an appropriate opening and closing, e.g. for *Emma Smith – acquaintance* the correct opening and closing salutation could be: *Dear Emma, Kind regards,*

5   Do five or six examples and let students compare their answers.

6   Check answers with the whole class and allow for variation where appropriate.

Think further

Elicit from learners any differences between these ways of opening and closing email messages in English language culture and their own. Point out there can be variation in English speaking cultures or even in different companies.

Notes

This activity could also be done as a Pelmanism game. The openings and closing could be put on cards. Students turn them over and when an opening and a closing match, they win the cards.

Rationale

At lower levels, students are often unsure how to begin and close an email message correctly. Close friends and a colleague that you report to are usually straightforward. The challenge is often with people who the writer knows, but not very well. In general, English language culture is becoming more relaxed in these openings and closings and, as noted in *Think further*, it can vary from one culture and workplace to another.

2.3 Odd requests

Outline Students write a request text message with some information obscured.
Level Elementary (A2) and above
Time 30 minutes (20 minutes if step 7 is done as homework)
Aim To practise writing text requests; to provide practice in reason linkers.
Preparation You will need to make different request message prompts available, one for each student (see *Example*). If teaching in a classroom, you may want to write individual prompts on pieces of paper to hand out to students.

Procedure

1 Give each student a prompt sentence that describes a situation. Students must write a request in response to the prompt.

2 Give an example:
Prompt – *We're having a party on Saturday evening.*
Request – *Can I borrow your portable speakers?*

3 Students write their request and then swap it with another student. They must not show the prompt sentence.

4 Elicit or teach the reason linkers *because* and *so that*. Students have to add a reason to the request they received. For example: *Can I borrow your speakers* <u>because</u> *my speakers aren't very good.*

5 Students add their reason to the request and then swap back their writing. They then read the situation, request and reason to see if it makes sense.

6 In feedback, ask for some examples – both ones that work well and some that are amusing because they don't make sense. You could show the example answers at this point.

7 Students can then write their own request text message that includes a reason for the request. Encourage them to think of a real request they would like to make. Students could send their requests to each other in class.

Example
Prompts
1 I missed the lesson yesterday.
2 I forgot to go to the supermarket today.
3 My computer is broken.
4 My car is at the garage for a repair.

Example answers
1 I missed the lesson yesterday. Can I borrow your coursebook so that I can check my answers to the exercises?
2 I forgot to go to the supermarket today. Could I borrow some flour from you because I have to bake a cake?

3 My computer is broken. Could I use your laptop so that I can finish my assignment?
4 My car is at the garage for a repair. Can I get a ride to work with you because the bus service isn't very good here?

Think further
Elicit from students the structure of a simple request email: situation request reason. Point out it is more polite when writing a request – even with friends – to provide a reason rather than just sending a direct request.

Notes
At higher levels, the sentence prompts could be less specific, and students could be encouraged to think of imaginary requests, for example, *I'm very worried* or *I don't know what to do*. Also, other reason linkers could be added, e.g. *in order to, so as to*.

Rationale

In spoken language, requests are often negotiated by means of a series of exchanges in which the speaker outlines the situation and gives a reason. A written request should ideally cover at least some of this.

2.4 Written whispers

Outline	Students send a message around a group by both writing and whispering and then compare the outcome with the original.
Level	Elementary (A2) and above
Time	10 minutes
Aim	To practise accuracy in noting down and relaying messages; to revise previously taught language.
Preparation	Cut up and distribute pieces of paper for students to write the message on.

Procedure

1   The first student in a group of students writes a message that is going to be passed from student to student until it reaches the final student in that sequence. It could be a personal message, a request or something to do with the topic of the lesson.

2   Student 1 passes the written message to Student 2 who reads it. Student 2 does not show the written message, but whispers the message to Student 3 who writes down what they hear.

3   The passing of the message continues in this way: write → whisper → write until the message arrives to the final student. If it arrives as a whisper, the student writes the message down and then reads it out; if it arrives as a written message, the final student just reads out the message. This final message is compared against Student 1's original message.

Think further

Ask the students who had to write the message down whether it was easy to understand what their partner was saying. Elicit expressions students can use for taking messages, e.g. *I'm sorry could you say that again? Could you repeat the last part? Can you spell that word?*

Notes

If you have a very large group of learners, you could divide the class groups and have two or three message sequences going at the same time. If you are concerned about the first student not coming up with an appropriate message, you could provide one. This activity is more suited to a face-to-face learning context.

Rationale

This could be used as a warm up activity with the first student encouraged to write something that uses previously taught language. This activity is a variation of a common speaking activity, but incorporating writing should make the message more stable, although this is not always the case: the end result can be surprising. Asking the first student to think of a message for the final student provides the activity with a more focused sense of audience.

2.5 Invitation generator

Outline	Students study some formulaic language used for a range of different invitations, then write their own invitations.
Level	Elementary (A2)
Time	20 minutes
Aim	To give students practice writing formulaic invitations to celebrations.
Preparation	Think about some common expressions for the kinds of celebrations that are going to be of most interest or relevance to your students (see *Example*).

Procedure

1   Establish with students some different kinds of celebrations you can invite people to, such as a birthday party, wedding anniversary, etc.

2   Show students some typical invitation phrases for celebrations without saying what kind of event it is. Students guess the party/celebration.

3   Elicit from students what other information they may need to include on the invitation, for example, the place, date, time and a phone number or email address to reply to. Some invitations might include the nature of the celebration, e.g. *dinner* or *drinks and snacks*.

4   Teach students *RSVP* meaning *please reply* (an abbreviation of the French phrase *répondez s'il vous plaît*).

5   Students write an invitation to a celebration then swap with their partner to make sure all the necessary information is included and clear.

6   Ask students what different events they have read about in their partners' invitations.

Example

1   I'm turning 20! Come to my . . .
2   You're invited to a . . . in honour of . . .
3   Join us to celebrate our 5th . . .
4   A new home! Let's have a . . .

Key
1 birthday party, 2 graduation party, 3 wedding anniversary, 4 housewarming

Think further
Establish from students how formal or informal different celebrations are in their own culture. Point out how the wording of the invitation differs in relation to how formal or informal the event is. For example, *Come to my . . .* is less formal, but *Join us to celebrate . . .* is a little more formal.

Notes

The celebrations focused on in this activity should be tailored to your students' interests and needs. With a class that needs more support, you can limit the number of celebration categories to just one or two. The invitation written in class can be considered a first draft. If desired, students could do a final draft as homework on computer, adding different fonts and images. The final invitations could be printed out and displayed in the classroom or uploaded to a Learning Management System (LMS).

Rationale

Invitations to celebrations may also be sent in email messages (see Activity 2.8 below). However, they are frequently written and word processed using formulaic expressions like the examples below with key information in note form. Digital tools have allowed people to be more creative and make invitations more personalised, hence the suggestion that learners try this out as a homework activity.

2.6 Email revision

Outline	Students write an email requesting advice. They read and revise an example email focusing on paragraphing and cohesive devices.
Level	Pre-intermediate (B1) and above
Time	50 minutes (30 minutes if step 1 is done at home)
Aim	To provide practice in revising the organisation and cohesion of an email; to highlight the benefit of clear text organisation.
Preparation	Find an email asking for advice and rewrite it without paragraph divisions and cohesive devices (see *Example*). Make the email available to your students.

Procedure

1 Students write an email using this writing prompt:
   Write an email to someone you don't know very well. Ask this person for travel advice about a place you're going to on holiday.

2 Show students an example of a similar email without any paragraphing. Tell them this is a first draft and needs to be improved.

3 In pairs, students decide how they can improve the example using their own emails as comparison.

4 Check students' ideas and suggest how the email can be divided into paragraphs (see *Example answer*).

5 Then ask students to improve paragraph 3 by adding linking words or phrases. Again, check and suggest answers.

6 Students write a second draft of their email requesting advice.

Example

● ● ●   Reply   Forward

Dear Julia

I'm a friend of your cousin Andy. He gave me your email address and said you can probably help me with some travel advice. I hope that's OK. This summer I'm planning to go to Argentina for a holiday. Andy said you went there last year and know a lot about it. There are two things I'd like to ask you about. What is the best accommodation to stay at – a hostel or is it better to rent a room in a flat? I don't want to spend too much, and I would like something flexible. I'm going for two weeks. What are some interesting things to see and do? Should I stay in Buenos Aires, or should I try – and is there enough time – to see more of Argentina? Looking forward to hearing from you.

Thank you.

Emma

Example answer

Dear Julia

I'm a friend of your cousin Andy. He gave me your email address and said you can probably help me with some travel advice. I hope that's OK.

This summer I'm planning to go to Argentina for a holiday. Andy said you went there last year and know a lot about it.

There are two things I'd like to ask you about. **First of all**, what is the best accommodation to stay at – a hostel or is it better to rent a room in a flat? I don't want to spend too much, and I would like something flexible. **Secondly**, I'm going for two weeks. What are some interesting things to see and do? Should I stay in Buenos Aires, or should I try - and is there enough time - to see more of Argentina?

Looking forward to hearing from you. Thank you.

Emma

Think further

Establish with learners that dividing the email into paragraphs not only makes it more clearly organised, but it also makes it easier to read. Long stretches of language without divisions can make a text seem more complex and challenging to read.

Notes

The first draft of the email could be done as homework. In this case, ask any students who have been unable to do the homework to work with two other students who have their first drafts. At a higher level, the language can be made more complex by making it more polite and cautious, e.g. *I hope you don't mind me asking ... I was wondering if you could make any suggestions ....*

Rationale

Making clear to students that the example email is just a first draft is a way of normalising models that are not perfect – the implicit message being that models can be improved. Students may be inclined to look for grammar errors, so the emphasis on organisation is a reminder that these broader, textual issues are also important to bear in mind when revising a text.

2.7 Text and match

Outline	Students send each other text messages and match adjacency pairs such as an invitation and reply.
Level	Pre-intermediate (B1) and above
Time	20 minutes
Aim	To practise adjacent pair text messaging.
Preparation	Tell students to bring their phones to class and check that they don't mind sharing their phone numbers with each other. Prepare a set of text message questions and prompts as well as replies (see *Example*). You could include texts with local place names and businesses.

Procedure

1 Divide the class into two groups – A and B.

2 Give each student in Group A one text message with either a question or a prompt, and each student in Group B one of the replies.

3 Students in Group A randomly text different students in Group B with their message. Group B students reply with their answer if it matches a text from a student in Group A. If not, they should reply 'no'.

4 Check with the class to see if the message questions and prompts have received the correct replies.

5 Students in A and B pairs can then text each other with messages of their own.

Example

Questions/prompts	*Replies*
what's yr address?	6 Mill Lane
pls get biscuits @ supermarket	OK will pick up a packet
meet u @ the gym?	already doing a workout!
r u on yr way?	sorry running 5 mins late
how r things?	great thnks
meet 4 coffee in 10 mins?	sure see u at café
can u help with homework?	no problem – tell me
remember dentist appoint. this a.m.	don't worry haven't forgotten

Think further

Elicit any abbreviations that students didn't know about in the examples. Point out that these are not consistently used, and some people use 'you' as opposed to 'u'. The predictive text function on many phones has made it easier to use full words. Suggest that students go online and find further examples of abbreviations.

Notes

If you think students will be uncomfortable sharing their phone numbers with each other, this can be done as a mingle and match activity in the classroom. Students move around saying their message, and when they meet the correct partner, they show each other the wording of the text. They then work in pairs to rewrite the text language exchange as a dialogue adding language and giving the full spelling of words.

Rationale

Text messaging often takes place synchronously and is like a spoken conversation with adjacent pairs. A question or a prompt of some kind is sent with the expectation of a quick reply. This activity highlights the interactive nature of text messaging while, at the same time, providing learners with examples of abbreviated text speak.

2.8 Looking for politeness

Outline	Students improve an invitation email by using expressions and phrases that make it more polite and friendly.
Level	Elementary to Pre-intermediate (A2–B1)
Time	20–25 minutes
Aim	To provide students with key phrases that add politeness to an invitation email; to highlight the importance of a friendly tone in social written communication.
Preparation	You will need to prepare an invitation email which needs to be improved and make it available to each student (see *Example*).

Procedure

1 Students read an invitation email that lacks the correct tone. Establish the relationship between the sender and receiver. In the example, Ellie and Alex are ex-classmates and probably know each other quite well. While the email is clear, it could be more friendly.

2 Show students some expressions that can be used to make the email more polite and friendly (see *Example sentences*). Tell students some phrases have a similar meaning and they can choose which they prefer.

3 In pairs, students write a new version of the invitation using the phrases they have selected.

4 Pairs exchange versions, note any differences and explain their choices. You can also show students an example answer.

Example

●●●   Reply   Forward

Hi Alex

Next week everyone from our Italian class last year is going out for a pizza. Do you want to come?

We're going to 'La Margherita' in the High Street on Thursday at 7.00pm. Tell me if you can come. I want to book a table.

Ellie

Example sentences

How are you?

How's it going?

I hope you and your family are well.

I hope everything is OK with your job.

Would you like to come?

Would you like to join us?

I hope so because it's going to be fun to see everyone again.

It'll be great to see everyone again.

Can you let me know if you would like to come?
Can you tell me if you can come?
I'm going to book a table.
I plan to book a table.
I hope you can come.
I hope you can join us.

Example answer

● ● ●   Reply   Forward

Hi Alex

How are you? / How's it going? I hope you and your family are well. / I hope everything is OK with your job.

Next week everyone from our Italian class last year is going out for a pizza. *Would you like to come? / Would you like to join us? I hope so because it's going to be fun to see everyone again. / It'll be great to see everyone again.*

We're going to 'La Margherita' in the High Street on Thursday at 7.00pm. *Can you let me know if you would like to come? / Can you tell me if you can come? I'm going to book a table. / I plan to book a table.*

I hope you can come. / I hope you can join us.

Kind regards / Best wishes

Ellie

Think further

Ask students if personal emails to friends are similar or different to spoken language. Point out that making their written language like conversation makes it sound friendly.

Notes

It's important for students to understand how to make an invitation coherent. Having selected the phrases they wish to use, the activity encourages them to think carefully about where they can be placed in the message. This is something you could usefully focus on in feedback. A follow up task could be to get students to write their own invitation email for an event of some kind. This activity can also be adapted for other functions such as requests and asking for a favour or help.

Rationale

At lower levels, students' personal written communication in English can often seem a little abrupt, as they tend to focus on the key function and overlook the nature of their relationship to the recipient. This can mean that students fail to consider using language that aims to establish a good rapport with the person they're writing to. In the activity, students are offered two phrases as options, to underline that there are always choices a writer can make with language.

2.9 What's news?

Outline	Students interview each other to learn news about their partner and then improve an example blog post before writing one of their own.
Level	Pre-intermediate (B1) and above
Time	45 minutes
Aim	To provide practice writing a news blog post; to revise the way present perfect and simple past work together in news stories.
Preparation	You will need to make available to students a class news blog post (see *Example*). It will probably be more motivating to create a class news blog using your students' names. Make sure your version is like the example below and avoids using the present perfect to announce the news.

Procedure

1   Put some notes on the board about some recent news about yourself and tell the class about it using the present perfect, e.g. *I've been to / made / finished / won* .... Invite students to ask you some follow up questions.

2   Students work in groups, make notes and tell each other news about themselves. (This could also be done as a mingle activity.)

3   Get students to tell you what they learnt about each other and write a few examples of their news on the board in note form, e.g. *Elif – buy – new bicycle*.

4   Students read a class news blog post. They improve the grammar to make it sound more natural.

5   Check students' ideas and suggest that the first sentence about each student would sound more natural in the present perfect.

6   Students write a class news blog post about three or four students using information they collected in step 2. Suggest they go back to the students they talked to for more information if necessary. The writing could be done individually or in pairs.

7   If you have a class LMS, you can post the news, or it can be put up around the walls of the classroom.

Example

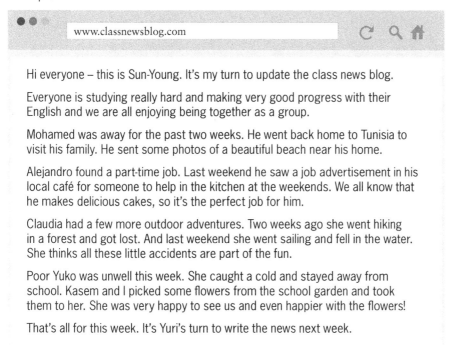

Hi everyone – this is Sun-Young. It's my turn to update the class news blog.

Everyone is studying really hard and making very good progress with their English and we are all enjoying being together as a group.

Mohamed was away for the past two weeks. He went back home to Tunisia to visit his family. He sent some photos of a beautiful beach near his home.

Alejandro found a part-time job. Last weekend he saw a job advertisement in his local café for someone to help in the kitchen at the weekends. We all know that he makes delicious cakes, so it's the perfect job for him.

Claudia had a few more outdoor adventures. Two weeks ago she went hiking in a forest and got lost. And last weekend she went sailing and fell in the water. She thinks all these little accidents are part of the fun.

Poor Yuko was unwell this week. She caught a cold and stayed away from school. Kasem and I picked some flowers from the school garden and took them to her. She was very happy to see us and even happier with the flowers!

That's all for this week. It's Yuri's turn to write the news next week.

Think further
Elicit the following grammar/discourse pattern: present perfect to announce the news followed by past simple to talk about details. Point out that use of the past simple to announce the news isn't always incorrect, but using the present perfect sounds more natural because it connects past events to the present and emphasises their relevance and news value.

Notes
If you have a learner group that you think would not be comfortable doing this activity, it could be reframed as a family news blog post and students could write about their extended family. Another possible variation is for students to invent outrageous news about themselves for a blog called *Crazy News*. There could be a prize for the student who comes up with the craziest news.

Rationale
The grammar point focused on in this activity is often focused on in the context of spoken language with a series of conversational exchanges between two speakers. *Think further* in this activity emphasises the idea of grammatical naturalness rather than accuracy in respect of tenses often used when giving news.

2.10 Yes and no reply

Outline	Students write invitations to each other with suggestions for things to do on a weekend stay, and then reply agreeing to one activity but not the other.
Level	Pre-intermediate (B1) and above
Time	60 minutes
Aim	To practise writing and replying to email invitations.
Preparation	If doing this as a paper-based activity, you could prepare pieces of paper to distribute for students to write on.

Procedure

1   Put students in pairs, but make sure they are not sitting close to each other. Show all students the following instruction:
    Write an email to your friend inviting them to stay with you this weekend. Suggest two fun things you can do with them while they are staying with you.

2   Students work alone and write the invitation to their partner.

3   Pairs swap their invitations. Show students a second instruction:
    Write a reply saying 'yes' to the invitation to stay and one of the suggested activities. Say 'no' to the other activity, and say why you don't want to / can't do it. Ask your friend a question about the weekend.

4   Students write their replies and then give it to their partner along with the original invitation.

5   Put students in new pairs (they can be sitting next to each other), so that they can tell each other about the weekend they have planned with their guest.

6   Ask the class as a whole whether they spoke to anyone who is planning to do a similar kind of activity at the weekend.

Think further

Ask students whether the replies they received to their invitation were polite and enthusiastic. Establish that replies accepting invitations need to show that you're looking forward to whatever you're invited to do. Elicit some appropriate expressions, e.g. *I'm really looking forward to ... I'd really love to ... Going to a concert sounds like fun ....*

Notes

A challenge for this activity is getting students to finish at more or less the same time. You will need to monitor students' progress carefully and, at a certain point, you might need to move on to the next step in the lesson even if not all students have finished. If students have online access and a digital device, the invitations can be emailed or sent via a messaging system. Alternatively, it can be done as a paper-based activity in the classroom.

Rationale

While it is not wholly authentic, this activity does provide learners with an audience and a sense of communicative purpose. Given that students will spend a large part of the lesson writing, the activity ends with a speaking activity to provide a change of focus.

Reference

This activity is based on a rubric in a sample writing test for the Cambridge B1 Preliminary examination.

Cambridge University Press & Assessment (2022) *Cambridge B1 Preliminary format* Available at: www.cambridgeenglish.org/exams-and-tests/preliminary/exam-format/ [Accessed September 2022]

2.11 Language problem

Outline	Students order an email asking for advice to a problem–solution pattern, before writing a similar email of their own.
Level	Pre-intermediate (B1) and above
Time	30 minutes (10 minutes if step 4 is done as homework)
Aim	To provide practice writing an email that requests help and to highlight problem–solution patterning.
Preparation	You will need to make an email for reordering available for your students (see *Example*). If you have a monolingual first language class, you could create a version of the email that refers to your students' first language and outlines typical needs of your learner group.

Procedure

1 Students read an email asking for advice with the order of three main paragraphs (1–3) scrambled. In pairs, they decide the correct order.

2 Check answers with the class.

3 Elicit from students a coherent order for the information:

situation (para. 3) → problem (para. 2) → solution (para. 1)

4 Students then write an email requesting help with their English language learning following the same problem–solution patterning. They can write to you or another fluent English speaker they know.

Example

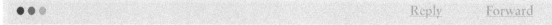

Dear Aldo

I'm getting in touch to ask for help with my Italian language learning.

¹Maybe one answer to my problem is to study more vocabulary so there are more words I can use for a wider range of topics. However, I still have to put the words together so they make sense, and that isn't always easy. Do you think this is a good idea or have you got any other ideas or suggestions?

²The trouble is that I always feel like I'm saying the same old things and having the same conversation. I'd like to be able to talk about different topics and have more interesting conversations.

³I've been studying Italian for about three years. I can usually survive quite well when I go to Italy on holiday. For example, I can have simple conversations with people in cafes and restaurants. Italians have told me that my grammar is OK and they can understand my pronunciation.

I'm looking forward to hearing from you.

Kind regards

Erica

Think further
Elicit from students how easy or difficult it was to understand the example email on first reading. Establish the idea that unclear organisation information of texts can make them difficult to understand even if all the grammar is correct.

Notes
This activity could also be used for requests that follow problem–solution patterning, e.g. for someone wishing to borrow an item of clothing because they've been invited to an important event. Another possible functional email following a specific structure is for an apology: *apology → excuse → promise*.

Rationale
Problem–solution patterning is often associated with business reports and memos. This activity aims to show it also underpins less formal written communication. It also emphasises to students that clear organisation of written text plays an important role in their communicative effectiveness.

2.12 Best thanks

Outline	Students evaluate two 'thank you' emails to determine an appropriate length and style, before writing one of their own.
Level	Pre-intermediate (B1) and above
Time	30 minutes (15 minutes if step 5 is done as homework)
Aim	To establish an appropriate level of detail in a thank you email.
Preparation	You will need to make available to half the students one 'thank you' email and to the other half of students a different 'thank you' email (see *Example*). You could include an event or situation that is relevant to your learner group.

Procedure

1 In two groups, students read two different 'thank you' emails. Group A students have to unscramble their email. Group B students read theirs to understand the reason for the email.

2 In the two groups, students discuss whether they think this was a good email or not according to the following criteria: *too much/little information, polite/impolite.*

3 In A and B pairs, students tell each other about their emails and their evaluation of them.

4 Check students' ideas and establish that the first email is too brief and is a little impolite, while the second is too detailed and includes unnecessary information.

5 Students write their own 'thank you' email. You can think of a basis for the email relevant for your learner group, or provide a rubric, such as: *Write a thank you email to a friend who gave you some free movie tickets.* This step could be done as homework.

Example
Group A

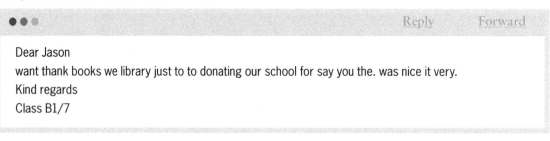

Reply   Forward

Dear Jason
want thank books we library just to to donating our school for say you the. was nice it very.
Kind regards
Class B1/7

Group B

Reply   Forward

Dear Olivia

It was very nice to meet you last Friday. We would like to thank you very much for coming to visit our class and giving a talk on your work as a music producer.

First of all, we would like to say that we don't have a lot of opportunities to meet and talk to native speakers of English. After you finished talking, we all felt a bit shy and embarrassed about saying anything. But you have a really friendly personality, and this made us feel much more relaxed and we felt we could ask you almost anything.

Secondly, it was really interesting to learn about how pop songs are produced. We didn't know anything about it. For example, the way you talked about some singers who just go into the studio and start singing a melody with no words was really surprising. We thought you needed to write everything down.

It was also interesting to find out a few stories about the way some pop stars behave. We thought they would all be quite arrogant and sure of themselves. We didn't realise that many stars just do what the producer asks them to do.

Anyway, we hope you enjoy the rest of your time in our country. And if you ever come back, we would love to meet you again. So, thank you very, very much. We are very grateful, and we really appreciated your visit.

Kind regards

Class B1/7

Key
Group A email unscrambled: We just want to say thank you for donating the books to our school library. It was very nice.

Think further
Establish with learners that including one piece of specific information about the subject of the thank you email is enough. For example, in the example email for Group B, the writer only needed to talk about one idea – the way pop songs are produced. Elicit that this is because in English-speaking culture, too much information can make a thank you email boring and perhaps seem insincere.

Notes
In the example, Group A's email is scrambled so it takes students more time to read and gives Group B enough time to read their longer email. With a class that needs a lot more support, you may want to add a third example email that gets the balance right and acts as a model. However, the combination of peer feedback and the inappropriate examples should provide enough guidance for most learner groups.

Rationale

This activity keeps students' focus specifically on the content – this is often an assessment criterion for evaluating written work. Students' perception of content is often linked to an idea of 'more is better' (which is not always the case). Clearly, though, there is a cultural dimension to this. If you are teaching in a context where the cultural norms for a thank you letter or email are different, you can compare and contrast these with the ideas in *Think further*.

2.13 Cut the announcement

Outline	In teams, students have a competition to edit tweets to reduce the character count.
Level	Intermediate to Upper intermediate (B1+–B2)
Time	30 minutes
Aim	To practise editing tweets to reduce character count.
Preparation	Find an online tweet character counter to direct your students to. Ask them to bring their phones to class to edit example tweets. You will need to make available to students some overlong tweets (see *Example*).

Procedure

1   Show students tweet 1. Explain that at 304 characters (including spaces) it exceeds the 280-character limit and requires trimming. Elicit suggestions from the whole class. Continue until the tweet is as short as possible.

2   Establish with students ways of reducing the character count, e.g. by cutting unnecessary details, omitting the subject pronoun, using a dash (–) or ampersand (&) instead of 'and', using contractions. But remind them that things like exclamation marks or emojis often remain because they show feeling.

3   Students read three more tweets and first guess whether the character is about right (see examples 2–4 below) – in all cases, they exceed the 280-character limit.

4   Students then work in small groups, editing the three tweets (ideally on their phones) and using an online character count tool to help them.

5   Set a time limit of six minutes, and groups compete to reduce the character count in each of the three tweets as much as possible, but need to ensure that the tweets still make sense.

6   When the time is up, each group reads out their tweets and states the number of characters used. The winner is the group with the fewest total number of characters, provided the tweet still makes sense. Students can then compare their tweets with example answers.

Example

TeamEnglish @TeamEnglish11

We are really happy to tell you all that our team has won the final match of the local championship with four wins from seven games. This was a fantastic victory! Everyone in the team played their very best. This means we will now go to the national finals next month. We are already training very hard.

2

Will&Elise @Will&Elise

We are really excited to announce that we are going to get married next year! We did not propose or anything – we just decided together that this was a great thing to do. There is no date for the wedding yet, but we just wanted to let you know we have made the big decision and we are really, really happy about it!

♡ 15   ◯ 2

3

Prospect English @ClassB2 Prospect English

We are all really pleased to welcome a new student to our class today. Her name is Indah and she comes from Indonesia. This means we now have a total of 15 students in our class. Indah is really friendly and we know that everyone is very happy to have her in our class. We think we are a friendly group so we hope Indah enjoys her time studying with us.

♡ 12   ◯ 5

4

Monica @MonicaS

I have just heard from the Marketing Manager of Product Solutions and I have got the job that I applied for as Marketing Co-ordinator in their online sales team. He told me more than 70 people applied for the job so I feel really lucky. I start at the beginning of next month and I can't wait. I am thrilled.

♡ 10   ◯ 2

Example answers

1

TeamEnglish @TeamEnglish11

Really happy to tell you we've won final match of local championship - 4/7 wins. Fantastic victory! Everyone played their best. We now go to national finals next month. Already training hard. (192 characters)

♡ 12   ◯ 3

2

Will&Elise @Will&Elise

Really excited to announce we're getting married next year! Decided together this was a great thing to do. No date for the wedding – just wanted to let you know & we're really happy about it! (193 characters)

♡ 15   ◯ 2

3

Prospect English @ClassB2 Prospect English

Really pleased to welcome a new student to our class today - Indah from Indonesia. We now have 15 students. Indah's really friendly & everyone's very happy she's in our class. We're a friendly group & hope Indah enjoys her time with us. (235 characters)

♡ 12   ⃝ 5

4

Monica @MonicaS

Just heard from the Marketing Manager Product Solutions - I've got the job - Marketing Co-ordinator. More than 70 people applied - feel really lucky. Start beginning of next month - can't wait. I'm thrilled! (208 characters)

♡ 10   ⃝ 2

Think further

Elicit from students that including feeling or emotion is usually more important in a tweet rather than a lot of information. Establish that this approach is more likely to attract Twitter followers.

Notes

With a lower-level group, you could provide more simple tweet examples and ask them to work on just one or two tweets.

Rationale

Tweets are a very specific genre and for learners one of the most challenging aspects of writing a tweet is knowing what can be left out and what must be included without the message losing sense. This activity gives practice in making those decisions. While the time limit adds a competitive element to the activity, it also represents what is often the real-time nature of writing tweets.

2.14 Prompted request

Outline	Students write an email request from prompts and then evaluate a partner's work before reading a sample answer.
Level	Intermediate (B1+) and above
Time	30–40 minutes
Aim	To practise writing an email for a significant request.
Preparation	Write a prompt and sample email request (see *Example*) appropriate for your students.

Procedure

1   Show students the following writing prompt:
Write an email asking to borrow a friend's car and give a reason. Say what you can do to thank your friend.

2   Students write the email.

3   In pairs, students exchange emails. They read and evaluate each other's writing based on the following questions:
Is the reason for the request detailed and clear?
Is the request specific and polite?

4   Students give each other feedback and then revise their own emails as necessary.

5   Show students an example answer and ask them what the differences are between their emails and the example.

6   For homework, students write another request email, for example, asking them to look after a pet while away at the weekend.

Example

Hi Rosie

This weekend my parents are coming here for a visit. They arrive by plane on Saturday. My mother has been unwell and I'd like to make their arrival as easy as possible. I think catching the bus from the airport to the centre of town could be tiring for her.

I was wondering if it would be possible to borrow your car on Saturday afternoon so that I can go to the airport and collect my parents. I would only need it for about three hours and I promise to return the car with a full tank of petrol.

If you need your car or it's not possible, that's fine, I understand.

Kind regards

Per

Think further
Elicit with learners the very polite nature of the request in the sample answer. Establish that while the email is to a friend, the language is more formal. The writer knows the request is significant and wants to show this to the reader, and therefore uses more polite language than they usually would.

Notes
For a class that needs more support, you could show the sample answer below as a model for a polite request email. Analyse it together, point out any useful language and then get students to write the email in class.

Rationale

Fluent users of English vary the level of formality of a request depending on how well they know the person they are communicating with. However, they also vary it in line with the degree of imposition involved with the request. This activity aims to highlight this point. It also aims to encourage evaluation of language use, although this is done in terms of its functional appropriateness rather than a focus on grammar.

2.15 Varied advice

Outline	Students add appropriate expressions to an email giving advice.
Level	Upper intermediate (B2) and above
Time	40 minutes (20 minutes if step 6 is done as homework)
Aim	To practise using a range of advice structures to soften the tone of and add interest to an advice email.
Preparation	You will need to prepare an advice email which lacks appropriate advice expressions and make it available for your students (see *Example*).

Procedure

1   Ask students to read an email giving advice and decide whether the tone is appropriate. (The only advice structure used in the example email is the imperative – highlighted in bold – so it comes across as quite abrupt.)

2   Tell students they need to amend the email and try to soften the tone by replacing the imperative forms with other more appropriate advice structures. Don't show the example structures below the text at this stage. Students should come up with their own examples.

3   In pairs, students compare their changes and give feedback to each other on the tone of the revision.

4   Show students a range of different advice structures (see examples below). Students should note which expressions – if any – they have already used.

5   Students do a second revision of their email using some of the suggested structures. If you think it would be helpful, they could then compare their email with a model answer.

6   Students write an advice email on a topic they are familiar with, e.g. a sport, a hobby, learning to do something, a job. This could be set as homework.

Example

● ● ●   Reply   Forward

Hi Julie

It was nice to hear from you. I'm pleased your studies have gone well this year. Good luck with your final exams – I'm sure you'll do well.

You asked about working as a nanotechnologist and what advice I could give. Overall, it's a fascinating area of work, and I find it really rewarding. However, it's not an easy field to get into.

Your biochemistry degree is definitely relevant, but it's only a start, so **continue** studying and do a Masters and then probably a PhD. There are now postgraduate courses in nanotechnology, so **consider** one of these. Also, bear in mind that nanotechnology incorporates engineering and computer science, so **be** flexible.

A nanotechnologist can either work in an academic context doing research or you can work in industry where you can use your knowledge and skills in a more practical way. In either case, it's not the kind of job where you work a regular 37-hour week. If that's what you'd like, then **don't follow** a career in nanotechnology!

Consider now whether you want to continue studying or not. **Look** in detail at a range of Masters programmes in biochemistry as well as nanotechnology. And **think** about whether you are more interested in the academic or the more practical side of nanotechnology.

Once you've done this, feel free to come back to me with more specific questions.

Kind regards

Mohamed

Advice structures

I would advise against	you'll need to	you should
my advice would be to	it helps to	I'd suggest you
it would probably be useful to	it's a good idea to	if I were you, I'd

Model answer

● ● ●   <u>Reply</u>   <u>Forward</u>

Hi Julie

It was nice to hear from you. I'm pleased your studies have gone well this year. Good luck with your final exams – I'm sure you'll do well.

You asked about working as a nanotechnologist and what advice I could give. Overall, it's a fascinating area of work, and I find it really rewarding. However, it's not an easy field to get into.

Your biochemistry degree is definitely relevant, but it's only a start, so you'll need to continue studying and do a Masters and then probably a PhD. There are now postgraduate courses in nanotechnology, so I'd suggest you consider one of these. Also, bear in mind that nanotechnology incorporates engineering and computer science, so it helps to be flexible.

A nanotechnologist can either work in an academic context doing research or you can work in industry where you can use your knowledge and skills in a more practical way. In either case, it's not the kind of job where you work a regular 37-hour week. If that's what you'd like, then I would advise against following a career in nanotechnology!

I think the key thing you need to consider now is whether you want to continue studying or not. If I were you, I'd look in detail at a range of Masters programmes in biochemistry as well as nanotechnology. And it would probably be useful to think about whether you are more interested in the academic or more practical side of nanotechnology.

Once you've done this, feel free to come back to me with more specific questions.

Kind regards

Mohamed

Think further

Elicit from students what the effect of using a range of advice structures has – it softens the tone of the email and makes it more interesting to read. Also point out that if the piece of writing were being assessed for an exam, using a variety of structures is evidence of grammatical range – a common criterion in the assessment of writing.

Notes

This lesson could be delivered using a more traditional text-based presentation, particularly if you feel students need more support. Students could be given both versions of the email to compare and then underline the advice structures used in the example answer. They could then go on to write their own email.

Rationale

At higher levels, students often need (and want) to begin using a greater variety of language, both grammatical structures as well as vocabulary. The methodological approach in this activity encourages students to use their own language resources before being provided with a range of expressions.

3 Writing to share ideas and opinions

The desire to share our ideas and opinions in writing can be both a natural and spontaneous impulse to communicate with people we know, or it can be a more measured wish that aims to communicate with, perhaps, a wider audience. We are likely to use different tools for each form of communication. A sudden need to tell friends and family about a great meal you have just eaten is most likely to be done via social media most suitable for a short message. However, a carefully reasoned contribution to a public debate might take the form of a blog post or an email (perhaps even a letter) to the editor of a newspaper that has been drafted and revised before being sent. Communicating our ideas and opinions, things that we know or believe, often involves the sharing of new information that we have accessed. It can also involve an attempt to persuade the reader – directly or indirectly – to align to our point of view. This is what is commonly called discursive writing: it typically considers several sides of an argument, albeit from a subjective, even opinionated, position (Content Writers Australia, 2021). It is also known as 'argumentation' (Grabe & Kaplan, 1996: p.139) or simply 'argument – stating your case' (Derewianka, 1990, cited in Grabe & Kaplan, 1996: p.136).

Functions, genres and patterns

Hyland (2019) indicates that text functions can occur at a primary and secondary level. The primary function of discursive texts is to persuade the reader of a particular opinion or point of view, but other functions will be embedded within the text. For example, an essay on the negative effects of climate change is likely to try to encourage readers to take action to reduce their carbon footprint. In doing so, it will describe different causes of climate change and the ensuing effects while reporting on a series of activities that either increase or inhibit the emission of greenhouse gases. A book review may either try to persuade or dissuade the reader to read the book, but will also probably outline at least part of the plot. And similarly, a blog that discusses current events or issues will doubtless include some reporting on what has taken place.

Writers can share their ideas and opinions across a range of genres, from a short tweet to a long article in a newspaper or magazine. While some genres share similarities to those focused on in Chapter 2, the broader aim in this chapter is less concerned with developing interpersonal relationships and more focused on conveying information (Biber & Conrad, 2019). While it could be argued that, in many cases, the writer knows the person or people they are addressing and are attempting to maintain an existing relationship, this is not the primary aim of this type of written communication.

The wide variety of genres used in opinion-based writing means attention needs to be paid to specific genre conventions. For example, a tweet has to adhere to a character count and the language needs to be succinct and direct, and often there is the expectation it will be humorous or witty. Crystal (2011) conducted a search of the Twitter database and noted that the largest category comprises tweets that give an opinion and often also include an aphorism or quotation. Conversely, a cause and effect essay can follow either a block structure which discusses causes, and then goes on to discuss effects, or a chain structure where different causes and effects are discussed in turn (Hyland, 2019).

The different genres are aimed at different audiences. Someone who writes an online review of a restaurant is likely to be thinking about future diners at the restaurant as well as the owners and staff working there. In writing their review, they are likely to consider everything that readers will be interested in, for example, the ambience, the food and the service. A student writing an essay in an examination setting will be thinking about the examiner of their written work and any formal expectations in terms of content and language that they need to include in their essay. Clearly then, writers who want to share their ideas and opinions need to take into consideration and adhere to genre conventions and reader expectations.

Puschmann (2013) contrasts two approaches to blogging: a topic-centric style and an author-centric style. A topic-centric blog tends to deal with broader concepts related to the external world. The language style usually tends to be formal, and the text is usually edited to some degree before it is posted online. Conversely, author-centric blogs usually focus on the writer's personal world and their daily experiences. The language here is less formal and often similar to spoken language because the writing tends to follow the writer's thinking and is more spontaneous. While there is a persuasive function in both approaches to blogging, a topic-centric blogger is more likely to try to inform their readers. By contrast, an author-centric blogger often actively reflects on the events they are writing about and tries to make sense of them. As a result, the effort to persuade is underpinned by a process of working things out as the blogger writes.

All three main discourse patterns, problem–solution, claim–counterclaim and general–particular, can be found in opinion-based texts (McCarthy, 1991). A political blogger might pose the question 'What's wrong with our city council?' and then provide a solution. An essay that aims to provide a balanced view of a topic such as government subsidy of sport might structure each paragraph according to a claim–counterclaim pattern. Finally, it is common to structure a paragraph according to a general–particular pattern, with the first sentence of the paragraph (often referred to as the topic sentence) outlining the main idea of the paragraph which is then discussed in more detail. As McCarthy (1991) indicates, these patterns co-occur in texts and can be embedded within one another.

Language

The range of genres that can be employed to share ideas and opinions means that there is also a wide variety of language that can be used. This can range from evaluative adjectives to complex sentences. Less formal written genres such as a personal blog or online forum are likely to use phrases for expressing opinions that are also used in spoken language, for example, *in my opinion . . . , I think that . . . .* In an academic essay, there is more likely to be less personal language, and expressions such as *It is generally agreed that . . .* are used to signal a point of view. These phrases that express an opinion are often used together with stance adverbials that give an indication of the writer's judgement of a proposition. In less formal texts, these adverbials are similar to those used in spoken language, for example, *honestly, obviously, no doubt* (Carter & McCarthy, 2006). In more formal genres, example stance adverbials are *apparently, arguably, evidently* (Carter & McCarthy, 2006). In a study that contrasted news reports with news editorials, Biber and Conrad (2019) state that there is a higher frequency of modals in opinion-based editorials compared to reports. They also note a higher incidence of hypothetical conditionals when speculating about future events and possible courses of action associated with the topic under discussion.

A key feature of neutral and more formal opinion-based writing is the use of cohesive devices. This includes pronouns that refer back and forward not just to nouns but also to ideas and concepts that might have been elaborated across a series of sentences. When *This* is used at the beginning of a paragraph, for example, it might be referring back to all the ideas discussed in a previous paragraph. Another key feature of cohesion is the use of linking adverbs and phrases. As such, the following words and phrases can be used to signal a cause and effect relationship between two propositions: *therefore, consequently, as a result, because, since, otherwise.* Alternatively, words and phrases that enumerate such as *first of all, secondly, finally,* etc. can be used to list a series of points. Some linkers are used in specific places within a text, for example, *in conclusion, to sum up, in summary* are used to sum up points previously made. Many linkers join two clauses together: *although* indicates a concessive relationship between two ideas, but it also links a main and subordinate clause. This joining of two clauses means that in neutral and more formal opinion-based writing, there is a greater use of complex sentences.

In the classroom

Opinion-based writing often has a prominent focus in English language classrooms because many students are following a course leading to an examination that requires students to write a discursive (discussion) essay. Cambridge English Qualifications and IELTS, for example, both include a discursive essay in the writing paper. Similarly, many general English programmes lead to EAP programmes and teachers see the value in beginning to focus on essay writing skills before learners join the EAP course. Teachers may well begin by focusing on individual paragraphs that outline an idea or express a point of view, rather than a complete essay.

Relative to thirty or more years ago, it is now possible for learners to share their ideas and opinions in English with a very wide audience through various forms of online delivery. This suggests a real need for teachers to help students develop critical tools so that they understand how their ideas might be perceived and what real-world feedback and reactions they can expect. The different genres associated with online delivery are often more straightforward in terms of the linguistic resources that learners will need to deploy, but a thorough focus on these genres is important for learners to understand English language conventions and cultural norms associated with such texts.

References

Biber, D. & Conrad, S. (2019) *Register, Genre, and Style Second Edition*. Cambridge, Cambridge University Press.

Carter, R & McCarthy, M. (2006) *Cambridge Grammar of English*. Cambridge, Cambridge University Press.

Crystal, D. (2011) *Internet Linguistics: A Student Guide*. Abingdon, Routledge.

Derewianka, B. (1990) *Exploring how texts work*. Rozelle, NSW: Primary English Teaching Association.

Grabe, W. & Kaplan, R. B. (1996) *Theory and practice of writing: an applied linguistic perspective.* New York, Longman.

Hyland, K. (2019) *Second Language Writing Second Edition.* Cambridge, Cambridge University Press.

McCarthy, M. (1991) *Discourse Analysis for Language Teachers.* Cambridge, Cambridge University Press.

Puschmann, C. (2013) Blogging. In: Herring, S. C., Stein, D. & Virtanen, T. (Eds.) *Pragmatics of Computer-Mediated Communication.* Berlin/Boston, Walter de Gruyter GmbH.

Content Writers Australia. (2021) *What is discursive writing?* Available from: www.contentwriters. com.au/blog/what-is-discursive-writing/#:~:text=%20There%20are%20six%20things%20 that%20typically%20make,has%20more%20than%20one%20argument.%20This...%20 More%20 [Accessed 23rd January 2022].

3.1 Tweet scramble

Outline	Students unscramble and order phrases from two opinion tweets then write one of their own.
Level	Elementary (A2) and above
Time	20 minutes
Aim	To present and practise example phrases and a structure for an opinion-based tweet.
Preparation	You will need to make scrambled tweets on two different topics available to students (see *Example*). These could be based on topics your students are familiar with.

Procedure

1   Show students the phrases from two simple opinion tweets about different topics.

2   Students unscramble the phrases and order them within a time limit (or you could make it a race to finish first).

3   Check answers with the whole class.

4   Ask students to name some things that they like and could tweet about, e.g. some new music, online game, gadget. Elicit different adjectives that can be used to describe these things.

5   Students write a tweet about an object or an activity that they like. They can send the tweet or just share with their classmates as a text message.

Example
[1]She's great in it.   [2]Try it soon!   [3]Really love the new film with Scarlett Johansson.
[4]The food is delicious.   [5]Go see it now!   [6]New Vietnamese restaurant Can Tho Café is fantastic.

Key
film = 3, 1, 5; restaurant = 6, 4, 2

Think further
Elicit from students the structure of an opinion tweet: general opinion → detailed opinion → recommendation. Point out that an imperative works well for the recommendation.

Notes
A way of making this activity more difficult is by having three or even four scrambled tweets. If teaching in a face-to-face context, the phrases could be placed around the room and students find, copy and order the two tweets. This could be done in pairs as a race. The language in the example tweets is suitable for a lower-level class, but the phrases can easily be changed to suit a higher-level class, e.g. *Am crazy about . . . Absolutely brilliant . . . Get there now.*

Rationale

Tweets are a user-friendly genre for lower-level students. The language can be kept simple and it's a way for students to begin communicating their opinions with a real audience. This activity provides some set phrases to get students started but also presents an example structure for the tweet, as outlined in *Think further*.

3.2 Review sentences

Outline	Students have a competition dividing up two reviews into sentences.
Level	Elementary (A2) and above
Time	15 minutes
Aim	To practise sentence punctuation of texts.
Preparation	You will need to make available to students an unpunctuated text of two reviews and model answer correctly punctuated (see *Example*).

Procedure

1 Show students the unpunctuated text and explain that they need to divide it into sentences and add punctuation to make two separate reviews.

2 Students work in teams of three or four with one secretary who writes or types for the team.

3 The teams race to divide up the two reviews into sentences.

4 The winner is the first group to finish with the most accurate version.

5 Show students the model answer, but accept alternatives, for example, the last two sentences of the second review in the example could be joined by a dash.

Example

> this is a very convenient hotel because it's close to all the most important tourist attractions the beds are very comfortable and the bathroom is really big the only problem was that the internet was really slow and it was almost impossible to do anything online the big rooms in this hotel are wonderful I also loved the views of the sea from the balcony the food was delicious and they have a beautiful swimming pool unfortunately the staff are not very friendly or helpful this was the one thing that wasn't perfect about our stay

Model answer

This is a very convenient hotel because it's close to all the most important tourist attractions. The beds are very comfortable, and the bathroom is really big. The only problem was that the internet was really slow, and it was almost impossible to do anything online.

The big rooms in this hotel are wonderful. I also loved the views of the sea from the balcony. The food was delicious, and they have a beautiful swimming pool. Unfortunately, the staff are not very friendly or helpful. This was the one thing that wasn't perfect about our stay.

Think further

Point to the sentences with the conjunctions *and* and *because*. Elicit which sentences can have a comma. Establish that a comma also comes after *Unfortunately* in the second review.

Notes

This activity is very adaptable for higher levels. A greater range of vocabulary, in particular adjectives, can be used and more complex sentences that include subordination can be included, e.g. *Despite the great amenities, the staff were unfriendly to the point of being rude.*

Rationale

This activity gives students practice in core punctuation. It demonstrates the challenge of making sense of text that is not clearly punctuated. Using a comma before *and* when it heads a new clause is sometimes seen as optional, and this shows how sometimes punctuation can involve making choices. The key point is that punctuation should make texts easier to understand.

3.3 Contrast research

Outline	Students research key linkers of contrast and concession in both *English Vocabulary Profile* and *English Grammar Profile* and compare notes to write sentences.
Level	Pre-intermediate to Upper intermediate (B1–B2)
Time	30 minutes
Aim	To practise linking ideas using contrast/concession linkers; to develop independent study skills using *English Profile*.
Preparation	Research the *English Profile* links suggested below to make sure you are familiar with the content. Ask students to bring digital devices to class to carry out online research. Make available to students some research notes (see *Example*). You could link the notes to a topic your students have been studying.

Procedure

1   Provide students with some research notes to develop into sentences that use subordination to make a contrast (see examples below).

2   Elicit from students the linking words *although, even though, despite* that they will use in the sentences.

3   Students work in two groups, A and B, and do research on these three linkers looking at rules and examples provided.

4   Group A goes to *English Vocabulary Online* www.englishprofile.org/wordlists/evp–. To see details and examples, they must click on the target word in the search result and 'Full view' on the top right of the page.

5   Group B goes to *English Grammar Profile Online* www.englishprofile.org/english-grammar-profile/egp-online. They should first search for a word, and then click on the 'Details' button on the right-hand side of the screen.

6   Students then work in A and B pairs and share the information they've learnt. They turn the notes into complete sentences using the linkers.

7   Check answers with the class. See the sample answers below, but accept variations.

Example

1   you think economics is not interesting – everyone should know how to manage money

2   high cost of living – many people want to live in Switzerland

3   having good qualifications is important – many successful people in business have not been to university

4   many people do not like paying taxes – they still think a good public health service is important

5   low salary – charity work is interesting and motivating

Sample answers

1   Even though you think economics is not interesting, everyone should know how to manage money.

2   Despite the high cost of living, many people want to live in Switzerland.

3   Having good qualifications is important although many successful people in business have never been to university.

4   Even though many people do not like paying taxes, they still think a good public health service is important.

5   Despite the low salary, charity work is interesting and rewarding.

Think further

Ask learners what they found most useful to read – the rules or the examples. Establish that both are important, and it is usually a good idea to check more than one source as they did with this activity.

Notes

English Profile also includes information on higher level ways of using these linkers, for example, the use of non-finite clauses after *although* (*Although feeling tired, he decided to go to the party*). The idea can be used to research different linkers associated with different areas of meaning, for example, cause and effect and comparison.

> **Rationale**
>
> Contrast/concession linkers of this nature are frequently used in opinion-based writing. A key focus of this activity is demonstrating *English Profile* to learners and alerting them to the fact it is a useful tool for independent study.

References

Cambridge University Press (2015) *English Vocabulary Profile Online – British English* Available at: www.englishprofile.org/wordlists/evp [Accessed September 2022]

Cambridge University Press (2015) *English Grammar Profile Online* Available at: www.englishprofile.org/english-grammar-profile/egp-online [Accessed September 2022]

3.4 Ongoing discussion

Outline	Students add successive replies to an online forum, agreeing or disagreeing with the post or the previous contributor.
Level	Pre-intermediate (B1) and above
Time	25 minutes
Aim	To practise language of agreement and disagreement in online discussion boards; to highlight simple cohesion and coherence in a chain of discussion board postings.
Preparation	You will need to make available for students the first post and replies on a discussion board (see *Example*). If doing the activity in a classroom, it may pay to have pieces of paper ready for students to write their replies on.

Procedure

1 Students read the first post of an opinion discussion board and tell their partner if they agree or disagree with it (see the example below).

2 Students read follow up posts and put them in a logical order.

3 Check answers with the class.

4 Students highlight expressions that show agreement and disagreement.

5 Elicit from students some other similar unwritten social rules and how these are sometimes broken.

6 Students choose a topic and write their opinion giving an example in support.

7 Students pass their initial opinion post to another student. The second student reads and adds a reply, either agreeing or disagreeing. Continue this for about five turns. The student who wrote the initial post on the forum can then read the replies and see how many were in agreement.

8 In pairs, students tell each other what they think is the most interesting reaction to their initial post.

Example

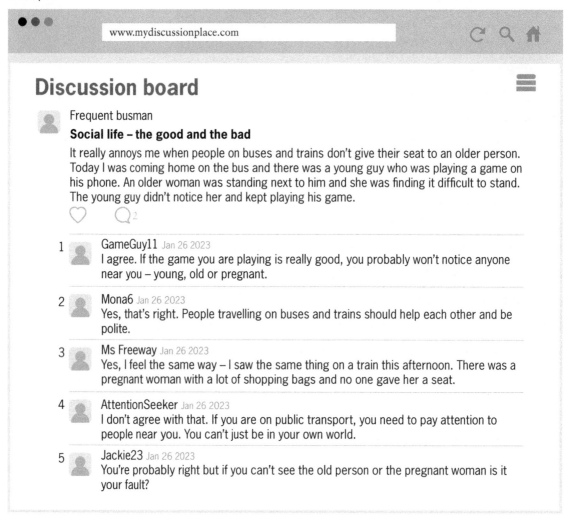

Key
Correct order: 3, 5, 1, 4, 2

Think further
Elicit from students that when they agree or disagree it is usually with the previous post and not the previous ones unless clearly indicate this, e.g. *I agree with Jackie23*. Also point out that this way of responding in writing is similar to a spoken discussion.

Notes

With a less confident class, the example posts could be given in the correct order, and learners go straight to underlining agreement/disagreement expressions. With a stronger or higher-level class, you could avoid using the follow up posts and just get students to write a series of posts of their own. This could be followed up with feedback on the range of agreement/disagreement expressions students use.

Rationale

This activity gives learners some simple language of agreement and disagreement that can be used in these kinds of online forums. The ordering task aims to get students focused on the cohesion and coherence in a chain of comments. This highlights the fact that the interactive nature of this kind of writing is like a conversation, as suggested in *Think further*.

3.5 Reason–result dictogloss

Outline	Students do a dictogloss of an opinion paragraph and add reason–result linkers to their writing.
Level	Pre-intermediate to Upper intermediate (B1–B2)
Time	40 minutes (25 minutes if step 5 is done as homework)
Aim	To practise using reason–result linkers in opinion-based writing.
Preparation	Prepare a suitable paragraph for a dictogloss (see *Example*). You could write a paragraph on a topic linked to your students' study.

Procedure

1 Show the following words: *so, because, as a result, consequently, therefore* and establish they are all ways to signal a reason or result.

2 Do a dictogloss of an opinion paragraph that contains reason–result linkers (see the example below).
   A dictogloss involves the following steps:
   a Students listen to the teacher read a paragraph. When the teacher has finished, students make notes of key words and phrases they remember, and check in pairs.
   b The teacher reads the paragraph again and students make notes again, but again only after the reading ends.
   c Students, in pairs or small groups, try to recreate the paragraph so it is as close to the original as possible.

3 Tell students that they should include the words from step 1 in their paragraph.

4 Pairs/groups swap and compare their finished paragraphs. Show the example answer if you think it's appropriate and/or useful.

5 Students write a paragraph on the value of learning a second language using reason–result linkers. This could be done as homework.

Example

Dictogloss

A lot of people don't believe it is a good idea to save minority languages <u>because</u> they think it is a waste of time and money. They argue that it costs a lot of money to produce videos and books in the language, and courses need to be set up to help people learn the language. <u>As a result</u>, a large amount of money will be spent, but just a few people will learn the language. However, other people say that saving a minority language is like saving a piece of culture in the same way we save historical buildings. <u>Therefore</u>, we need to spend time and money to rescue these valuable languages. They also argue that a language is a way of understanding our world <u>so</u> if we lose one, we lose part of our ability to see the world in a new light. <u>Consequently</u>, we can find it difficult to understand different cultures and different ways of living.

Think further
Establish with students that the reasons and results in the paragraph they wrote are not the main opinion – they support these ideas.

Notes
With groups that need more support, you can show fewer linkers to include, e.g. *so, because, therefore.* With higher levels, you can include extra words and expressions, e.g. *since, otherwise, for this reason.* Alternatively, you could not show any linkers and ask students to include some.

Rationale

Dictogloss activities are very good at getting students to draw on the linguistic resources they have in order to recreate a version of the original paragraph. Introducing the reason–result linkers at the beginning of the activity encourages students to focus on them as they recreate the paragraph. As indicated in *Think further*, these linkers are commonly used in opinion-based writing to back up or support main ideas.

3.6   Reviewing and planning

Outline	Students read a mind map for a review, then organise the information into a coherent plan before planning their own review.
Level	Intermediate (B1+)
Time	40–45 minutes
Aim	To highlight the value of planning before writing; to present a generic structure for a review.
Preparation	You will need to make a mind map and review plan available for each student (see *Example*).

Procedure

1   Students read a mind map with notes for a review but including one point that is unlikely to be used in the review itself. (In the example mind map, the point about the birthday present is unlikely to be used in the review.)

2   In pairs, student sort the notes into a coherent review plan with four paragraphs.

3   Check ideas with the class and show an example review plan.

4   Individually, students then make a mind map for a review of one of the following subjects: film, book, website, podcast, TV programme.

5   Students swap mind maps with a partner and check each other's work for any points that might not be appropriate to include.

6   Students pass back the mind maps and then write review plan notes.

7   In new pairs, students read each other's plan to check that the organisation of the review is clear.

8   Students write the review as homework.

Example

Mind map

eco soldiers on mission to find nuclear fusion formula

excellent sound design – feels like you're in the scene

was a birthday present from my parents

design sometimes makes climate change look like a fantasy – not a reality

same great characters – real & surprising

Video game: *Nerthus Patrol* version 2

fights & battles based on player's skill not kind of weapon used

2 new characters – both women – better gender balance now

more interesting than most other games

some fight sequences too easy – not enough challenge

recommended creative revision of first version & link to famous myth adds layer

---

Review plan

Introduction

Nerthus Patrol version 2 – eco soldiers on mission to find secret of nuclear fusion – similar scenario but new challenges

Positive points

same great characters – real & surprising – 2 new characters both women – now good gender balance

fights & battles based on player's skill – not the kind of weapons used

excellent sound design – feels like you're in the scene

Negative points

some fight sequences too easy – not enough challenge

design sometimes makes effects of climate change look like a fantasy world and not a reality

Recommendation

overall, a creative revision of the first version – the linking of climate change to a famous myth adds layer – more interesting than most other games

---

Think further

Elicit from students the differences between doing a mind map and a plan. Establish that making mind maps is a freer activity and they can write down anything that comes to mind. Irrelevant points can be cut when they come to writing the plan.

Notes

If you feel your students need support at step 2, you can give them headings for the four paragraphs. Not doing so is a way of evaluating their competence in the skill of organising ideas into paragraphs. If students have obvious needs in this area, then it would pay to do some revision of the typical organisation of a review.

Rationale

The broader aim of this activity is to develop students' awareness of the value of planning before writing – generating ideas at the mind mapping stage and then shaping these ideas into a coherent plan.

3.7 Essay kitset

Outline	Students follow a planning task that presents two models of organisation for a discursive essay and select the most appropriate linkers.
Level	Intermediate (B1+) and above
Time	50 minutes (15–20 minutes if step 7 is done as homework)
Aim	To provide students with a model of how to plan the content and consider the organisation of a discursive essay; to present core linkers for the essay.
Preparation	Prepare a worksheet similar to the one below for each student. If you wish to focus on a different topic, you will need to create a set of notes that have reason–result connections.

Procedure

1   Show students notes that can be used for a discursive essay (see ex. 1 in worksheet on the topic of driverless cars). These should include reason–result relationships.

2   Students select points *for* and *against* the topic of the essay. Check answers.

3   Students now connect notes together in reason–result relationship (ex. 2) – do an example on the board, e.g. *driverless cars follow the road rules – fewer traffic accidents* (not all points can be paired). Check answers and allow for reasonable alternative suggestions.

4   Show the different ways of organising the essay (ex. 3). Organisation A would discuss only points for <u>or</u> against, but organisation B would discuss points for <u>and</u> against.

5   Students work alone and choose the kind of organisation they prefer for the essay topic. In pairs, they tell each other what organisation they prefer and why.

6   Put students in pairs/small groups who have all chosen the same kind of organisation. Show linking words and expressions that can be used for one essay structure, the other or both. Check answers on the board.

7   Students can write the essay in class or as homework. Encourage them to develop the notes further and add their own ideas.

Key

ex. 1 *For:* 1, 4, 5, 7, 11; *Against:* 2, 3, 6, 8, 9, 10

ex. 2 2–10; 4–1; 5–11; 8–3

ex. 3 Students' own ideas

ex. 4 A: first of all, secondly, finally

B: on one hand, on the other hand, whereas, while

Both A and B: a key point in favour/against, in summary, another point, in conclusion

Think further

Establish with students that both ways of broadly organising the essay follow claim–counterclaim discourse patterning. In the first organisation, there is a claim and counter claim with each point. With the second organisation a series of claims are included in one paragraph and counter claims in the next.

Notes

Some students find these models of organisation overly formulaic, so it's worth pointing out they are likely to be useful if they ever do an English language exam with a writing paper. At higher levels, you could give even less support in the notes and get students to come up with their own ideas.

Rationale

Many students are unfamiliar with different ways of organising a discursive essay in English because the approach is different in their first language. This activity supports students by giving them ideas on content while suggesting and allowing them to choose a way of organising these ideas. It also gives students suggestions on linkers that will make their essay more cohesive.

▲ *Worksheet 3.7*

1 Which points are *for* and which are *against*?

   [1] fewer traffic accidents

   [2] can be hacked like a computer

   [3] people lose jobs

   [4] people don't drive after drinking alcohol

   [5] save people time

   [6] a long time before they're widely used

   [7] driverless cars always follow the road rules

   [8] decrease in number of taxis and ride share programmes disappear

   [9] a mix of driver and driverless cars means more accidents

   [10] whole transportation system could break down

   [11] spend driving time doing useful things or relaxing

2 Which points in ex. 1 can be paired in a reason–result relationship?

3 Choose your organisation, A or B.

   A Introduction
       ↓
      Point 1
       ↓
      Point 2
       ↓
      Point 3
       ↓
      Conclusion

   B Introduction
       ↓
      Points for
       ↓
      Points against
       ↓
      Conclusion

4 Choose the linking words and phrases you will use.

   a key point in favour/against   another point   finally   first of all   in conclusion   in summary
   on one hand / on the other hand   secondly   whereas   while

From *Teaching and Developing Writing Skills* © Cambridge University Press 2023   PHOTOCOPIABLE

3.8 Topic sentence secret ballot

Outline	Students write a topic sentence for a paragraph and vote for the best one, before revising their own.
Level	Intermediate (B1+) and above
Time	20 minutes
Aim	To practise writing clearly focused topic sentences.
Preparation	You will need to make available a paragraph without a topic sentence for each student (see *Example*).

Procedure

1 Students read a paragraph without a topic sentence and identify that the topic sentence is missing.

2 In small groups, students write a topic sentence for the paragraph.

3 Display all the topic sentences on the board or on screen.

4 Each group votes for the topic sentence they like best, but they cannot vote for their own topic sentence.

5 You could also show the paragraph's original topic sentence and compare it with the winner. Then hide/remove all the topic sentences.

6 Students then revise their topic sentence in light of the examples they have seen.

Example

> Some critics of solar panels have pointed out that it requires energy to produce them, in particular, in the manufacturing of the panels as well as shipping them to people who buy them. However, it is generally agreed that a solar panel pays back this energy cost after about four years. Furthermore, new materials and methods used in the production of solar panels have helped reduce the energy cost. For example, the use of a material called perovskite in a panel, as opposed to the more traditional silicone, requires less energy input in production and makes the panel more efficient. It is also a very flexible substance that can be used on a wide range of surfaces. As a result, solar energy remains a key way of reducing carbon emissions and reducing our carbon footprint.

> *Topic sentence*
> Solar panel production does involve an energy cost, but there are new methods that ensure it is still an eco-friendly source of renewable energy.

Think further

Elicit from students the characteristics of a good topic sentence: it introduces the reader to the main idea of the paragraph and outlines what information it aims to cover.

Notes

An alternative activity would be to provide a series of topic sentences for students to vote on what they think is the most effective.

Rationale

A focus on topic sentences can be useful for groups of learners that struggle with coherence in their paragraph writing. Getting students to work on topic sentences on their own can be challenging for many learners, so this activity aims to make it co-operative and introduce a game element. In step 5, the suggestion to remove all the topic sentences is a way of ensuring that weaker groups don't make a direct copy. Having seen some examples, they should try to improve their own version.

3.9 Discursive retell

Outline	Students read an opinion article, retell it to another student and then rewrite the article in a less formal style.
Level	Pre-intermediate to Upper intermediate (B1–B2)
Time	40–45 minutes
Aim	To give students practice adopting an appropriate style for an opinion article that is aimed at a less formal audience.
Preparation	You will need to prepare two opinion paragraphs for an online forum (see *Example*), one for students for each half of the class.

Procedure

1 Divide students into two groups: A and B. Each group reads an opinion paragraph on a different topic. Put these questions on the board for students to answer:
   Where can you read a text like this?
   Who might be interested in reading it?
   Is the style formal or informal?

2 Check students' ideas and establish that in both paragraphs the style is formal and could come from an essay or article for a general readership.

3 Students imagine the point of view in the paragraph is their own. They read the text again and make notes of key points before turning the text over.

4 Working in A and B pairs, students tell each other about the information in their paragraphs using their notes only and as though it were their own opinion.

5 Students then work alone and rewrite the paragraph for an online forum in a similar tone to their spoken retelling.

6 Now pair students with a partner who has the same article to read each other's paragraph. They can give feedback to each other on how personal the language is. You could also show sample answers.

Example

Paragraph A
Many people have had the experience of a company offering to save personal data after an online purchase. They promise easy, straightforward shopping in the future. However, many people now no longer give their details to online shops. They say they are worried about what companies do with the data and how safely it is stored. There are many reports of people having their personal information, including credit card details, stolen from online shops. This suggests that it is important to keep your personal information safe and think carefully about giving it to online companies.

> *Paragraph B*
> It is possible to read many reports about Artificial Intelligence (AI) and the range of extraordinary tasks it can do. AI is able to store large amounts of information and make decisions in less than a second. There are questions about whether the decisions it makes are good ones. The algorithms it uses are improving all the time and this increases the range of tasks AI can perform. Some reports show that AI may have the possibility of taking control of humans. Many people now believe that governments need to start making laws about how AI is used. Otherwise, they might lose control, as was the case with social media.

Sample answer A

I'm sure you've all had the experience of a company offering to save your personal data when you make a purchase. It's supposed to make online shopping easier for you in the future. Well, I've stopped doing this. Why? I worry about what these companies do with the data and how safely they store it. A friend of mine had all his data hacked from an online shop, including his credit card details. I think everyone should keep all their personal data safe and never let online companies save it.

Sample answer B

I keep reading articles about Artificial Intelligence (AI) and all the amazing things it can do. It can store so much information and make decisions in less than a second. And who knows if the decisions they make are always good ones? The algorithms that are being created are better and better and can do more things. It looks like computers might have the power to take control of humans. So I think governments need to start making laws about how AI is used. If not, it could end up like social media and get out of control.

Think further

Remind students that in the activity, they spoke about the information before writing. Elicit from them other online genres that are less formal and similar to spoken language, for example, social media and blog posts as well as tweets.

Notes

It's important to make sure students can't read aloud from the written paragraph – it should be covered or taken away from them. This helps students make the transition to a less formal style. Students could record the spoken retelling using a smartphone and refer to this as they rewrite the paragraph. A variation of this activity could be to reverse the focus, so students read a less formal online forum comment and then change it to something more formal and aimed at a more general readership.

Rationale

A lot of discursive writing is written either for the students' teacher or for an anonymous audience such as an examiner. Online forums provide students with a real audience. However, the style of writing that is most suitable for these opinion pieces is less formal than an essay and closer to spoken language. Getting students to retell the point of view in each paragraph is a way of loosening up the language they might use. Talking it through in pairs gives students a greater sense of a real audience before they begin writing.

3.10 Sentence swap

Outline	Students identify misplaced sentences in two paragraphs from a discussion essay then reorder the sentences to make the paragraphs more coherent.
Level	Upper intermediate (B2) and above
Time	20 minutes
Aim	To develop students' awareness of coherence by means of a logical development of ideas in discursive text.
Preparation	You will need to prepare two paragraphs from a discussion essay with misplaced sentences, one for students for each half of the class (see *Example*). You could find or write two paragraphs from a discursive essay on a topic relevant to your learners and swap a sentence from one paragraph to the other.

Procedure

1   Divide students into two groups: A and B. Each group reads a different paragraph from a discursive essay and identifies sentences that don't fit in their paragraph (see examples below).

2   In pairs within the same group, students first decide which two sentences don't fit in the paragraphs.

3   Now pair students: one from Group A and one from Group B. They tell each other about the sentences that don't fit in their paragraph and decide whether they can swap them (they can).

4   Students copy the ill-fitting sentences from their partner and decide where they can fit in their own paragraph.

5   Check the correct order of sentences with the class.

6   Ask students how they decided on the correct sentence order and point out how ideas in a piece of writing need to relate to each other.

Example

Paragraph A

[1]There are many arguments in favour of using GMOs (genetically modified organisms). [2]Scientists can engineer crops to be more resistant to threats such as pest invasion or weather extremes such drought, frost or very heavy rainfall. [3]These problems usually have a negative effect on the food supply because crops are damaged. [4]Already in many parts of the world, large areas of land are less fertile than they used to be because of bad irrigation practices. [5]It is also possible to put genes into core crops such as rice and wheat so they become a more nutritious source of food. [6]Plants can be modified so that they restore nutrients to the soil. [7]In general, GMOs offer an effective solution to problems associated with the quantity and quality of food supply around the world.

Paragraph B

[8]Another positive outcome of using GMOs concerns the environmental impact of agriculture. [9]If crops can be modified so they become more productive, then less land will need to be used. [10]Furthermore, farmers may not need to search for new land in which to cultivate their crops. [11]Genetic engineering can give plants a better chance of surviving natural threats and ensuring there is plenty for everyone to eat. [12]Plants can be modified so they can survive in these areas. [13]It would also be possible to use GMOs to improve the quality of the soil in land that has been damaged in some way. [14]An example of this is Golden Rice, which has an increased quantity of vitamin A and solves a serious health problem in the developing world. [15]These are all ways of minimising the negative impact that farming can have on the environment.

Key

Sentences that don't fit in Paragraph A: 4, 6; Paragraph B: 11, 14
Paragraph A: 1, 2, 3, 11, 5, 14, 7
Paragraph B: 8, 9, 10, 4, 12, 13, 6, 15

Think further

Ask students when they think is the best time to develop ideas – when they are planning writing or when they are writing a first draft. Ask them to give reasons.

Notes

The example paragraphs are best suited for B2 level or above, but the design of the activity could be adapted for lower levels with paragraphs using more straightforward language and with just one sentence that doesn't fit.

Rationale

Often the use of grammar and vocabulary in students' writing is mostly correct. Nonetheless, the writing may still be difficult to understand because the ideas have not been developed in a logical way and the text, therefore, lacks coherence. Learner attempts at discussion essays can sometimes seem like a series of random ideas jotted down, not fully and logically developed. This activity helps to underline for students that incoherent writing is problematic and also focuses them on sense relationships within a paragraph.

3.11 Using devices

Outline	Students improve the introduction of an article by replacing noun and verb phrases with referring cohesive devices.
Level	Intermediate (B1+) and above
Time	25 minutes
Aim	To practise using referring cohesive devices as a means to making writing more natural.
Preparation	You will need to make available to students a paragraph similar to the one below (see *Example*). If you use your own paragraph, you will need to rewrite it replacing cohesive devices with noun and verb phrases.

Procedure

1   Students read an introduction to an article in which the cohesive devices have been replaced by full forms. They decide if the introduction reads naturally or not.

2   Establish with the class that the paragraph isn't very natural and ask them to work in pairs and improve it.

3   Students work for about three or four minutes. Then suggest a few words that might be useful to improve the paragraph, but tell students they don't have to use them if they don't want to. For the example below, you could suggest *it* and *they*.

4   After another three or four minutes, suggest some more words – for the example: *this, we*. Then after two or three more minutes suggest the final cohesive devices – for the example: *one, so*.

5   Students finish improving their paragraph and compare their rewritten version with another pair.

6   Show students the example paragraph with the cohesive devices underlined and allow them to ask you questions about any differences.

Example

Most of the readers of this article are superstitious to some degree. Being superstitious can range from fear of what might happen if you break a mirror through to small habits that readers carry out each day, for example, the need to always put on your left shoe before your right shoe. By contrast, the world of Information Technology (IT) is technical and very logical, and readers of the article can probably safely assume the world of IT isn't full of superstitious belief. However, the assumption about IT and superstitions is not the correct assumption. Many people talk to their computer when the computer doesn't do what people want the computer to do, and people are not talking to any kind of voice-activated assistant like Alexa or Siri. Then there are other people who believe in clearing the browsing history when other people are looking for a good deal online. Clearing the browsing history is meant to help you get a better price, but clearing the browsing history doesn't. Just like any other world, IT has its fair share of superstitious beliefs.

Paragraph with cohesive devices

Most of <u>us</u> are superstitious to some degree. <u>This</u> can range from fear of what might happen if you break a mirror through to small habits that <u>we</u> carry out each day, for example, the need to always put on your left shoe before your right <u>one</u>. By contrast, the world of Information Technology (IT) is technical and very logical, and <u>we</u> can probably safely assume <u>it</u> isn't full of superstitious belief. However, <u>this</u> is not <u>so</u>. Many people talk to their computer when <u>it</u> doesn't do what <u>they</u> want <u>it</u> to do, and <u>they're</u> not talking to any kind of voice-activated assistant like Alexa or Siri. Then there are other people who believe in clearing the browsing history when <u>they</u> are looking for a good deal online. <u>It</u> is meant to help you get a better price, but <u>it</u> doesn't. Just like any other world, IT has its fair share of superstitious beliefs.

Think further

Elicit from students some of the features of the cohesive devices used. For example, the use of 'we' and 'us' as a means of including the reader in the topic under discussion, and the way 'this' refers back to an idea mentioned in a previous sentence whereas 'it' more commonly refers to a specific noun phrase.

Notes

It's important to emphasise that it is optional to use the suggested words in step 3. This activity could be done by taking a paragraph from a text that students have recently read in class. You could make the activity easier be highlighting the nouns and phrases that need to be replaced by cohesive devices. The example material is an introduction, but any paragraph from a discursive text can be used – the key consideration is that it includes a range of cohesive devices.

Rationale

As referring cohesive devices are frequently used in opinion-based writing and most other genres, students need consistent practice in their use. Some learners may repeat noun or verb phrases more than necessary because they feel the need to be specific, while others may leave out pronouns because they are not required in their first language. The drip feeding of the cohesive devices aims to get students to come up with their own improvements, thereby making the activity a little less prescriptive than a straightforward substitution activity.

3.12 Unscrambling the genres

Outline	Students unscramble sentences of two short texts on the same topic but of different genres, then use notes to extend the texts.
Level	Upper intermediate (B2) and above
Time	35 minutes
Aim	To practise identifying the register of two different genres of opinion-based writing; to practise recognising cohesive ties in a short text.
Preparation	You will need to make a worksheet available such as the one below, half for Students A and half for Students B. You can create your own scrambled texts, but make sure the differences in register are clear.

Procedure

1   Students work in A and B pairs. Explain that each has a set of sentences that come from two texts. The sentences are all on the same topic (emotional and social learning), but the examples are a mix of two genres. Students read their examples aloud to each other (but must not show them) and sort the sentences into two coherent texts.

2   Check answers as a class and show the correct versions of the two texts.

3   Elicit from learners the different registers of the two genres (text 1 is a less formal opinion article, perhaps an online blog/forum, and text 2 is more formal and academic).

4   Students use the *Extra notes* to continue the text. Students A continue text 1 in a less formal register and Students B text 2 in a more academic register.

5   Working A and B pairs, students swap their continuations and give feedback to each other on the appropriateness of the register.

Key
Correct order of texts: A = 3, 6, 2; B = 5, 1, 4

Correct texts

Text 1
Of late you hear a lot more about the subject of social and emotional learning in school. It's all about the way kids deal with their feelings and emotions and get on with other people. If they do this, they'll be better prepared to live in the real world when they grow up.

Text 2
In the past few years, there has been a greater emphasis on social and emotional learning. This aims to help school children manage their feelings and emotions in a positive way and develop good relationships with other people. These skills will allow them to meet the challenges of daily life effectively.

Think further
Elicit from students examples of language that helped them to determine which genre each text belonged to, for example, *it's all about* ... vs. *It aims to help* ...; *kids* vs. *children*; the use of *you* in the less formal text.

Notes

A homework extension for this activity would be to get students to research the topic of the texts online and develop their writing into a complete essay (for the students who extended the formal text) or a complete online article (for the students who extended the less formal text). This activity can be simplified by making available all six scrambled sentences together for students in pairs to unscramble.

Rationale

Apart from developing awareness of the register of the two genres, this activity also indirectly focuses students on cohesion within the two short texts. The initial information gap activity is a way of introducing speaking into the activity – students get spoken fluency practice as they negotiate the correct genre and sentence order.

 Worksheet 3.12

Student A

Sentences

[1]This aims to help school children manage their feelings and emotions in a positive way and develop good relationships with other people.

[2]If they do this, they'll be better prepared to live in the real world when they grow up.

[3]Of late you hear a lot more about the subject of social and emotional learning in school.

Extra Notes
- some adults think too much time is spent on social and emotional learning – academic subjects ignored – parents should teach life skill
- teachers say children need life skills for connected world, e.g. deal with bullying – understand different cultures

- - - - - - - ✂ -

Student B

Sentences

[4]These skills will allow them to meet the challenges of daily life effectively.

[5]In the past few years, there has been a greater emphasis on social and emotional learning.

[6]It's all about the way kids deal with their feelings and emotions and get on with other people.

Extra Notes
- some adults think too much time is spent on social and emotional learning – academic subjects ignored – parents should teach life skill
- teachers say children need life skills for connected world, e.g. deal with bullying – understand different cultures

From *Teaching and Developing Writing Skills* © Cambridge University Press 2023   PHOTOCOPIABLE

3.13 Toning it down

Outline	Students revise a strongly worded opinion piece, then write their own opinion pieces that are revised for tone by a partner.
Level	Upper intermediate (B2) and above
Time	45 minutes
Aim	To highlight and practice editing the tone of opinion-based writing.
Preparation	You will need to make available to students a paragraph similar to the one below (see *Example*). If there is a topic you think would be motivating for your students, write a strongly worded opinion piece on that, which they can revise with a more neutral tone.

Procedure

1   Students read a strongly worded paragraph and decide if it voices a forceful opinion or not (see the example below in which it does).

2   Tell students the text needs to be revised for a context where such a strong opinion isn't appropriate, for example, for an online magazine aimed at songwriters.

3   Students work on their revision and then compare their versions in pairs.

4   Show students a sample revision (see below) and get them to compare it to their own paragraphs.

5   Elicit key features of the revision: the cutting of extreme adjectives and adverbs, use of less forceful modal verbs and the qualifying phrases *it seems that, in some ways, in my opinion.*

6   Students then choose a topic that they feel strongly about (or you could provide topics for them to choose from, e.g. online advertising, electric scooters, smartphone addiction) and write a very strongly worded opinion paragraph, similar to the one they revised.

7   Students then swap their work and tone down the strength of opinion to make it more appropriate for certain contexts.

Example

> Sometimes when I read the credits for a hit song, I see that the ridiculously unbelievable number of up to 20 people have been involved in the writing of it. If you were in the studio when the song was being recorded and you made just the smallest idiotic suggestion, you get a credit. This is nothing but the madness of song writing by committee. I also think it means that a lot of hit songs sound utterly identical to one another because there is no completely individual and totally unique quality that the song has. We absolutely have to go back to the days when only one or two people are involved in writing a song. Two people who are dependent on help from ten more people need to get a new job.

Sample revision

Sometimes when I read the credits for a hit song, I see that up to 20 people have been involved in the writing of it. It seems that if you were in the studio when the song was being recorded and you made a small suggestion, you get a credit. I'm not sure you can even say this is real song writing because it seems more like something put together by a committee. I also think it means that a lot of hit songs can end up sounding similar to one another because there is no individual and unique quality that each song has. In my opinion, we should go back to the days when only one or two people are involved in writing a song. If two people often need help from ten more people then they might be in the wrong job.

Think further

Check with students whether they would post a strongly worded opinion to an online forum that anyone could read. Establish the idea that if they do so, they need to be prepared to receive equally strongly worded or even abusive replies. Underline the importance of thinking carefully about how an audience will react to strongly worded opinions.

Notes

This activity can be simplified by providing students with the two versions of the text and getting them to identify the differences in the use of language. It's possible to manage steps 6 and 7 across two lessons: students write their strongly worded paragraphs as homework and the editing takes place in the next lesson.

Rationale

At all levels, students need to be alert to different styles of writing, but perhaps particularly at higher levels where they are more likely to be studying for an exam or in an EAP context. Although less formal opinion-based writing can be more expressive, students will still need to consider the appropriacy of the tone. This activity also focuses indirectly on qualifying phrases and modality as a means to making an opinion less categorical.

4 Writing to get something done

The kind of writing focused on in this chapter is transactional in nature, the intended outcome being the receipt of goods or information, the discharge of a service or the performance of a procedure. For example, a message is sent to a hotel requesting a room with a balcony, or a person emails or messages a telecommunications company to query their invoice. Given that many of these goods and services transactions are now carried out online (and perhaps across borders), communication between businesses and customers is often written where it once might have been spoken. For example, many businesses encourage their customers to make a product enquiry by sending an email or by completing an online form on their website. Trying to contact someone by telephone can be difficult and take time. Of course, not all transactional writing is business related, often it can have an interpersonal dimension. For example, a person might share a recipe with a friend or send them a message requesting to borrow something.

Functions, genres and patterns

In transactional writing, there is likely to be more of an emphasis on a range of micro functions such as requesting, advising, warning and explaining. For example, an instructional guide explains steps in a process, an email of enquiry requests further information, and completing an online form might be some kind of application. Embedded in this transactional writing will be other text functions. As such, a message that gives positive feedback on a successful service encounter may also narrate the story of what happened, and an email of complaint about a product will describe the problem.

Each of the texts focused on in the activities in this chapter could be considered an instance of a specific genre. Given that these genres include some kind of transaction, there is often a specific person that the text is aimed at. Writers may not personally know their audience, but they will know something about the kind of role the receiver of a message performs. The clearest example of this is sending a request to a company knowing that the message will be read by a customer service representative. This means the writer needs to consider what information is necessary for the audience, and what is the clearest way of conveying it in a written message in the absence of knowing exactly who the reader will be. For example, if we want to change a restaurant booking, we need to ensure we include our name, contact details, the date and time of the original booking as well as the request for a new day and/or time.

Biber and Conrad (2019) suggest that transactional email messages between two people who do not know each other tend to be longer because the writer often needs to provide more information. For example, people who rent out their apartment for a short period of time to people they do not know usually provide very detailed instructions indicating where appliances are and how they work. By contrast, if the instructions were written for close friends of the owners who know the apartment well, they would include less detail because the owners would assume their friends' familiarity with their home.

There are often specific conventions that underpin transactional writing. Hyland (2019: p.18) suggests that these conventions are 'beyond the page' and are determined by the social context in which the writing takes place. The context can include the writer's reason for writing, the relationship they have with the audience and the amount of information they feel is necessary to convey. A message complaining about a defective product would include information about the date and place of purchase, a description of the fault and an indication of the complainant's expected course of action (a refund, replacement or repair).

Two of the three main discourse patterns, problem–solution and general–particular, are often found in transactional texts. A letter of complaint about service will state the problem and often then outline a solution that would remediate the problem in some way. General–particular patterning is often inherent in online order forms. Having clicked on a product they wish to buy, the consumer may then go on to select specific features of that product such as the size or colour, perhaps even adding a specific comment in a relevant field. Claim–counterclaim patterning is less likely, but could perhaps be included in texts that aim to advertise a product, for example, *our competitors say … but we say …* .

Language

The specific function of a transactional text will often determine the kind of language used. It is noted by Biber and Conrad (2019) that the language of task-focused email messages is often similar to spoken language. The utterance *I'd like a table on the terrace* used when booking a restaurant table could be made on the phone to someone in the restaurant taking the booking, or could equally be written in an online booking form. However, this is not always the case. Warnings and advice, for example, can be stated directly in writing using imperatives (*Don't bring food and drink into the library*), but they are more likely to be expressed using modality in spoken language (*Sorry, but you can't bring food and drink into the library*). Biber and Conrad (2019) also point out that imperatives are often used in email communication, such as *Please advise when I can expect a reply*. Some transactional texts include formulaic chunks of language associated with that specific genre. For example, a product complaint is likely to include phrases such as *under guarantee* and *I've attached the receipt*.

Given that many transactional genres outline some kind of process, linking words and phrases that either enumerate, order or list are used, for example, *first of all, then, after that* or *the first step, the next one, the final step*. As noted above, imperatives are frequently used in written guidelines and instructions and are not perceived as too direct or impolite by readers as they might be if they were spoken. In fact, they are often preferred as being a clear and efficient way of communicating.

If a transactional text involves description, adjective phrases are often used. For example, when someone is writing an online advert and describing the condition of something they want to sell. Such a description might also involve a degree of ellipsis, so that *It's in very good condition* becomes *In good condition*. Many transactional genres also employ specific language and layout choices. A recipe writer, therefore, is very likely to use imperatives to explain the process of making a dish in bullet points or numbered steps.

In the classroom

Many of the activities in this chapter are suitable for lower levels, but are easily adaptable for higher-level learners. Some of the genres are frequently included in the writing syllabus of courses books (for example, a recipe, a letter of complaint, a request for information), but, more importantly, many texts might be useful in learners' daily lives outside the classroom because they may engage in online transactions outside their country of residence and may need to use English in order to do so. While specific genres in this chapter are not common in English language written examinations, they will sometimes be embedded within another genre. For example, in B2 Cambridge First part 2, students can choose to write an email to someone and this email could involve giving instructions or explaining.

References

Biber, D. & Conrad, S. (2019) *Register, Genre, and Style Second Edition*. Cambridge, Cambridge University Press.

Hyland, K. (2019) *Second Language Writing Second Edition*. Cambridge, Cambridge University Press.

4.1 Expanding race

Outline	Students expand special request notes for a hotel online booking form.
Level	Elementary (A2) and above
Time	30 minutes (20 minutes if step 6 is done as homework)
Aim	To provide practice in expanding notes into complete written requests.
Preparation	You will need to make a set of notes available to students similar to the one below (see *Example*). You could come up with your own ideas for hotel special requests, or you may prefer to use another online sales/service context, such as booking travel, buying clothes online, making an IT support request.

Procedure

1 Elicit information required for an online booking at a hotel (name, email, stay dates, etc.) or show an example.

2 Establish that the final field in an online form is usually for special requests – elicit examples of what these might be.

3 Show the following request phrases to students: *I'd like . . . Could/Can I/we . . . ?* and elicit some example oral requests.

4 Show students notes for hotel requests (see examples below). In small groups, students then have a race to write full requests from the notes. They need to use all three request phrases from step 2.

5 The first team to write complete requests that are correct wins.

6 Students write a special request for some other kind of online booking or order – let them choose their own context that they think they're likely to use outside the classroom. This could be done as homework.

Example

```
1   quiet room – not near lift
2   room – sea view – possible
3   use hotel pool & spa
4   late check out – cost
5   sign into – Netflix account – TV – your hotel
```

Sample answers

1 I'd like / Could/Can I have a quiet room that's not near the lift. (?)
2 I'd like / Could/Can I have a room with a sea view if (it's) possible. (?)
3 I'd like to / Could/Can I use the hotel pool and spa. (?)
4 I'd like / Could/Can I have a late check out and is there a cost. (?)
5 Could/Can I sign into my Netflix account on the TV at your hotel?

Think further

Establish with learners that forms have made online shopping and booking services in English easier, but sometimes they need to write some kind of note or request. Elicit other examples where this is necessary, for example, online order delivery instructions, special food requests at restaurants, course enrolment request for a late start, etc.

Notes

For a higher-level class, you could cut step 3 in the procedure. You could also reduce the notes to one word or phrase for students to expand with their own ideas. For example, *quiet room – not near lift* could just be *quiet room*.

Rationale

As *Think further* indicates, some degree of writing is often required for automated online forms. This activity alerts students to this necessity and gives them practice doing it. Making this a race aims to add a degree of motivation by adding a competitive element.

4.2 Complete form

Outline	Students do an information gap activity correcting problems in an online course application and write follow up questions or comments.
Level	Elementary to Pre-intermediate (A2–B1)
Time	30 minutes
Aim	To practise proofing skills for written accuracy; to practise writing clear follow up questions and comments for online applications.
Preparation	You will need to make available a completed online application form for Students A and a baggage tag for Students B similar to the ones below (see *Example*). Preferably, the application form is in digital format to add authenticity to the task. If the language course context isn't suitable for your students, create your own application form for a course that might motivate your students, for example, a course on video game design and an alternative label in place of the baggage tag.

Procedure

1   Elicit from students the kinds of problems that can arise when completing online forms, e.g. misspelling, giving incorrect numbers, the auto-fill function filling the wrong fields.

2   Student A has a course application form with errors. Student B has a baggage label with correct information. Without showing each other their information, Student A checks the details with Student B and corrects their application form. Set a five-minute time limit.

3   Check corrections with the whole class.

4   In the same pairs, students write one question and one comment in the final box of the application form.

5   Sets of pairs (i.e. a group of four) then compare answers and decide on one question or comment they would like to share with the whole class – the one they agree is most relevant for a language course.

6   Each group writes their chosen question or comment so the whole class can see it. Ask other students to improve these if necessary.

7   Students complete the same application form with their own details imagining it's for an English language course.

Example
Online application form

Baggage tag

Key
first and last names in the wrong field; wrong house number and street name; 'Hillmorton' is the suburb not the town; the town is 'Parkway' not 'Parkvale'; post code is 0487 not 0587; phone number is 857314 not 856314; email missing an extra 'e'

Think further

Elicit from students problems that can result from giving incorrect information online, for example, you can't be contacted, you can be sent incorrect goods or information. Establish with students the importance of carefully proofreading information they type into online forms.

Notes

With lower-level learners, it would pay to check useful language for this activity, for example, *How do you spell that? What's the name of . . . ? What's the second/third number?* The level of challenge for this activity can be raised by asking students to write two questions and comments in step 4.

Rationale

Editing and proofreading are a key part of the writing process, particularly when accuracy is important. Digital tools sometimes lull writers into a false sense of security with a false expectation that writing will be auto-corrected. This activity is a reminder that typing into online fields needs to be done with accuracy. The writing of questions or comments encourages students to consider the relevance and clarity of what they write in this field.

4.3 Order change

Outline	Students assume the role of customer service representatives and write a reply to a request for compensation.
Level	Pre-intermediate (B1) and above
Time	30 minutes
Aim	To provide practice responding to a written request; to highlight the idea of audience in written service exchanges.
Preparation	You will need to make available a request email for each student (see *Example*). You could write a request resulting from any kind of change in service.

Procedure

1 Elicit examples of businesses making changes to booking, such as flights, hotel reservations, entertainment. Establish that many companies have 'terms and conditions' that allow them to do this.

2 Students read a message complaining about a change of service and a request for compensation (see example below regarding a flight time change).

3 Tell students they are customer service representatives and they need to write a reply which should:
   a fully agree to, partially agree to or refuse the request
   b give reason(s) for the decision – you might encourage students to be imaginative
   c be polite

4 In pairs, students decide on their approach and write a reply.

5 Students then work in groups of six to ten and read each other's replies. If you feel it is appropriate for your students, you could ask each group to choose the most original, the most co-operative and the least co-operative reply, and read them aloud to class.

Example

●●●   Reply   Forward

I'm writing to complain about the change of my flight time from the morning to the afternoon. This means I will have less time to spend with my friends and family when I get to Dublin.

I know that your terms and conditions say you can change flight times up until a week before the departure, but I don't think this is fair. It also gives your airline a bad reputation.

I would like some compensation for this inconvenience, for example, upgrading my ticket to business class and letting me use the VIP lounge before my flight.

I look forward to hearing from you.

Regards
Liam Walsh

Think further

Ask learners of any examples they may have had when dealing with customer service or if they have worked in customer service. Were they polite when they wrote to them? What was the outcome? Does playing the role of a customer service agent in the activity and responding to a written complaint change their point of view at all?

Notes

To ensure a selection of responses, students could be placed in three groups to write their replies: one to fully agree, one to partially agree and one to refuse. The activity can be extended by students swapping their customer service replies and then writing a customer response.

Rationale

Having learners respond to a request or demand in a customer service role is a way for them to consider an unknown audience they are addressing. Encouraging students to be imaginative in their customer service response can be a way of making the activity fun and motivating.

4.4 Recipe clarity

Outline	Students read or listen to instructions for a recipe and then rewrite them using a recipe format.
Level	Pre-intermediate (B1) and above
Time	30 minutes
Aim	To practise writing a set of instructions using imperatives.
Preparation	You will need to prepare a transcript or oral instructions for a recipe, or you could make a recording of someone explaining a recipe.

Procedure

1   Students read a transcript or oral instructions for a recipe. Alternatively, you could read the instructions aloud and ask them to make notes. They should only note the most important information.

2   Elicit or remind students of the format of a recipe: a list of ingredients followed by instructions in the imperative form.

3   In pairs, students use their notes to write a recipe.

4   Sets of pairs compare their versions and note any differences. You could also show students the model recipe.

Example

Transcript

So, if you're cooking for two people, this is what you'll need. A couple of zucchini – medium size – and a can of tomatoes. And I use a small onion – if you've got a large one cut it in half. Then some oregano – about a teaspoon and, of course, salt and pepper. Then for the pasta – I like to use penne – about 200 grams, but really you can use any pasta you like.

Well, the first thing you do is cut the onion into very small pieces and then cut the zucchini into small chunks – about 2 centimetres long. Then get a saucepan and put in the olive oil. Let it get hot and add the onion. I usually let it cook for maybe two to three minutes. Don't let it burn and add in the zucchini. You need to fry them for maybe three or four minutes. You know, until you can see the zucchini are getting a bit soft. Then at that point you add the tin of tomatoes. Oh, I forgot to say – when you put the onions in the oil, add a bit of salt and when you put in the zucchini, I add more salt, some pepper and most importantly, the oregano.

OK, so once you've added to tomatoes, wait until it all begins to boil, then turn the heat down to low or medium. It usually takes about 20 minutes and then it becomes a nice, rich tomato sauce. In the meantime, you can put water for the pasta on the stove and get that to boil. How long you cook the pasta depends on the instructions on the pasta packet. That's it – once it's all cooked, mix together and serve.

Model recipe

<u>Ingredients for 2 people</u>

2 medium-sized zucchini	1 small onion
1 can of tomatoes	1 teaspoon oregano
Salt and pepper	200 grams of pasta

- Cut the onion into very small pieces. Cut the zucchini into small chunks (about 2cm long).
- Heat the olive oil in a saucepan. Add the onion with a little salt. Fry for 2 to 3 minutes.
- Add the zucchini with the oregano and a little salt and pepper. Fry for 3 to 4 minutes – until the zucchini is beginning to get a bit soft.
- Add the tin of tomatoes to the fried vegetables. Wait until it begins to boil.
- Turn down the heat to low or medium. Let the tomatoes cook gently for about 20 minutes until they become a sauce.
- Cook the pasta separately in a large pot. Follow the cooking time instructions on the pasta packet.

Think further

Establish with students that the spoken description of the recipe in the transcript includes linkers like *first, then, once,* etc. Elicit that this is not necessary with a written recipe because the format shows the order. Ask students to compare the imperative instructions of the recipe with the transcript and note that linking words may add clarity for other kinds of daily processes, for example, assembling kitset furniture, repairing appliances, carrying out simple IT tasks.

Notes

This activity could be adapted for other sets of instructions. With stronger groups, doing step 1 as a listening adds more challenge. A possible follow up homework task would be for students to write their own recipe.

Rationale

The specific genre for this activity is one that students might engage with if they share recipes with English speaking friends. The activity focuses on the format and the way in which this helps make instructions clear. It also highlights differences between spoken and written instructions.

4.5 Still processing

Outline	Students write an enquiry message to find out what has happened to an undelivered package, and write a reply to a partner's enquiry.
Level	Pre-intermediate (B1) and above
Time	35 minutes
Aim	To practise writing an enquiry message.
Preparation	Make available for each pair an online package delivery tracker (see *Example*). You could include local places.

Procedure

1   Students read an online package delivery tracker where the delivery is running late, and identify the current date and the latest reported date (see the example below where the package has been processing for 11 days).

2   Tell students they are waiting for the package. In pairs, they write a message to the courier company to ask what has happened.

3   Pairs swap messages and now take the role of customer service officers for the courier company. They read the enquiry message and write a reply. Give the following instructions:
   • If there's not enough information in the message, ask for more in your reply to the customer.
   • If there's enough information, say what you will do.

4   Pairs swap back their messages and replies and decide if they are satisfied with the reply from the courier company: Is it polite? Does it include enough information?

5   Ask students how satisfied they were and whether they have any suggestions to make to the courier company.

Example

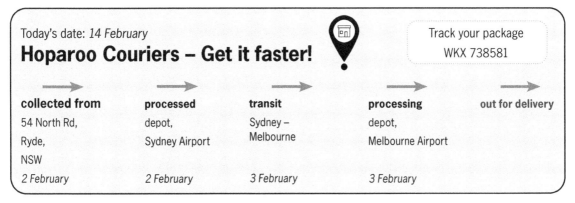

Think further
Establish with learners that enquiry messages of this kind need to include all relevant information. For example, with this message the package number, the current status of the package and all relevant dates should be included.

Notes
If your students need more support, you could elicit/establish what should be included in the initial message at step 2. This means at step 3 students just reply saying what they will do (the *Think further* section would reinforce this). At higher levels, the writing and replying could be done by students working alone.

Rationale

This activity places students in both the writer and audience roles. By writing as if they were customer service officers in step 3, they learn what information is necessary in an enquiry of this nature in order to be able to reply.

4.6 Thinking it through

Outline	Students read an example email, then listen to a visualisation of arriving in an English-speaking country and respond by writing their own email requesting information.
Level	Pre-intermediate (B1) and above
Time	30 minutes (15 minutes if step 7 is done as homework)
Aim	To provide students with thorough preparation in order to write an email requesting further information.
Preparation	You will need to make the offer email available to students (see *Example*). You could write an email offer about another English language learning context that contains few details (e.g. free exam fees) and an associated visualisation.

Procedure

1 Students read an email that offers some kind of scholarship or English language learning opportunity (see the example below). Ask them if they would like to receive something like this.

2 Elicit or point out that the email gives very little detail about practical arrangements and that it would be necessary to reply and ask for more information. Elicit one or two examples of things they would need to ask about.

3 Tell students you are going to read out some sentences about the experience of the language learning opportunity. They should try to imagine the situation and think of things they would like to know – they can make notes.

4 Read the visualisation and make sure you pause often and long enough for students to make notes.

5 Put students in small groups to pool their ideas and turn them into questions.

6 Elicit a range of questions from the class.

7 Students write an email directed to the school asking for more information.

Example
Offer email

● ● ●   Reply   Forward

Congratulations! You've won the scholarship for a free four-week English language course in Vancouver, Canada. The scholarship also includes flights and homestay. Here's important information:

Course dates: 3–28 March

School: The Pacific School of English, central Vancouver.

Homestay: Dan and Sally Paterson, W 2nd Ave, West Point Grey, Vancouver.

We hope you have a great time!

Best wishes

Scholarships Overseas

Visualisation

You arrive at Vancouver Airport and go through passport control and customs. It's Sunday.

You travel from the Airport to Dan and Sally Paterson's house.

You arrive at Dan and Sally's house.

They show you to your room.

You go to bed early – you start school the next day.

You get up, have breakfast and go to the school in central Vancouver.

Think further

Establish with students other contexts where imagining a situation they are going to write about is something they can do on their own. In small groups, ask them to make a list of different email messages/letters where this can be useful.

Notes

Students can write the email as homework. Visualisations can be created for different situations. For example, you could get students to visualise the experience of receiving a damaged product they ordered online. The key is to provide enough information to generate thoughts and/or questions, but not too much so that it pre-empts their own imagination.

Rationale

This activity aims to give learners confidence in asking for more information in response to a written communication that fails to provide enough detail. It encourages them to think through the context in detail by means of visualisation. This can be a useful strategy when planning emails that send or request information.

4.7 Information transfer

Outline	Students use information from an email to write an online ad, then analyse a partner's online ad about a different product and give feedback.
Level	Pre-intermediate to Intermediate (B1–B1+)
Time	40–45 minutes
Aim	To provide practice drafting a descriptive online advertisement; to practise giving peer feedback on writing.
Preparation	You will need to prepare a worksheet such as the one below for your students. You could write emails and ads about products you know your students are interested in.

Procedure

1 Elicit the idea of online auction sites such as eBay where people can buy secondhand goods.

2 Divide the class in half and provide Students A and Students B with the relevant email and online ad (see worksheet below).

3 Students read their email and the online ad, and then with a partner from the same group, write a new online ad using information from the email. All students must write the ad – they will need it for the next stage.

4 Put students in A and B pairs. They swap ads and compare their partner's ad with the example they have on the worksheet. They should give feedback to each other – both positive and negative – and not simply show the example ad.

5 Students discuss whether they would buy either of the products for sale.

Think further

Ask students about online ads in their first language and whether they use complete sentences or just phrases like in the examples. Establish that ads like these need to be clear and direct and emphasise the most appealing aspect of the product for sale.

Notes

Encouraging students to give feedback rather than just show the example answer means that students need to focus on both the example and their partner's writing. It also requires them to prioritise strengths and weaknesses in their partner's writing. A follow up activity for homework could be for students to write an online ad for something they want to sell.

Rationale

This lesson contrasts the level of description of an object in an email in relation to what is included in the ad. Students also need to consider the communicative purpose of this kind of text – it has to try and sell, so key features of the product need to be emphasised. The peer checking means students get immediate feedback on their draft.

⬆ **Worksheet 4.7**

Student A

● ● ●   Reply   Forward

Hi Stefania

Do you remember that blue portable speaker I have? Well, I'm going to sell it. I've had it for about a year now, but there's a new BBT model that's a bit smaller and is a bit more powerful so I'm going to buy that.

If you know of anyone who would like to buy my old one, tell them to get in touch with me. It's in good condition and there are just a couple of small scratches on it. And it's really small and light – I carry it around in my backpack all the time. It's also really easy to use – the Bluetooth connects with any smartphone and it has about 12 hours of play time before you need to recharge it.

The thing I really like about BBT speakers is the sound quality – it's excellent. And it's waterproof – remember we took it the beach last summer?

I've still got the original USB cable. And the price? I'm hoping to get £40 for it.

Thanks
Hans

On-the-Go Action Camera

£200

- Black
- Like new condition. Bought 6 months ago and almost never used.
- Very small – fits in your pocket.
- Easy to use for streaming or recording.
- High-quality video recording and it's waterproof to 10 metres.
- Comes with case, headstrap and extra battery.

Student B

Reply   Forward

Hi Frank

I've decided to sell that black On-the-Go action camera I bought 6 months ago. I've almost never used it and I don't think I ever will. I've realised I'm not so keen on videoing everything I do in life!

Are you interested in buying it? I'd be happy getting £200 – they're worth about £350 brand new. It's in like-new condition. It's very small – you can easily fit it in the pocket of a jacket or jeans.

Although I haven't used it much, it's easy to use if you want to record something, or you can also use it to stream live. It produces high-quality video, and you can even film things underwater – it's waterproof down to 10 metres. And I've still got the original case, headstrap and an extra battery – all in the same new condition.

So if you're interested or your know someone who is, let me know.

Thanks
Mia

BBT Portable Speaker

- Blue
- In good condition. 1 year old with only two small scratches.
- Small and light – easy to carry in a backpack.

- Easy Bluetooth connection with 12 hours of play time.
- Excellent sound quality and it's waterproof – take it to the beach!
- Comes with USB cable.

£40

From *Teaching and Developing Writing Skills* © Cambridge University Press 2023   PHOTOCOPIABLE

4.8 Scripting the board

Outline	Students match the steps of a video storyboard to the correct part of script, add phrases to improve the narration, and then script their own video storyboard.
Level	Pre-intermediate (B1) and above
Time	60 minutes
Aim	To practise writing an explainer video script; to highlight the use of deictic phrases to add clarity to the script.
Preparation	You will need to make available to students a video storyboard and jumbled script sentences similar to those below (see *Example*). You could choose another topic and find or create your own storyboard – there are many examples and templates available online – and write a script.

Procedure

1   Show students a video storyboard for a simple instructional video (see the example storyboard below for how to make a paper plane). Students talk through what's happening in each stage.

2   Students match the jumbled script sentences to the correct steps in the storyboard.

3   Show students the following phrases: *like so, like this, like this one, this way, now you can see* which they should add to the script sentences. Monitor and check students' work (see a sample answer below, but many variations are possible).

4   In small groups, students decide on a topic and create a rough storyboard for a simple instructional video.

5   Two groups work together explaining their storyboard to each other and giving feedback on how clear and easy to follow the steps are.

6   Each group now writes the script for their storyboard followed by a presentation to the whole class.

Example
Video storyboard

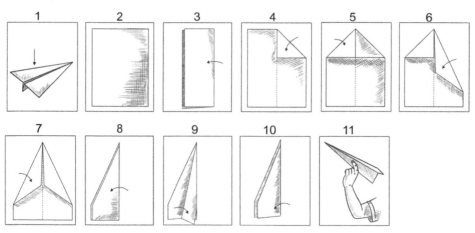

Jumbled script sentences

a.	Now fold the top right corner to the centre to make a triangle.
b.	And fold the outside edge on the left in the same way.
c.	I'm going to show you how to make a simple paper plane.
d.	Do the same thing with the top left corner for the nose of the plane.
e.	Now make the wings. On one side, fold the top edge to the bottom.
f.	Take a sheet of paper.
g.	Fold the outside edge on the right to the centre.
h.	Now your paper plane is ready to fly.
i.	Turn the paper over and do the same to make the other wing.
j.	Fold the paper in half so it makes the shape of a plane.
k.	Fold the paper in half to make a central line and then open it again.

Key
1–c, 2–f, 3–k, 4–a, 5–d, 6–g, 7–b, 8–j, 9–e, 10–i, 11–h

Example answer
1 I'm going to show you how to make a simple paper plane, **like this one**.
2 Take a sheet of paper **like this**.
3 Fold the paper in half to make a central line and then open it again **like so**.
4 Now fold the top right corner to the centre to make a triangle.
5 Do the same thing with the top left corner. **Now you can see** the nose of the plane.
6 Fold the outside edge on the right to the centre **like this**.
7 And fold the outside edge on the left in the same way.
8 Fold the paper in half **this way** so it makes the shape of a plane.
9 Now make the wings. On one side, fold the top edge to the bottom.
10 Turn the paper over and do the same to make the other wing.
11 Now your paper plane is ready to fly.

Think further
Establish with learners that the phrases focused on in step 3 help to make the connection between the script and the images clearer. They can also make the narration simpler by, for example, showing and saying 'like this one', which avoids a long description or explanation.

Notes

Some groups may find step 2 challenging. One way to make this easier is to give students the storyboard with some of the sentences of the script pre-matched. If your group is strong, they could write their own script and you could then get them to add to deictic phrases if they are missing. Students could try and film the instructional video they have scripted perhaps in another lesson or for homework.

Rationale

This activity aims to highlight the usefulness of deictic phrases. The script of a video is likely to be more typical of spoken language, so steps 1 and 5 aim to make the connection between what students say and what they write.

4.9 Complaint chunks

Outline	Students improve an email of complaint by replacing some language with formulaic chunks.
Level	Intermediate (B1+) and above
Time	35 minutes
Aim	To present and practise formulaic chunks of language that can be used in a message complaining about a product.
Preparation	You will need to make available to students an email of complaint and have ready to show relevant language chunks similar to the those below (see *Example*). If you focus on a different product, you can add some formulaic language associated with that product, for example, for clothing: *it doesn't fit*, or a household appliance: *it doesn't work*.

Procedure

1   Students read an email of complaint that is unnatural (see the example below regarding a pair of faulty earbuds).

2   In pairs, students work on improving the email. As they do so, you can gradually show language chunks that are useful (see examples below).

3   Pairs compare their revisions, and then check their drafts against the model answer.

4   Students write an email of complaint about a product they have bought recently, or they imagine a problem. They use as many of the language chunks as appropriate.

5   Pairs read each other's emails and compare the way they have used the language chunks.

Example

> I bought earbuds from your internet shop – see a copy of the receipt. After about 10 days I started hearing static in the right earbud. In the beginning, I could hear it only occasionally, but in the past week the problem is bad. I think the wiring is wrong in the earbud.
>
> There's still a guarantee, so fix or give me new pair. Tell me the solution.

Language chunks

to begin with	what should I do next?
under guarantee	the problem has got worse and worse
I bought X online	get them either fixed or replaced
there's something wrong with	I've attached

Model answer

I <u>bought earbuds online</u> from you about a month ago – <u>I've attached</u> a copy of the receipt to this message. After about 10 days I started hearing a noise in the right earbud. <u>To begin with,</u> I could hear it only occasionally, but in the past week <u>the problem has got worse and worse</u>. I think <u>there's something wrong with</u> the wiring in the earbud.

The earbuds are still <u>under guarantee</u>, so I'd like to <u>get them either fixed or replaced</u>. Can you tell me <u>what I should do next</u>?

Think further

Establish with learners that the language chunks you showed in step 2 (and any others you noticed when monitoring) can be used when complaining about problems with different online product purchases. Point out that sometimes it's a good idea to learn complete phrases or expressions that can be used in a range of similar situations.

Notes

At step 2, monitor and see if students are using any of the expressions you aim to feed into their writing. If they are, you could draw attention to this to illustrate that some of the expressions are already known. With a group that needs more support, all of the expressions can be shown at once in step 2.

Rationale

The genre of making a written complaint is frequently focused on in coursebooks and something that students are likely to use in their daily lives if they are living in an English language speaking country, or they have bought goods online from a company that transacts in English. The activity aims to focus on the formulaic nature of much of the language appropriate for making written complaints. The drip feeding of the chunks aims to give students some room to come up with their own ideas as they improve the message. If they do, only provide expressions that are necessary.

4.10 Gallery guidelines

Outline	Students simplify the language of a set of guidelines then write their own for a context they are familiar with.
Level	Intermediate (B1+) and above
Time	45 minutes
Aim	To practise writing guidelines that are straightforward and clear for the intended audience.
Preparation	You will need to make available to students a set of guidelines similar to the one below (see *Example*). Alternatively, you could write over-elaborated guidelines for another context you think would be more suitable for your students.

Procedure

1   Students read visitor guidelines for an institution (see the example below for an art gallery), and decide if they are typical for institutions in their own country.

2   Establish that the guidelines are written for a brochure and are longer than they need to be. They need to be rewritten to be clearer for a range of visitors including those who don't have English as their first language. Suggest students use bullet points.

3   In pairs, students rewrite the guidelines within a word limit of 150–170 words.

4   In pairs, students compare their versions. You could show a model answer.

5   Students write guidelines for another context where rules need to be followed, for example, going to a swimming pool or gym.

Example

Reply   Forward

Welcome to our gallery. To make sure everyone has a safe, enjoyable visit, remember you must follow our guidelines.

You are free to stay as long as you like and, of course, we want you to take your time and see as much as you can. However, we ask that you avoid touching any of the artworks because your touch can damage the artwork. And also be very careful to keep a safe distance between you and the works of art as well as other visitors. We don't want someone to accidentally knock into any of the artwork.

We're sorry, but you cannot take any food or drink into the gallery. However, we do have a café and you are welcome to go there during your visit. We also ask you not to take any bags with you into the gallery. There is a cloakroom where you can leave your bags and which is a free service.

You may wish to bring a smartphone or another digital device with you into the gallery. As you are probably aware, our wi-fi is free and you can use it during your visit. However, if you are planning to take any photos in the gallery, you are not allowed to use the flash on your camera because this can damage the artwork. At the same time, if you want to listen to music during your visit, you must use headphones. Not everyone has the same taste and your music could be annoying for some other visitors.

(253 words)

Model answer

●●●   Reply   Forward

Welcome to our gallery. To make sure everyone has a safe, enjoyable visit, remember to follow our guidelines.

- Stay as long as you like and take your time to see as much as you can.
- Don't touch any of the artwork – it could be damaging.
- Keep a safe distance between you, the artwork and other visitors to avoid any accidents.
- Don't take food or drink into the gallery, but feel free to visit our café during your visit.
- All bags must be left in the cloakroom – it's a free service.
- Bring a smartphone or other digital device and use our free wi-fi.
- Don't use flash if you take photos in the gallery because this can damage artwork.
- Use headphones if you want to listen to music during your visit.
(130 words)

Think further

Establish with learners that using imperatives and bullet points are clearer. Point out that imperatives in written form are appropriate for people the writer doesn't know, but often may be too direct when speaking to someone.

Notes

While one of the aims of this activity is to highlight the changes in language for the sake of clarity, an alternative approach could be to provide rules in note form from which students write the guidelines. For example:

✓	✗
stay long time, bring smartphone/digital device, etc.	*touch artworks, any food or drink, etc.*

Check students' use of the imperative form and teach this grammar point if appropriate. At a higher level, you could include more varied forms in the example answer, for example: *If you touch artworks, you can damage them.* However, bear in mind that the aim is clarity so they shouldn't be too complex.

Rationale

Writing guidelines of this nature is a common writing activity in English language classes, but often students' texts are more complicated and long-winded than necessary. This can be the result of trying to write more complex language more suited for an essay. This activity emphasises clear and direct written communication for certain genres of writing.

4.11 Question guided instructions

Outline	Students think of practical questions associated with looking after someone's home, then use these to write instructions for someone looking after their home.
Level	Pre-intermediate (B1) and above
Time	45 minutes
Aim	To practise writing a set of instructions; to demonstrate how reader expectations can guide coherence of a text.
Preparation	No preparation is necessary other than thinking of some relevant linking words and phrases (see *Example*) unless you want to write a model text for a group that needs more support.

Procedure

1   Ask students to imagine they are coming to stay in your home to look after it for two days while you are away. In pairs, students think of practical questions to ask you about the way your home works, for example, an alarm code, wi-fi code, rubbish.

2   Elicit different questions and put them on the board or on screen.

3   Ask students to imagine someone is coming to stay in their home while they are away. Are there any other things the person might need to know about? Elicit some examples.

4   Show students some useful linking words and phrases they can use.

5   Working alone, students use the questions to write a list of important, practical points to the person staying in their home needs to know. Tell them to order the information in a logical way and use the linking words and phrases.

6   Pairs swap their instructions and give feedback on how clear they are.

Example
Linking words and phrases

you asked about	finally
after that	as I mentioned in my email
I'll start by talking about the most important thing	by the way

Think further
Ask students if they wrote their instructions from their point of view or the point of view of the reader. Establish the value of writing this kind of instructional text from the reader's point of view as this will help them organise their writing in a logical way. With this context, a good approach is to imagine how the person staying will move through the home once they are inside, and what they might find or need.

Notes
If you feel your students need more support, you could show them a model text at the end of step 4. With a stronger group, you could begin this activity at step 3 and skip step 4 and ask students whether their partner's instructions would benefit from the use of linkers.

Rationale

This activity emphasises the connection between coherence and reader expectations. There is a very tangible relationship between the two, but in all writing, it helps if students write with the target audience in mind. The linking words and phrases show how cohesive devices can underpin and strengthen coherence.

4.12 Service request

Outline	Students choose phrasal verbs and their collocations to write a service request for a product or service, then write a request.
Level	Intermediate (B1+) and above
Time	40 minutes
Aim	To provide practice writing online service requests; to highlight the use of phrasal verbs and their collocations associated with household goods and services.
Preparation	You will need to prepare word roses for students such as the ones below (see *Example*). You could produce word roses with different phrasal verbs and collocations on a different topic, for example, plumbing: *fill up / sink; connect up / pipe; turn on / tap.*

Procedure

1   Show students a pair of word roses on a specific topic, one rose contains phrasal verbs, the other words they collocate with (the example focuses on IT).

2   In pairs, students look at the words in the roses and think of a problem with a product or service associated with the topic. They then write a service request message asking for help with a problem, but they must use at least two phrasal verbs and their collocates from each rose.

3   Display all the messages so students can see them (either pin them up around a room or show on screen).

4   Each pair chooses another pair's message and writes a reply that includes a suggestion on how they can deal with the issue.

5   The answers are posted, and each pair decides if the reply (or replies) to their initial message is helpful or not. Pairs who receive no replies can write a follow up message to say they have now fixed the problems and describe how they did this.

6   Ask the class for examples of useful advice and ask those who received no help why they think they didn't.

Example
Word roses: IT

Think further

Establish with learners that many phrasal verbs can be associated with a specific topic and they will often collocate with specific nouns, for example *pull down* collocates with *menu* in the context of computer software, but the meaning changes if it collocates with the word *building*. Suggest students record phrasal verbs in topic areas with words they collocate with.

Notes

If you want to make this easier, you could provide students with a choice of possible options for students to choose the correct collocate, for example, *click on – icon / ~~cable~~ / application*. Alternatively, you could show just the first word rose and ask students to think of their own collocations for the topic.

Rationale

In their daily lives, students may need to engage with help desks for products and services that may not be based in their home countries, and perhaps even use English to communicate the problem. The focus on phrasal verbs and collocations aims to encourage students to use context as a means of recalling vocabulary. The interactive nature of this activity is a way of providing a sense of audience for their initial message.

4.13 Email evaluation

Outline	Students evaluate three problematic competition entries before writing their own version.
Level	Intermediate (B1+) and above
Time	45 minutes
Aim	To practise evaluating the content and tone of emails for a volunteer work opportunity.
Preparation	You will need to make an advertisement for a volunteer work opportunity and a relevant email available to each student (see *Example*). You could think of a different kind of advertisement, for example, for a competition, and write an invitation and three example entries in which the writing is problematic. You can vary the nature of the problem.

Procedure

1   Students read an invitation to apply to do volunteer work (see example below). Check for any unknown vocabulary.

2   In small groups, students discuss what information they would include in their email.

3   Put students in to three groups: A, B and C. Students in each group read an email application for the volunteer opportunity (see examples below), and decide what the problem is with it. Make sure each student has a copy of their email.

4   Check answers individually with each group – not as a whole class.

5   Students work in new groups of three with one student each from groups A, B and C. They tell each other about their emails and explain the nature of the problem.

6   In the same groups, students collaborate to write their own email for the competition entry. They can then share their versions with other groups. Students could check their email against a model answer.

Key
Email A = too enthusiastic, not enough information about the writer's background;
Email B = the tone is too confident and overly assertive, and the description of experience has no detail;
Email C = the information is given randomly and lacks coherence.

Model answer
I'd like to apply for the opportunity to go to Bali and work with Reef Savers to help save coral reefs.

   I've been interested in environmental issues, particularly the marine environment, since I was about 14 years old. There's no doubt that coral reefs play an important part in the ecosystem of our oceans. They are also beautiful environments and need to be maintained for future generations.

   I don't have any experience cleaning and replanting coral reefs, but I have been involved with several environmental projects aimed at protecting our oceans. For example, last summer I worked in a team cleaning up plastic waste. I've also given talks to high school students about these projects.

   I have a diving licence and four years' experience diving. I believe I am a suitable person to work with Reef Savers and would be really excited to do so.

Example

Opportunity to save a coral reef!

Reefer Saver is a coral reef protection programme based in Bali. Apply for a six-week stay with the *Reef Saver* team to help save and restore coral reefs. You will receive the following:

- return flight to Bali
- three-day training programme
- all diving equipment provided
- all food and accommodation for the six-week stay

During your stay you will:

- clean and replant coral
- give short webinars on your work with Reef Savers

To apply you need to send an email (maximum 150 words) and tell us about the following:

- why you would like to take part in the Reef Saver programme
- what past experience you have that makes you the right person

Please note: all applicants must have a current diving licence.

Send your email to: competition@RST.com

● ● ● **Email A** Reply   Forward

I'd like to apply for the Reef Saver volunteer position and work with the team in Bali.

I think saving coral reefs is one of the most important things we can do to protect marine life. A coral reef is a key part of underwater ecosystems and plays a central role in the well-being of planet Earth. It takes hundreds of years for a reef to grow and then a fishing boat can destroy everything in a matter of minutes. I can hardly believe how this destruction is possible.

As a result, I can see how important it is to try and save as many coral reefs as possible and I can see Reef Saver is doing an amazing job. I'd love the opportunity to fly to Bali and join the team for six weeks. I'm very hard working and enthusiastic, and I don't think you would regret choosing me.

Email B

Reply   Forward

I want the job with Reef Saver. The reason I want it is that I think I'm one of the best people to help repair the coral reef because I've got lots of experience.

I've done this work before and everyone said I was good at it. I was in Australia and worked on the reef there. It was a mess – people just don't care enough about these things. Anyway, we cleaned things up and did some replanting.

I've got a diving licence and I've done a lot of diving. You don't need to worry about that. And, by the way, I want to go to Bali – it looks like a fun place to go for a while. I just hope the accommodation and food is OK. Please choose me – I'd be the best.

Email C

Reply   Forward

I don't have any experience cleaning and replanting coral reefs, but I have been involved with several environmental projects aimed at protecting our oceans.

I believe I am a suitable person to work with Reef Savers and would be really excited to do so. I've given talks to high school students about these projects.

There's no doubt that coral reefs play an important part in the eco system of our oceans. I've been interested in environmental issues, particularly the marine environment, since I was about 14 years old.

I have a diving licence and four years' experience diving. Coral reefs are also beautiful environments and need to be maintained for future generations.

Think further

Elicit from students key points that need to be observed when writing job applications for paid or volunteer work, for example, include all relevant information requested, make sure your tone is polite and enthusiastic, and make sure your email is logically organised. Point out these are all points to consider when evaluating their own writing of this nature.

Notes

If you feel students need more support, the points in *Think further* could be elicited/established either at step 3 or step 5. Another alternative would be to show the sample answer as a model and provide students with a new competition invitation.

Rationale

This activity aims to develop students' evaluation skills with a specific focus on information and the tone used in this kind of email. Students need to ensure they include all relevant information that is requested, and that it is presented in a clear and logical way. They also need to bear in mind the audience they are writing for and show enthusiasm without being too forceful.

5 Writing expressively

This chapter focuses on writing that provides students with opportunities to express themselves and explore their creativity. This is sometimes known as 'creative' or 'free' writing; in this chapter, the term 'expressive writing' is used. Compared to activities in other chapters, there is more of a sense of the teacher stepping back and giving students the room to explore their own ideas and imagination, the importance of which is recognised by Hyland (2019). This suggests a more open-ended, playful and humanistic approach to developing students' writing skills. Teachers are less likely to provide model texts unless they act as a spark to generate ideas and creativity. However, this does not mean that all expressive writing takes place in a 'genre-free' environment. Students' ideas and feelings can sometimes be explored within the conventions of fictional and other literary genres. Likewise, close attention to language can help students express their creativity effectively in writing.

Functions, genres and patterns

Expressive writing involves direct communication of the writer's view of a subject they are writing about, which conveys a specific emotion or feeling. This writing usually provokes an emotional response in the reader – humour, wonder, fear – or it may cause them to think and reflect. Expressive writing can do this using a variety of means. It can narrate a story, which can either be based on a real event or be entirely fictional. For example, a writer can tell the story of a childhood memory and say why it still has meaning for them now, or they could invent a story that aims to impart a message or perhaps has the sole purpose of amusing the reader. Some expressive writing describes the physical world and explores its meaning for the writer, or a description could involve feelings and sensations associated with the writer's internal world. Expressive writing can also encompass some kind of discussion or argumentation. For example, two characters in a novel may argue two different points of view on a subject. The writer can also be in discussion with themself. Many of Shakespeare's sonnets are personal meditations in which he explores different points of view (Edmondson & Wells, 2020).

Expressive writing is either very genre-bound or not at all. If a writer is recalling a childhood memory in a diary, they are not likely to be concerned with specific genre conventions in the same way they might be if the memory were written as a blogpost where genre conventions and a sense of audience could influence choices about the content and language used. Also, the audience that they are writing for is most likely themself. Conversely, expressive writing that is fictional often aims to respect specific genre conventions, and at the same time, the writer is very aware of making the story interesting for the reader – the audience. Biber and Conrad (2019) note the genre conventions of novels: they are usually character-based stories of conflict that build to a climax that is then resolved. Within the novel genre, there are also sub-genre categories with more specific conventions. For example, fantasy fiction is expected to contain some kind of supernatural element, an unreal physical setting and a conflict that is usually associated with competing power structures. Often expressive writing is literary in nature, and the conventions can be historical and very specific. A writer wishing to express their thoughts and feelings in poetry, for example, can choose from a variety of poetic forms such as sonnet, ballad, haiku, elegy, limerick, etc. all of which have conventions associated with stanzas, lines and metre as well as the physical layout of the poem on the page. These different forms aim to shape what the poet wishes to express and communicate. Plays or scripts are another literary form that differs from other written genres in that they are written specifically to be performed in front of an audience (Biber & Conrad, 2019).

While a piece of expressive writing can encompass any of the three main discourse patterns discussed in the Introduction (problem–solution, general–particular, claim–counterclaim), they are unlikely to be of primary concern in the act of expression. A classic example of macro problem–solution patterning, for example, is a whodunnit crime story. Likewise, a piece of expressive writing that is descriptive writing often begins with some kind of overview of a scene – the general – and then moves on to examine specific details in the scene – the particular. Discourse patterns tend to be used as tools for analysing expressive writing rather than providing frameworks that guide the form of expression.

Language

The prevalence of storytelling in much expressive writing means there is frequent use of narrative tenses. It could be argued that expressive writing should be very free and less concerned with grammatical accuracy than writing in other, more formal or instrumental texts. However, there are instances when grammatical accuracy adds clarity to an expressive text, for example, an ability to deploy narrative tenses effectively when telling a story allows the writer to sequence events in a dramatically interesting way. Narrative tenses in stories are often used together with time adverbials such as *after that, suddenly, immediately*.

Expressive writing can also involve a lot of descriptive language. Writers will often choose adjectives and adverbs carefully so that the event or experience they are writing about is clearly described. Sometimes descriptive language has a strong emotional charge in order to invoke a specific feeling in a reader. The language can also be playful and involve rhyme, alliteration or repetition. While this could suggest the language of a children's nursey rhyme, it also evokes the limerick form, an example of adult playful language. Although clearly a quite specific genre with a very targeted audience, it is interesting to note that advertising, too, will often use playful language to engage prospective customers.

Expressive writing that is descriptive will include a variety of noun and adjective phrases. In order to describe a scene or a feeling or sensation, writers often strive for the exact words to render what they see and feel. These very specific lexical choices are even more critical when the expressive writing is a literary genre. This suggests writers need to be able to draw on a wide range of language.

In the classroom

Hyland (2019: p.9) suggests that the personal nature of expressive writing means that it is 'learnt, not taught'. In effect, writers learn to write by writing in the same way they can learn to speak by speaking. As a result, there is not likely to be directive instruction for this kind of writing, rather teachers provide students with activities that encourage them to use their imagination and express themselves in writing. There is sometimes no expected outcome in the form of a specific product (email message, article, report) and teachers may wish their students to engage with expressive writing because they see it as part of an on-going process of developing a students' ability to write in English. As such, it could be argued that expressive writing benefits students indirectly and underpins their ability to engage with a wide range of non-expressive genres.

Some teachers also see expressive writing as an opportunity for students to develop life competency skills, in particular, skills associated with creative thinking (Cambridge University Press, 2020). It allows students to express their feelings and explore their identity and so teachers are able to use writing activities to integrate life skills within English language classes.

References

Biber, D. & Conrad, S. (2019) *Register, Genre, and Style Second Edition*. Cambridge, Cambridge University Press.

Cambridge University Press (2020) *The Cambridge Framework of Life Competencies*. Available at: www.cambridge.org/gb/cambridgeenglish/better-learning-insights/cambridgelifecompetenciesframework [Accessed 22nd March 2022].

Edmondson, P. & Wells, S. (eds.) (2020) *All the Sonnets of Shakespeare*. Cambridge, Cambridge University Press.

Hyland, K. (2019) *Second Language Writing Second Edition*. Cambridge, Cambridge University Press.

5.1 Future selves

Outline	Students write a description of their future self as an English language user.
Level	Elementary (A2) and above
Time	35 minutes
Aim	To practise writing a description of future learning; to find out about students' long-term goals.
Preparation	No preparation is necessary unless you want to make available for students a sample answer (see *Example*). Students are likely to be motivated by reading or listening to a paragraph about your own future self associated with another language you may be learning.

Procedure

1   In pairs, students tell each other why they are learning English and what they want to do with it in the future.

2   Show the heading *My future English self* together with some prompts like the following:
I will ... I'll be able to ... speak ... talk to ... read ... write ... understand ...
You can also show them an example – see below a Norwegian speaking future self.

3   Students write a description of their future English self – they can imagine anything they like.

4   Students work in small groups of four to six students. They read each other's future selves and find similarities between them.

5   In open class, ask each group for examples of similarities.

Example

> In the future, I will speak Norwegian very well. I'll go to Oslo and Bergen and meet a lot of different people. I'll be able to understand everything they say. I'll be able to read Jo Nesbø's crime novels in Norwegian and talk about them with Norwegian friends. And I'll write a blog about my time in Norway in Norwegian.

Think further

Establish with groups that their future selves may be far in the future, but it's good to have an ideal, ultimate goal. In the meantime, they can have more achievable goals such as being able to talk about family, friends and hobbies in English.

Notes

This activity is very suitable at the beginning of a course. Before step 3, students could talk in pairs about their future selves before writing the description. At higher levels, students will need less support

Rationale

Getting students to focus on learning goals can involve short-term, achievable objectives, but it can also include a longer-term dream. Both can be important in keeping motivation alive. While learners could talk about this, getting them to write down their future self gives them a bit more time to think about what different possibilities and opportunities might be available to them. It also means the teacher can collect in these descriptions and get a broader view of students' English language learning goals.

Reference

This activity is based on an idea from:
Hadfield, J. & Dörnyei, Z. (2013) *Motivating Learning*. London, Routledge.

5.2 Imaginary weekend

Outline	Students imagine a perfect weekend and then write about it as though it were a past event.
Level	Elementary (A2) and above
Time	35 minutes
Aim	To practise writing fluency; to practise writing a personal narrative.
Preparation	No preparation is necessary.

Procedure

1   In pairs, students tell each other about their perfect, imaginary weekend. They have plenty of money and should choose at least three things to do from the following categories: *people you meet, an outdoor activity, entertainment, food, something you buy, a social event.*

2   Students work alone and write about their perfect weekend as though it happened last weekend – as a past event. Let them know they will share their writing with other students.

3   Students work in small groups of three to five students (it's better if the pairs in step 1 aren't in the same group). They read about each other's weekends and decide whose weekend is most different from theirs.

4   Students ask follow up questions about the weekend, for example, why they chose to do one activity or another.

Think further

Ask learners if the writing would have been more or less difficult without step 1 of the lesson. Establish that it often helps to think and then talk about the content of writing before they write. This applies to both imaginary ideas and real events.

Notes

With a class that needs more support, it may help to give your own example of an imaginary weekend to act as an oral model for the speaking. It might also help to get students to make notes of their ideas before they begin writing.

Rationale

A key aim of this activity is to practise writing fluency, but contextualising the writing as a past event is a way of giving practice of narrative tenses. In this regard, the activity could be diagnostic or it could provide revision of previously taught language. Getting students to imagine a perfect weekend is a way of generating ideas. Often if students are asked to write about their own past weekends, they will say they didn't do anything interesting and have nothing to write about. The group work in steps 4 and 5 means there is an audience for their writing as well as providing spoken fluency practice.

5.3 The thing I love the most

Outline	Students write a description of something they own and love without saying what it is. They read their descriptions aloud and students guess what it is.
Level	Elementary (A2) and above
Time	30 minutes
Aim	To provide freer practice of writing a description of an object.
Preparation	No preparation is necessary.

Procedure

1 Show students the following phrases:
   It's made of ... It's (colour) ... It's (shape) ... I use it to ...
   I bought it in ... It cost/didn't cost ... It was given to me by ...
   I've had it for ... I like it because ...

2 Students think of something they own and write a paragraph about it using the phrases in step 1. However, they should not say what the object is.

3 Students work in small groups and read aloud their paragraph – other students guess what the object is. Students can ask follow up questions to help them guess, e.g. *Is it something you can play? Do you use this in the kitchen?*

4 Each group chooses one of the descriptions to read to the whole class, who guess what the object is.

Think further

Elicit from learners what they felt was the most difficult part of the description. Ask for some example sentences and write them on the board. Elicit or give improvements, if necessary, or leave as good examples.

Notes

If your class needs more support, you can change some of the phrases in step 1, for example, *it was given to me by ...* can be replaced with *[person] gave it to me ...*. You could also elicit or give colours and shapes. At higher levels, you could do the activity with just prompts rather than phrases, for example, *material, colour, shape, time of possession*, etc. If you have an LMS where students can post writing, they can post their paragraph with a picture of the object. If the lesson is being conducted online, students could show each other the object they have described in step 4.

Rationale

This activity provides students with a framework for describing objects which has potential crossover to different genres, for example, describing a faulty product in a letter of complaint (see Chapter 4). This activity can also be included in an early course 'getting to know each other' phase. The description of a loved object reveals something about the owner.

5.4 Word story

Outline	Students write a fictional story from three words prompts, and then read and try to identify the words in a partner's story.
Level	Elementary (A2) and above
Time	40 minutes
Aim	To provide fluency practice writing a fictional narrative.
Preparation	You will need to make available to students a simple framework for them to complete. If using hard copies in the classroom, it may help to make enough copies for every pair in your class. Alternatively, you could get students to copy the rubric from the board on to a blank piece of paper.

Procedure

1 Tell students they are going to write a story from words. Give pairs the following framework:

verb	noun	adjective

2 Each pair writes a verb in the first box and then pass the rubric to another pair. The second pair adds a noun then passes to a third pair who completes the adjective box.

3 A fourth pair receives the completed rubric. They think of, and then write a story in which all three words are included. Ask students to write an imaginary story. It may pay to set a time limit.

4 Two pairs work together (make sure neither of the pairs have contributed words to the rubric). They read each other's stories without looking at the rubric and try to identify the three words in the story that they had to include.

5 Ask students if they read a story by another pair that they enjoyed. The story can be read aloud, and all students try to guess the words.

Think further

Ask students which word or words gave them the main idea for their story. Elicit examples of how individual words can suggest ideas, for example, a verb might suggest an event, a noun an object and an adjective could suggest a person. Establish that using prompts like words or pictures or sounds can be a good way to start a story.

Notes

A class that needs more support could be shown a range of words for each word class and students select a word rather than having to come up with one. At higher levels, two words can be placed in each column. Alternatively, with a class that enjoys fictional writing and is confident, the activity could be done by students working on their own. This activity can also be done using online automatic word generating tools such as: www.thewordfinder.com/random-word-generator/ or https://randomwordgenerator.com/.

Rationale

This activity offers students the chance to use their creativity and show how random prompts can help generate a fictional story (also see Activity 5.10). It also offers students an opportunity to practise narrative tenses.

References

This activity is adapted from 'Developing a Story' (Stanley 2013).

Stanley, G. (2013) *Language Learning with Technology*. Cambridge, Cambridge University Press.
The Word Finder Available at: www.thewordfinder.com/random-word-generator/
Random Word Generator Available at: https://randomwordgenerator.com/

5.5 Fill the bubble

Outline	Students complete the speech bubbles for a cartoon then pool their ideas with other students to create a final draft.
Level	Elementary (A2) and above
Time	35 minutes
Aim	To provide free practice writing dialogue; to encourage peer collaboration for writing.
Preparation	Search online for a cartoon with blank speech bubbles that you think will be suitable for your students. A search with the terms 'comic strip blank speech bubbles' will result in freely available templates. If you are good at drawing, you could draw your own cartoon.

Procedure

1 In pairs, students discuss the pictures of a cartoon with blank speech bubbles. They talk about the following questions:
  - Who are the characters?
  - Where are they?
  - What's happening between them?

2 Pairs write the first draft of dialogue in the speech bubbles.

3 Two sets of pairs then work together and compare their dialogues. They write a second draft incorporating ideas from both first drafts.

4 Final drafts are displayed for the whole class to read. Students decide on the version that is closest to theirs and the one that is most different.

Think further

Elicit from students what improvements they made to their first drafts when they worked with a new pair. Establish that it can be useful to collaborate on writing projects and get ideas from each other as well as make improvements to the text.

Notes

It is important to choose a blank cartoon that is suitable for the level of the class. The right illustrations can provide an opportunity to revise previously functional language. However, with some groups it might be more motivating to use a more genre-based cartoon (for example, science fiction, fantasy) that appeals to their creativity.

Rationale

Writing dialogue for a cartoon offers an alternative for students who are less motivated by writing prose. The visual element of cartoons is also likely to motivate students who respond well to visual stimuli. Step 3 of the activity aims to give students insight into the benefits of peer support when writing.

5.6 That old sensation

Outline	Students describe a memory associated with a specific sensation. Groups swap texts and guess who, in the other group, wrote each text.
Level	Pre-intermediate (B1) and above (see *Notes*)
Time	30 minutes
Aim	To provide free practice of descriptive writing.
Preparation	Think about an example sensation memory from your childhood. If teaching in a face-to-face classroom context, you may wish to provide pieces of paper for students to write on to facilitate the groups swap in step 3.

Procedure

1   Tell students about a sensation memory from your childhood and then show the prompt: *The sight / sound/ small / taste of . . . reminds me of my childhood.*

2   Students work alone and use the prompt to begin writing about a sensation memory from childhood. They add more detail, for example, they describe the sensation, when and where it took place, the people involved.

3   Put students in groups of 5 to 8. They collect their texts and swap them with another group.

4   Students read the other group's memories and guess which student wrote it.

5   Groups work together to check their guesses.

6   Check with the whole class if they found any memories that were very similar.

Think further

Elicit from students which of the memories they read were very clear to them and why this was the case. Establish simple criteria for descriptive writing, for example, varied use of adjectives, giving clear detail. Suggest that it helps to form a picture in their mind before they write.

Notes

With classes that need more support, you can ask for less detail in step 2, for example, they just write about where and when the sensation took place. With higher levels, you can ask students to write a complete paragraph. There's also the option of focusing on sentence starters before students write. These could be included in your oral memory and then pre-taught. Examples are: *I [distinctly/ vaguely] remember + that-clause or -ing; I can still hear/see/smell . . . ; It always brings back memories of . . . / makes me feel. . . ; The sight/sound/smell/ taste of . . . reminds me of . . . .*

Rationale

This activity gets students focused on descriptive writing and building a full picture of a feeling associated with a specific event. The guessing in step 4 adds a game element to the activity as well as providing an opportunity to share. The group swap means that students are unlikely to feel shy about the reading of their memory alongside others in this sharing stage of the lesson.

5.7 After the cliff hanger

Outline	Students read or watch a story until its cliff hanger ending, then write a continuation of the story and share in small groups.
Level	Pre-intermediate (B1) and above
Time	40 minutes
Aim	To provide freer practice writing an imaginary narrative; to show how to create interest in storylines.
Preparation	You will need to make available a story with a cliff hanger climax for each student (see *Example*). You could find a story or a scene from a TV programme or film that you think will be suitable for your students.

Procedure

1 Elicit or teach the term 'cliff hanger' with reference to a key dramatic point in a storyline.

2 Students read part of a story or watch a scene from a TV programme or film with a cliff hanger ending.

3 In pairs or small groups, students discuss ideas about what might happen next.

4 Students work alone and write the continuation of the story.

5 In small groups, students read and compare their endings and decide which is the most surprising, the funniest, the most dramatic and/or any other categories they can think of.

6 With the whole class, ask students to read out three or four example endings.

Think further

Elicit from students why writers of stories and scripts use cliff hanger endings at certain points in a story – in order to keep their readers/viewers engaged. Point out that the general idea of having key points in a narrative is a way to create interest for the reader – even narratives about personal experiences.

Notes

If using a scene from a TV programme or film, you will need to find something that none of the students have seen or know the ending to. The continuation could be written as dialogue rather than a narrative. This activity can be very effective if you use a graded reader that students are reading as part of their course as they will already have a good understanding of the characters and context of the story.

Example

Josh and Melinda had both had a long and busy day. They ate their meal and did the dishes in silence. Melinda then collapsed on the sofa, turned on the TV and changed from one channel to the other every two or three minutes. Josh found this irritating and went off to use the computer in their study. He surfed the internet looking at different cake recipes. He imagined baking and eating each cake.

They had been married for just over a year now. They had a comfortable and spacious apartment filled with everything they needed. But after the excitement of planning the wedding and their honeymoon, married life wasn't everything they had hoped it would be. It felt like they had nothing more to say to each other.

Each night, they both lay awake trying to understand what had changed. They both noticed that the apartment made strange sounds. It was in an old building so they thought this was the reason for the noises. Josh sometimes almost felt like there was another person in the apartment. Melinda sometimes felt there was a movement of the air even though the windows weren't open. These feelings and sensations kept them awake at night and made them feel even more tired and alone. But they never said anything about them to each other.

As Melinda was watching a documentary on TV and Josh was reading a rich chocolate cake recipe, the power suddenly went off. Melinda sighed, pulled herself off the sofa and found some candles and matches in the kitchen.

'What is it?' asked Josh.

'I don't know,' replied Melinda. 'Probably the fuse box on the landing. Can you come with me and hold the candle while I look?'

Josh took the candle and they moved towards their front door. Melinda opened the door and what they saw in front of them in the candlelight was the thing they feared most.

Rationale

Students often enjoy the opportunity to give free rein to their imagination and develop a narrative, without the restrictions imposed by more formal written genres. Apart from giving freer practice of writing a narrative, the activity also directs students to the strategy of creating interest and sense of drama in a narrative.

5.8 Don't mention the snake

Outline	Students transcribe part of a role play, edit it and rewrite it imagining a snake has been introduced into the role play context.
Level	Pre-intermediate (B1) and above
Time	50 minutes (see *Notes* for option to spread activity across two lessons)
Aim	To practise improving and adapting scripted written language.
Preparation	Find a role play that you think would be suitable for your students' level and the nature of this activity, for example, buying clothes in a shop or two friends meeting in a café to catch up. Alternatively, you could invent your own role play scenario and instructions, perhaps something that revises previously taught language.

Procedure

1   Put students in pairs and give them a situation which is familiar to them for a short role play. Students do the role play and record themselves.

2   Students then listen to themselves and transcribe a part (or all) of the role play – between 30 seconds and a minute of dialogue.

3   Each pair then edits their dialogue improving the language and perhaps making it more interesting.

4   Ask students to imagine a snake suddenly appearing at some point in their role play. Each pair now rewrites the dialogue with this in mind, but must not make any direct mention of the snake.

5   In groups of 6 to 10 students, students perform their scripted dialogue for each other. Although the snake is not mentioned in the dialogue, they should try and show the characters are aware of it when they perform.

6   Invite two or three pairs to perform their dialogue for the whole class.

Think further

Elicit from students what language they improved at step 4 of the activity. Establish that transcribing language and editing it in this way can be a useful way for improving overall language accuracy.

Notes

The snake is only one possible external element that can be introduced – this can be varied according to the teaching-learning context and level. With higher-level classes, two external elements could be introduced, for example, *you are in the back of a hot taxi and can't open the windows, and the driver is driving very dangerously*. The lesson could be divided up into two parts: step 1 could be done in a first lesson and steps 2 and 3 could be done as a homework activity with the remainder of the activity carried out in a subsequent lesson.

Rationale

Getting students to transcribe the role play has two functions. It is an opportunity for self and peer correction of language, and also gives students dialogue to work with for the second part of the activity. This is often easier than writing a script from scratch. The introduction of a dangerous external element is a technique used in dramatic improvisation. It adds a creative layer on the activity and introduces an element of fun.

5.9 This was when

Outline	Students write a paragraph caption for a photo that shows a memorable event or occasion and then read and edit each other's paragraphs.
Level	Pre-intermediate (B1) and above
Time	40–45 minutes
Aim	To provide freer practice writing about past events; to practise peer editing of texts.
Preparation	Before the lesson, ask students to bring a personal photo (digital or hardcopy) of a past event or occasion that was memorable to them.

Procedure

1   In pairs, students show a picture from their past associated with a memorable event or occasion and tell each other the background to the photo. (If some students have forgotten to bring a photo, they can just describe the event.)

2   Show students the following instructions for writing a paragraph caption for their photo.
   a   Begin with *This photograph was taken when* ...
   b   Explain what happened before and after.
   c   Describe how you felt.

3   Students work alone and write a paragraph. Set a time limit and move to the next stage if there are just a few students who have not quite completed their paragraph.

4   In new pairs, students exchange and read each other's paragraphs. They ask each other more detailed questions about the event or occasion.

5   Remind students of the following narrative tenses: past simple, past continuous and past perfect.

6   Students now edit the tense used in each other's paragraph and give feedback.

7   Students revise their paragraphs. They can add more information as a result of the questions their partner asked and/or they can improve the tense use.

8   If appropriate, students can 'publish' their photos and paragraphs on a class blog/LMS or on a notice board.

Think further

Elicit or establish from students other language areas they could have given feedback on in step 6. For example, the use of adjectives to describe the scene and the feelings the writer felt, or the use of linking words and expressions to indicate time, e.g. *after that, next, suddenly*. Also point out that the questions students asked each other in step 4 is a way of editing the content by pointing out to the writer what interesting or useful information is missing from the paragraph.

Notes

A class that needs more support could be reminded to use the narrative tenses at step 2. With a stronger class, you could add an extra activity after step 7. Students work in new pairs and swap their revised paragraphs and photos. They then write a response to the photo or paragraph – what it reminded them of and how it made them feel.

Rationale

Apart from providing freer practice of using narrative tenses, this activity aims to give practice editing each other's texts. The main focus is on editing language, but there is also indirect editing of content as suggested in *Think further*. This activity would work well at an early stage in a course as it allows students to find out about each other's pasts.

5.10 Blended narrative

Outline	Students brainstorm a narrative based around four objects or four characters, then work in groups to merge the two narratives into a single, imaginary story.
Level	Pre-intermediate (B1) and above
Time	45 minutes (25 minutes if step 7 is done as homework)
Aim	To prepare students to write a fictional narrative and provide them with ideas for the story.
Preparation	Decide which kind of fictional genre would interest your students most (crime, fantasy, adventure, horror, romance, science fiction) and choose pictures of four objects and four people to give to students. For example, for a crime story the objects could be: *a rope, a key, an umbrella, a motorbike*; and the people could be: *a tough-looking young woman, a shy-looking young man, a sinister-looking middle age man, an old woman with a kind face.*

Procedure

1   Give half the class pictures of four objects and the other half pictures of four people. Make sure the two groups can't see each other's pictures.

2   Tell students they're going to create a story and tell them what the genre is.

3   In small groups (photos of objects only and people only – don't mix at this stage), students think of a story in which their objects or people are part of a narrative. Students make notes of the ideas, but don't write the story. Set a time limit.

4   When most groups have finished, put students in new groups of four, with two students from an object group and two students from a people group.

5   Students tell each other the stories they have created so far. They then work to blend the stories together to create one story, making notes – they will need to change some of their original ideas.

6   Ask each group for one example of a change they made when they mixed the two stories together.

7   Students could either write the stories in class in pairs from the same group or write their own version alone as homework.

Think further

Establish with students that it's important to have interesting characters in a story. Elicit the idea that the objects can help get a story started, and other prompts such as pictures of a place can do the same thing.

Notes

The interaction of this activity is based around small groups. Trying to do it with pairs could be challenging if one student is unable to contribute very much. At higher levels, introduce a third group at step 1 with a different set of stimuli, for example, pictures of different kinds of clothing.

Rationale

As noted in Activity 5.4, expressive writing can be a refreshing change for students. To support students who might struggle to come up with ideas for a fictional narrative, the group dynamic means that ideas are pooled and shared.

5.11 Differently ever after

Outline	Students rewrite a classic fairy tale with a modern setting and a change to the story.
Level	Intermediate (B1+) and above
Time	40 minutes
Aim	To provide fluency practice of narrative and descriptive writing; to develop creative thinking skills.
Preparation	Select and familiarise yourself with one or two classic fairy tales in the event you need to provide the stimulus in step 1.

Procedure

1 Elicit examples of popular fairy tales that your students know. Then either tell one fairy tale or get students to recall a fairy tale in pairs.

2 In their pairs students rewrite a fairy tale (either the one you told or one they remember) doing two things:
   a giving it a modern setting (for example, the characters can use mobile phones)
   b making one major change to the story (for example, Cinderella decides to have a night in, or Little Red Riding Hood has a picnic with the wolf)

3 Three or four sets of pairs then work together (if possible, pairs who have rewritten the same fairy tale) and read each other's revised fairy tale. They decide on one to share with the class – the funniest, the craziest, the most original, etc.

4 Each group reads aloud their chosen story.

Think further

Establish with learners that thinking of an alternative version of the story in this activity is a useful, transferable skill. It requires creative thinking to question accepted ideas and consider alternatives.

Notes

In some contexts, it may be a good idea to focus on the one fairy tale in step 1. Doing so may help some classes who need more support because you can choose a fairy tale with more manageable vocabulary and pre-teach any words that you know will be difficult for students. In multi-lingual/multi-cultural contexts, it may be difficult for students to choose fairy tales they both know about. At higher levels in a multi-cultural context, students could work alone and choose a fairy tale that is very specific to their culture. They could tell the traditional version to other students and write the alternative version.

Rationale

Fairy tales often form the basis of contemporary stories, for example, the Oscar winning film *The Shape of Water* is a mix of *Beauty and the Beast* and *The Little Mermaid*. Apart from practising narrative and descriptive writing, this activity is potentially an entertaining way of providing an opportunity for creative thinking, as indicated in *Think further*.

5.12 Genre switch

Outline	Students write a piece of prose based on a poem, compare it with the original, and then write a poem based on a piece of prose.
Level	Upper intermediate (B2) and above
Time	45 minutes
Aim	To provide students with an opportunity to express their ideas in poetic form; to highlight differences between prose and poetry.
Preparation	You will need to prepare and make available for students two short extracts from an original descriptive prose text, and a poem based on the first extract. (In the example below the extracts are taken from Katherine Mansfield's short story, *At the bay*.)

Procedure

1 Students read a poem based on a first extract of the descriptive prose text (see example poem and extract 1 below).

2 Show students just the first couple of sentences of the original prose text and, in pairs, they rewrite the poem as prose. Set a time limit.

3 When time is up, show students the complete original extract and get them to compare it to their text – encourage them to focus on the way the information is conveyed rather than specific grammar points.

4 Ask for examples of differences between their own text and the original. Also ask students if they prefer the prose text or the poem.

5 Students read the second extract of the text and, in pairs, write a poem based on it. Again, set a time limit.

6 In small groups, sets of pairs compare their poems (or poems-in-progress). They decide on one example to read aloud to the class.

7 For homework, students could write a descriptive poem of a scene of their choice. Suggest they first try writing the description as prose and then turn it into a poem.

Example

At the bay

Very early morning,
sun not yet risen,
big bush-covered hills of the bay
smothered
under white sea-mist.
Gone the sandy road
and paddocks and bungalows.
No white dunes,
no mark between beach and sea.
Nothing.

Grass-blue, heavy dew
and big drops on bushes –
they do not fall.
Silvery, fluffy toi-toi
limp on long stalks.
All the marigolds
and all the pinks
bowed down to earth
with wetness.

Glossary

toi-toi (also spelt *toe-toe*) (n); a variety
    of thick grass found in New Zealand

Extract 1

Very early morning. The sun has not yet risen, and the whole of Crescent Bay was hidden under a white sea-mist. The big bush-covered hills at the back were smothered. You could not see where they ended and the paddocks and bungalows began. The sandy road was gone and the paddocks and bungalows the other side of it; there were no white dunes covered with reddish grass beyond them; there was nothing to mark which was the beach and where was the sea. A heavy dew had fallen. The grass was blue. Big drops hung on the bushes and just did not fall; the silvery, fluffy toi-toi was limp on its long stalks, and all the marigolds and the pinks in the bungalow gardens were bowed down to earth with wetness . . . .

Extract 2

Ah-Aah! sounded the sleepy sea. And from the bush there came the sound of little streams flowing, quickly, lightly, slipping between the smooth stones, gushing into ferny basins and out again; and there was a splashing of big drops on large leaves, and something else – what was it? – a faint stirring and shaking, the snapping of a twig and then such silence that it seemed someone was listening.

Think further

Elicit from students that one of the differences between the poetic and prose versions of the text is the use of ellipsis in the poem to focus on key words that convey meaning. Establish that this focus on meaning-filled words in poetry is what can make it seem more vivid. Also establish that the choice and arrangement of the words on the page can make the language poetic by isolating and foregrounding key ideas or sensations.

Notes

If you would like to provide your students with more support (or you would like to reduce the lesson time), you could provide them with the original prose that matches the first verse of the poem and students write a prose version of the second verse only.

Rationale

It's important to cater to the interests of all learners from time to time, and while most students don't join English language classes to learn to read or write poetry, there are learners who wish to develop their skill in understanding English literature. However, more generally, this activity also gives students practice in writing descriptive language and demonstrates its flexible nature when considering the two genres.

5.13 The way I see it

Outline	Students retell a narrative. Half the class do it from the perspective of one character, the other half from the perspective of a different character. Students then compare their retelling of events.
Level	Intermediate (B1+) and above
Time	35 minutes
Aim	To highlight the way in which a writer's point of view affects a narrative.
Preparation	You will need to write a description of a series of events as well as Character A and B cards similar to those below (see *Example*). You could use a narrative that students have read in the course materials you are using.

Procedure

1   Make available to half of the class the Character A card and to the other half the Character B card. Students read the character description, the context and the events.

2   In pairs (both with the same character card), students discuss and write their version of events using the first person. It's important that both students write down their story. Set a time limit – if any pairs with the same character card finish early, they can read each other's versions.

3   Students work in Character A and Character B pairs. They read their partner's story and decide if it's the same set of events as theirs. They try to guess whether the other person's character knows the people in the story or not.

4   Students tell each other their impressions of each other's stories.

Example

> *Character A*
>
> You live opposite the Marsh family – Will and Ella Marsh and their young son, Lucas. Recently poor Ella had to go to hospital for an operation. Will took time off work to look after her, but today he had to go back to work. Will told you Ella's sister had kindly offered to come and collect Lucas to take him to school. Poor Lucas has been very upset by his mother's illness.
>
> This is what you saw this morning …
>
> A car pulls up in front of a house. It is driven by a man. A woman gets out from the front passenger seat and hurries into the house. After a short time, she comes out of the house with Lucas who is crying. The woman guides him to the car. Lucas is reluctant to get into the car and the woman has to insist he gets in. She gets in beside him in the back seat of the car. The door slams shut and the man drives off quickly.
>
> Describe the scene you saw this morning. You can add details and imagine how the people in the story must have been feeling.

Character B

You were parked in Walker Road this morning – you had come to pick up your friend Jack to give him a ride to work. When you were waiting in the car, you saw another car drive up quickly. A young boy was picked up. Everything looked very suspicious to you. Just lately, you've read a lot of articles online about parents getting a divorce and then fighting over the custody of children. The adults just think about themselves and don't care for the children.

This is what you saw this morning …

A car pulls up in front of a house. It is driven by a man. A woman gets out from the front passenger seat and hurries into the house. After a short time, she comes out of the house with a young boy who is crying. The woman guides the boy to the car. The boy is reluctant to get into the car and the woman has to insist he gets in. She gets in beside him in the back seat of the car. The door slams shut and the man drives off quickly.

Describe the scene you saw this morning. You can add details and imagine how the people in the story must have been feeling.

Think further

Elicit from students why their stories were different. Establish that a writer's point of view and attitude can completely change a story, and the writer's choice of language will differ significantly, particularly the choice of verbs (e.g. _helped_ him towards the car vs. _dragged_ him towards the car) and adjectives (*Ella's _kind_ sister* vs. *a very _determined-looking_ woman*). Point out this is often the case with news stories.

Notes

If your class needs more support, you could give them two sentences on their character cards to get their narrative started. With a stronger group, you could suggest they write the description of events according to their character's perspective, but that they write it using the third person.

Rationale

While providing practice of writing a narrative, this activity demonstrates to students the way in which a person's subjective point of view can alter the telling. It suggests that narrative is never neutral, and the language choices writers make help to convey their point of view.

5.14 What's it all about?

Outline	Students read and then write an enigmatic dialogue before performing it for other students to guess the context.
Level	Upper intermediate (B2) and above
Time	30 minutes
Aim	To practise writing natural dialogue; to highlight the use of ellipsis as a feature of natural-sounding dialogue.
Preparation	You will need to make available to each student a dialogue similar to the one below (see *Example*). You could write a dialogue that refers to (but doesn't indicate) a context you know your students are familiar with or motivated by.

Procedure

1 Students read a short dialogue where the context, characters and topic of conversation aren't specified. They guess who's speaking and what they're talking about – (in the example, a teenage child (A) and parent (B) are talking about breakfast).

2 In pairs, students write a similar short dialogue. They think of a context, characters and a topic of discussion but make no reference to these things in the dialogue.

3 Pairs practise performing the dialogue together.

4 Either as a whole class activity or with students working in large groups, each pair performs their dialogue and other students guess the characters, context and topic.

Example

A: What do you call this?
B: Same as always.
A: Exactly!
B: Is there a problem?
A: If there weren't, I wouldn't have said ...
B: So ungrateful!
A: So predictable.
B: But you like your routine. That's what you say.
A: I know, but ...
B: C'mon. You know what to do.

Think further

Elicit or establish with learners that the non-specific nature of these dialogues is as a result of ellipsis. For example, the second line of the example dialogue could be 'It's the same breakfast as you always have'. Point out that authentic spoken language contains a lot of ellipsis – speakers understand each other from the shared context. Including this feature of spoken language in written dialogue is a way of making it sound more natural and it can also add an initial sense of mystery, which is a way of engaging an audience reading the text or watching the drama.

Notes

In step 1, you could perform the dialogue together with a confident student. In step 3, a layer of complexity can be added for stronger groups by getting them to think of an adverb that indicates how they will perform the dialogue, for example, 'frenetically', 'lazily' or 'knowingly'. The audience guesses the adverb as well as the context.

Rationale

Some students may not initially see the value of writing dialogues as in this acitivty, although the obvious association with film and TV scenes will have appeal. The focus on ellipsis is a way of suggesting to students it's often preferable not to have too much obvious exposition in a dramatic scene, but also makes students give careful consideration to the language they should and should not include.

5.15 Regular thoughts

Outline	Students maintain a personal journal for the duration of an English language course which is monitored by the teacher.
Level	Elementary (A2) and above
Time	On-going during a course – a set time during some lessons
Aim	To develop students' ability to express themselves in writing with greater fluency.
Preparation	You will need to set up either hard copy or digital journals that you can have occasional access to.

Procedure

1 Early in the course, tell students you would like them to keep a regular written journal. Either ask them to buy a notebook for this purpose, or set up a digital notebook for each student within a Learning Management System. You and the student will be the only two people who will have access to the journal.

2 Tell students how often you want them to write something. You could devote 5 to 10 minutes of class time once a week to this.

3 Provide students with a series of topics they can write about in their journal which could include:
   - things they do with friends and family
   - opinions of films, TV programmes books, music
   - opinions of sports matches, events, players
   - comments on their English language learning
   - reactions to news events
   - future plans, ambitions

4 Give students regular reminders and read their journals from time to time. Comment on what they write, but only respond to their ideas and don't correct the language.

Think further

Towards the end of the course, ask students to reflect on their journal. What topics did they feel most motivated to write about? To what extent do they feel they have made progress in their writing?

Notes

With a group of students that is reluctant to engage with a project of this nature, you will probably need to spend more class time to get it going in the early stages and set journal writing as a homework activity on a regular basis. This also means you will need to be more vigilant and active monitoring their use of the journal. It also helps if you keep a journal and allow students to access this.

Rationale

A project of this nature can be very beneficial for a group of students that needs to develop their writing skills for a particular purpose, for example, preparing for an English language exam with a writing paper or planning to study English for Academic Purposes. The strong fluency focus in maintaining a journal will develop their ability to get started with writing – something many students struggle with – and to normalise writing in English regularly, in the same way that many students learn to speak English by speaking.

6 Writing for academic contexts

Writing is usually perceived as a key language skill for learners studying English for Academic Purposes (EAP) (de Chazal, 2014). In English-language academic settings, students are likely to be asked to write more than they will be required to speak. Written academic discourse is a register with its own conventions and demands, and students need to develop specific skills in order to be able to produce texts deemed appropriate in the wider academic community. The kinds of texts they are required to write can differ from one academic discipline to another. A student who intends to study history and another who wants to study engineering will have slightly different needs. Certain genres may be predominant in different disciplines. For example, the history student will probably write more argumentative essays while the engineering student will probably write more case studies. Furthermore, each discipline will have its own sub register with specific jargon (Biber & Conrad, 2019). In many contexts, a distinction is now made between English for General Academic Purposes (EGAP) and English for Specific Academic Purposes (ESAP).

In a book of this nature, it is impossible to cover every aspect of the wide-ranging breadth of EAP. This chapter therefore provides an overview and a sampling of writing for academic contexts with activities that it is hoped teachers will be able to adapt to their students' specific needs. Some of the activities in Chapter 3 which focus on sharing ideas and opinions may also prove useful.

Functions, genres and patterns

A core function of almost all academic writing is to persuade a reader towards a particular point of view or the viability of a research conclusion (de Chazal, 2014). This means that the main thrust of most academic texts is discursive and argumentative. In order to persuade, writers may consider and evaluate both sides of an argument before arriving at the position they wish to defend. In doing so, the text will probably also report on background theory associated with the topic of the essay, and perhaps describe some original research carried out by the writer. Academic texts can also explain ideas, demonstrate how a conclusion is reached and narrate a series of events. All these micro-functions feed into the broader aim of an academic text to convince the reader.

While we can perceive academic writing as a genre in and of itself, it is made up of a variety of different sub genres. Biber and Conrad (2019) note the following sub genres: argumentative essays, personal narratives, self-reflection essays, lab reports, case studies, literature reviews, research reports and research proposals. For our purposes in the chapter, however, we will refer to these sub genres simply as 'genres'. The functional aim of these different genres varies. For example, a lab report will provide statistical information on a practical experiment while one of the likely aims of a literature review is to demonstrate that the writer has done sufficient background reading on a topic. Each genre has its own set of conventions, and these are often determined by the discipline and/or the institution in which the academic writing takes place. These specific genre conventions signal the role of the audience in academic writing. Students are largely writing for tutors or supervisors who expect arguments to be cogently discussed. Students are also expected to adhere to conventions within different disciplines. If a student finishes their study and goes on to pursue an academic career, they are likely to write and publish articles and books that will be read by the wider academic community.

More broadly, all academic writing adheres to specific conventions associated with acknowledging sources in the form of citations (de Chazal 2014). Academic writers need to give evidence and provide examples from background literature that supports their argument. There are specific ways in which this information is included and presented in an academic text. Perhaps the most well-known set of citation guidelines is the one determined by the American Psychological Association (APA). These outline very specifically how direct quotes and paraphrases are to be included in the text.

One of the key aims of citation is to acknowledge the intellectual property of other writers and researchers. Failure to do so is perceived as an act of plagiarism. However, in an age of digital tools that can facilitate writing, it has become harder for academic teaching staff to determine the degree to which an academic text is the writer's own work and the level of support that a student might have had in writing an essay. While there is software that aims to detect plagiarism, Artificial Intelligence is capable of producing texts that this software is unable to recognise as plagiarised work (Davies, 2022). Chandrasoma, Thompson and Pennycook (2004) argue that the notion of plagiarism is largely outdated and suggest it would be more useful to conceptualize the use of external sources on a continuum of transgressive and nontransgressive intertextuality. They suggest that a number of contextual factors, such as the student's background, the requirements of the assignment and the nature of the discipline should be taken into account in order to determine an instance of transgressive intertextuality.

The complex nature of academic writing means that discourse patterns can be embedded within each other in a macro-organisational structure (de Chazal, 2014). For example, a paper reporting on research might begin by outlining a problem that the research aims to address. The description of the problem will probably begin with a general overview and then go into more particular detail. The report may then go on to discuss the way in which previous researchers have investigated the problem and outline the different claims and counterclaims that have been made in the literature that focus on the topic of the report. In EAP classes, learners tend to focus on discourse patterns one at a time, in line with the genre they are focusing on at different points in their course. For example, claim–counterclaim discourse patterning is relevant when learners are writing a discursive essay. Similarly, in ESAP there is often an emphasis on specific discourse patterns. Business essays often focus on problem–solution case studies while earth science reports are likely to include a lot of general–particular description.

Language

As Carter and McCarthy note (2006), written academic language is more complex and formal than every day written communication, and it is also less personal. They list a series of grammar and discourse features that foreground noun phrases and the degree to which verbs and adjectives are often turned into nouns. Other key features are also detailed, such as passive constructions, impersonal constructions using *it*, hedging expressions that include modality, linking adverbials, and the pronouns *it, this* and *that* used to signal cohesive ties in a text. This syllabus largely matches a corpus study carried out by Biber and Conrad (2019) that compared academic prose with news reports and conversation.

When building an argument in an essay, there are two sub functions that academic writers often need to use: comparison and contrast, and cause and effect. Comparison and contrast language involves comparative adjectives and adverbs, linking adverbials (*in contrast, however, although*), and lexical phrases (*the difference between, when compared to*). Cause and effect language includes individual nouns (*cause, reason, result*), conjunctions (*so, because*) as well as adverbial linkers (*therefore, consequently*). As is the case with comparison and contrast language, cause and effect relationships can be signalled by lexical phrases (*is/are due to, as a consequence*). Hinkel (2004: p.39) signals the value of such lexical phrases in academic writing in general and cites research that indicates they are largely stable forms. Focusing on these fixed expressions in an EAP writing programme can result in greater learning efficiency.

In a corpus study that focused on student writing, Biber and Conrad (2019) noted a high incidence of structures that indicated the writer's stance, for example, *we would argue that, it is our aim to, it is important to note*. They also noted a large number of evaluative adjectives such as *central, pertinent, important*.

It is useful to note here a milestone piece of research into academic language that has resulted in an invaluable resource for teachers and learners alike. Coxhead's (2000) Academic Word List contains 570 word families of the most frequent words found in an Academic Corpus of approximately 3,500,000 words. The main list contains headwords, which are the stem forms of academic word, and 'sublists' contain different forms included in each word family.

In the classroom

When teaching EAP first emerged, classes were typically offered at intermediate (B1+) level and above. However, now it is possible for students to begin studying academic written language at beginner (A1) level. Pitching EAP lessons at low levels has answered the needs and preferences of learners who know early in their English language learning that they want to study English-medium university courses in their chosen discipline.

In his summary of academic writing methodology, de Chazal (2014) notes that teachers eventually develop an approach that draws on a range of methodological ideas and is adapted in light of their learners' needs. He suggests that EAP writing classes need to take into consideration the genre of a text and its purpose, the coherent use of language, the content of the text and the kind of research learners might need to carry out. The importance of critical thinking skills in both the planning and writing of a text are also signalled.

Many EAP courses have a twofold aim. They endeavour to prepare learners for an English-medium academic context, and they also aim to provide adequate preparation for some kind of assessment or examination that will either allow students to proceed to a higher level of EAP or give them direct entry to an undergraduate or postgraduate programme of study. Assessment can involve different combinations of marked course tasks and in-house final examination, but might also require students to sit an external examination, such as IELTS, and achieve a requisite score.

References

Biber, D. & Conrad, S. (2019) *Register, Genre, and Style Second Edition*. Cambridge, Cambridge University Press.

Carter, R. & McCarthy, M. (2006) *Cambridge Grammar of English*. Cambridge, Cambridge University Press.

Chandrasoma, R., Thompson, C. & Pennycook, A. (2004) Beyond Plagiarism: Transgressive and Nontransgressive Intertextuality. *Journal of Language Identity & Education*. 3/3, 171–193.

Coxhead, A. (2000) *The Academic Word List*. Available from: www.wgtn.ac.nz/lals/resources/academicwordlist [Accessed 3rd March 2022].

Davies, W. (2022) How many words does it take to make a mistake? *London Review of Books*. 44/4, 3–8.

de Chazal, E. (2014) *English for Academic Purposes*. Oxford, Oxford University Press.

Hinkel, E. (2004) *Teaching Academic ESL Writing: Practical Techniques in Vocabulary and Grammar*. Mahwah, New Jersey, Lawrence Earlbaum Associates.

6.1 Compounding things

Outline	Students use conjunctions and their own ideas to write continuations of sentences.
Level	Elementary to Pre-intermediate (A2–B1) (or above – see *Notes*)
Time	20 minutes
Aim	To practise using simple conjunctions; to write compound sentences.
Preparation	You will need to prepare six non-complex sentences for students to continue (see *Example*).

Procedure

1 Show students six sentences.

2 In pairs, students copy the sentences and write continuations using their own ideas. For three sentences, they should use *and,* and for the other three *but.*

3 Two sets of pairs work together and compare their sentences. They decide on one *and* example and one *but* example to read aloud to the class.

Example

1 Social media can be dangerous.
2 Many parts of the world are now very dry.
3 E-readers are small and light.
4 Tourism means that some towns and cities can earn a lot of money.
5 Top sports athletes train many hours a day.
6 Many employees say they prefer working from home.

Think further

Elicit from students the term conjunction for the way *and* and *but* are used in these sentences. Point out that a comma is used before the conjunction.

Notes

With a class that needs more support, it's a good idea to elicit examples on the board. With stronger classes, you could add *because* and perhaps *so* to the list of conjunctions to be used. At a higher level, you could ask students to use more formal linking words such as *however, moreover* and *furthermore.* This would mean the continuation would result in a new sentence.

Rationale

At lower levels, students are often reluctant to try making their written language a little more complex. This activity aims to focus students on the need to explore their grammatical range to some degree in academic writing.

6.2 The right support

Outline	Students order information in note form as the basis for a coherent paragraph and then write a first draft of the paragraph.
Level	Pre-intermediate to Intermediate (B1–B1+)
Time	40 minutes
Aim	To practise ordering information in a paragraph in a coherent way; to revise using topic and supporting sentences in paragraphs.
Preparation	You will need to choose (or write) a model paragraph and make a set of scrambled notes available to each student (see *Example*). You may wish to focus on a paragraph in teaching materials you are using. If you are teaching in a face-to-face context, it may help to cut up sets of the scrambled notes so they can be physically reordered.

Procedure

1   In pairs, students read scrambled notes and decide on a coherent order.

2   Put pairs into groups of six or eight students to compare their ordering of the notes and agree on a group answer.

3   Check answers with the class and identify the first and final note as being a basis for the topic sentences and concluding sentence of a paragraph.

4   Students work alone and write the paragraph before comparing their drafts in pairs.

5   Show an example model of the paragraph and allow students to ask you questions about the model or their alternative versions.

Example

Scrambled Notes

1	in a video game – lot of visual information – players keep eye on characters & objects – which can move quickly
2	choosing best solution to problem – a way of teaching critical thinking – need to prioritise
3	a key feature video of games: present players with problem & different solutions
4	parents worry children spend too much time playing video games – research shows children develop useful life skills
5	gaming not just fun activity – hobby with educational benefits
6	video games involve both hand-to-eye co-ordination & an ability to solve complex problems – useful offline in real world
7	an ability to follow visual information – good exercise for children's brains – quick to notice & observe what's around them in physical world

Key
Correct order of notes: 4, 6, 1, 7, 3, 2, 5

Model paragraph

Parents often worry that their children spend too much time playing video games online, but research has shown that children can develop useful life skills from gaming. Playing video games involves both good hand-to-eye co-ordination skills as well as an ability to solve complex problems, and these are both useful offline in the real world. In a video game, there is a lot of visual information that players have to keep their eye on, and characters and objects can move very quickly. An ability to follow all this is good exercise for children's brains and can make them quick to notice and observe what is around them in the physical world. A key feature of video games is to present players with a problem and a range of possible solutions. Choosing the best solution is a way of teaching children critical thinking skills and the need to prioritise. This shows that gaming is not just a fun activity but also a hobby that has educational benefits for children.

Think further

Elicit from students the difference between the first and second sentence in the model paragraph. Establish that the topic sentence makes a broad statement while the second sentence provides more detail. The rest of the paragraph provides supporting information until the concluding sentence.

Notes

Step 4 could be set as a homework activity and pairs compare their writing in the next lesson. If your class needs more support, it may pay to teach or remind them of the information structure of a paragraph before they reorder the notes.

Rationale

Students often struggle to get a good grip of the information structure of a coherent paragraph. By getting students to read and order the scrambled notes, they are encouraged to focus on information rather than language. The pair and group discussion provides students with an opportunity to check their answers and get help from peers if necessary. It also suggests that taking time to think about the correct order of information is an important part of planning a piece of writing.

Reference

Source for ideas in the *Scrambled Notes* section from *The Conversation* website available at:
https://theconversation.com/is-gaming-good-for-kids-153774

6.3 Comparison edit

Outline	Students brainstorm ideas to compare two topics, and then write a report before revising it with a focus on comparative language.
Level	Pre-intermediate (B1) and above
Time	45–50 minutes
Aim	To practise writing a comparative report; to extend students' range of comparative language; to practise editing for language improvement.
Preparation	No preparation is necessary apart from thinking of two topics that can be compared that would be motivating for your students.

Procedure

1   Students work in two groups, A and B. Group A brainstorms ideas for a report on one topic, and Group B brainstorms a different but related topic (the two topics will be compared later). Some related topic examples are: face-to-face and online learning, solar power and wind power, two kinds of cuisine, two styles of music, etc.

2   Students discuss and make notes on their topic, such as: key features and qualities, strengths/ advantages, drawbacks/disadvantages, possible problems and solutions. Each student needs to make notes for the next stage in the activity.

3   Students work in A and B pairs, comparing their notes and looking for similarities and differences between the two topics.

4   Each pair then writes a draft of their report comparing the two topics.

5   When most pairs have finished their drafts, show the following language:
    *different from, similar to, like, unlike, difference(s), similarity(-ies),
    both, neither ... nor, while, whereas*

6   Still in their pairs, students revise their reports adding any of the language from step 5 as appropriate.

7   Sets of pairs can then swap and give feedback to each other focusing on comparison language.

Think further

Ask students which words and expressions in step 5 (as well as other examples of language of comparison) they find difficult to use. Elicit two or three examples of usage to share with the class. Praise correct examples and elicit correct versions of examples that need reformulation.

Notes

With a class that needs more support, you could include fewer words and expressions at step 5, while with a stronger class you could add more, for example, *differ, in contrast, on the other hand*. The activity could be spread across two lessons and step 4 could be set as a homework activity.

Rationale

Students are likely to use comparative adjectives and adverbs as well as simple linkers such as *but* in their first draft. This activity encourages them to use a greater range of comparative language. Getting them to write a draft first means students have a context in which to use the language. It also demonstrates the value of editing and revising to make language more correct and more interesting.

6.4 Spot the reference

Outline	Students proofread a set of publication references looking for omissions and errors and then write three example references.
Level	Pre-intermediate (B1) and above
Time	25 minutes
Aim	To practise accurate referencing of text sources; to practise proofreading.
Preparation	Before the lesson, remind students to bring a digital device to the lesson so they can search online for resources to reference. You will need to make available to students a set of publication references containing omissions and errors (see *Example*). If your institution recommends a particular referencing guide for students to use, then it's preferable to set your references in that style. Otherwise, it might be a good idea to locate a freely accessible online referencing guide for students to use (the example below is based on Harvard referencing style). It may also be a good idea to create a reference list using publications students have referred to for assignments.

Procedure

1 Students read a set of references with omissions and errors – set a time limit for them to find them.

2 Check answers with the whole class and elicit suggestions for what should or can be added to correct the references.

3 Working alone, students choose an area of study that they are involved or interested in, and search online for three different kinds of relevant sources: a book, a journal article, website article.

4 Students write references for these sources using a reference guide.

5 Pairs exchange their references (and reference guides, if different) and check that all the information is included and all punctuation is correct.

6 With the whole class, allow students to check any uncertainties with you.

Example

> Salviati, S. *What's coming our way? Future climate and weather conditions*. Natural World Papers.
>
> Radley, L. M! (2005) *Weather Patterns and Urbanization (Edition)*. Boston.
>
> Chambers, C. (2018) drought climatology, weather patterns and climate change. In: Taylor, B. P. & Zhang, (eds.) *Climate Variability in the New Era*. Melbourne: Yarra Publishing.
>
> Shiba, A. (2042) Extreme weather and projected changes in weather patterns on the Eastern Seaboard. *International Journal of Applied Climatology*. pp.272–284.
>
> World Weather Institute (2022) *Climate change and the long-term outlook for the planet*. from: www.woweins.org/Assets/art-pub/cc-longterm-outlook. [Accessed: 19th December]

Key

Salviati, S. (1998) *What's coming our way? Future climate and weather conditions.* Devon: Natural World Papers.

Radley, L. M. (2005) *Weather Patterns and Urbanization (Second Edition).* Boston: Saunders Press.

Chambers, C. (2018) Drought climatology, weather patterns and climate change. In: Taylor, B. P. & Zhang, J. (eds.) *Climate Variability in the New Era.* Melbourne: Yarra Publishing.

Shiba, A. (2022) Extreme weather and projected changes in weather patterns on the Eastern Seaboard. *International Journal of Applied Climatology.* 15(2), pp.272–284.

World Weather Institute (2022) *Climate change and the long-term outlook for the planet.* Available from: www.woweins.org/Assets/art-pub/cc-longterm-outlook. [Accessed 19th December 2022].

Think further

Elicit from students the importance of proofreading references clearly to make sure all the information is included and correctly punctuated. Point out that there are many websites that provide support and, for example, Harvard or APA referencing are commonly used – they can do an internet search to find them.

Notes

You can adjust the time limit in step 1 in line with your students' level of ability. If there is a specific aspect of referencing that your students find challenging, you can adapt the example material accordingly and make sure you include plenty of incorrect examples you give to students.

Rationale

While students at B1 may not be doing a lot of referencing of their written work, it is a good idea to get them into the habit of being accurate with references at an early stage in an academic English programme. This activity also focuses on proofing for errors and omissions – a useful subskill in academic contexts.

6.5 Graph kitset

Outline	Students complete a step-by-step approach to writing an explanation of data in a graph focusing both on structure and appropriate language.
Level	Pre-intermediate to Intermediate (B1–B1+)
Time	45 minutes
Aim	To practise writing a coherent, paragraph-long explanation of a graph using a good variety of language.
Preparation	You will need to prepare a graph and make it available to students along with examples of useful language (see *Example*). You can use the approach described in the activity with different kinds of graph and might also choose to vary the useful language in light of your students' needs.

Procedure

1 Show students a graph that indicates simple increases and decreases in data (the example is on the viewing habits of New Zealanders).

2 In pairs, students discuss the information shown in the graph.

3 They then brainstorm examples of useful expressions for describing the data in a graph. With the whole class, ask for examples, but don't write them up.

4 Students then put the following steps in order for a generic structure for a paragraph describing data in a graph.
   a. Explain the most noticeable changes.
   b. Suggest a reason(s) for the changes.
   c. Introduce the graph and what it shows.
   d. Explain other changes.

5 In pairs, students write the first draft of a paragraph to describe the information in the graph.

6 After they have written their first draft, show students some examples of useful language (see examples below).

7 Pairs revise their first drafts trying to use a wider variety of language. Remind them to use the correct tense of verbs.

8 Sets of pairs then swap their second drafts and give feedback on the variety of language and correct use of verb tense. If appropriate, students can compare their work to a model paragraph.

Think further

Elicit from students some of the examples of new language they used from step 6. Suggest that it would be a good idea to record this in a notebook so they remember to use it in future. Establish the idea that using a variety of language makes the description more interesting.

Example

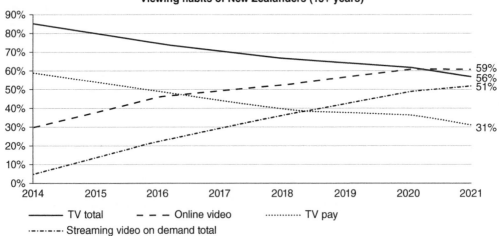

Viewing habits of New Zealanders (15+ years)

Legend:
— TV total   – – Online video   ·········· TV pay
·–·–·– Streaming video on demand total

Values shown at right: 59%, 56%, 51%, 31%

Useful language
verbs and adverbs

increase rise decrease fall	sharply dramatically noticeably gradually slowly	(by X%) (from X% to Y%)

nouns and adjectives

a (more / less) the (most / least)	sharp dramatic noticeable steady gradual slow	increase rise decrease fall	(of X%)

more adverbs

about   almost   nearly   (just) under   (just) over

Key
Correct order for structure of paragraph: c, a, d, b

Model paragraph

This graph shows the viewing habits of New Zealand adults over the age of 15 between the years 2014 and 2021. During the seven years, there was a move away from watching traditional TV to viewing material online. Viewing regular TV gradually decreased from about 85% in 2014 to 56% in 2021. Not surprisingly, the most noticeable increase was in watching on demand streamed video, from just over 5% to 51%. There was a less dramatic increase in the viewing of general online video such as YouTube and Facebook. There was also a sharp fall of about 50% in the number of New Zealand adults who watched pay TV. It would seem that the growth of TV streaming services that offer viewers a wide choice of material at a low price is a key reason for the change in viewing habits.

Notes

If you think your students will struggle to come up with language examples at step 3, you could provide some of the language that is shown at step 6. With a stronger class, you could skip step 4 that focuses on paragraph structure and just remind students to present the information in a logical way.

Rationale

The activity takes a drip-feed approach to writing a description of a graph. First, students discuss the information as a way of making sense of it. They then recall language they already know in preparation for the first draft and are provided with a logical structure for the information. Once they have written a first draft, they are provided with extra language examples as a way of increasing the range. Students tend to use verb phrases more than noun phrases. The activity suggests to students that looking for and using different language is something they can do when revising a first draft.

6.6 More to less

Outline	Students rewrite unpacked noun phrases for an essay introduction, then write their own introduction using noun phrases to convey key information.
Level	Intermediate (B1+) and above
Time	50 minutes
Aim	To practise writing noun phrases in order to convey key information more efficiently; to practise writing an essay introduction.
Preparation	You will need to prepare an introduction to an essay with the noun phrases unpacked and make it available to each student (see *Example*). You could choose or write an essay introduction associated with a topic your students have been studying. If students are not currently working on an essay, you will need to find the body of a short essay for which students can write an introduction.

Procedure

1   Students read an introduction to an essay in which some of the noun phrases have been unpacked. They decide what the problem is with the phrases (i.e. they are too long and the information isn't given efficiently).

2   With the whole class, do an example of rewriting one of the phrases in the paragraph as a condensed noun phrase. Students then complete the rest and compare their answers in pairs.

3   Check answers with the class and accept any correct variations.

4   If students are working on an essay, ask them to write an introduction for it. Alternatively, you could give them the body paragraphs of a short essay and ask them to write an introduction, using noun phrases.

5   In pairs, students compare and give feedback on their introductions.

Example

> Until recently, [1][*there have been sport's scholarships and the public have an understanding of them*] has been that top performing athletes have their study costs paid. However, in some colleges, there is now [2][*a trend and it is growing*] of offering monthly 'expenses' to these athletes. In 2015, the National Collegiate Athletic Association (NCAA) allowed some universities to pay athletes [3][*some money and it's a small sum and this helps athletes with things like costs related to living*]. However, it is not considered or called a 'salary' (Kludt & Chang, 2021). In 2021, the organization allowed these athletes to make [4][*money that can be made when athletes appear in advertisements and agree to sign autographs*]. Some older athletes worry that the financial rewards will mean universities will expect more from their athletes, and it will leave them little time for study. They also worry the new regulations destroy [5][*the status of college football which has always been amateur*]. In this essay, we will explore [6][*the fact that there are consequences and they can be both positive and negative*] of allowing college scholarship athletes the opportunity to earn as they study.

Key
1 the public's understanding of sports scholarships
2 a growing trend
3 a sum of money to help with the cost of living
4 money from advertisements and signing autographs
5 the amateur status of college football
6 both the positive and negative consequences

Think further
Ask students why there are often a lot of noun phrases in the introduction to an essay. Establish that the introduction usually contains a lot of key ideas and terms that will be explored in the essay, and these are normally expressed concisely as noun phrases. Also point out that noun phrases are a feature of academic writing.

Notes
If your students need more support, you could let them know the head noun in each noun phrase. An alternative for some groups might be to provide the words in the noun phrase scrambled, and students have to put the words in the correct order. For example, the first noun phrase would be given as *public's sports the understanding of scholarships*. Some groups may be interested in further analysing the noun phrases, for example, identifying the head nouns and the elements before and after each one.

Rationale

Writing complex noun phrases is one of the key grammatical challenges in academic writing. Introductory sections of essays and articles often include a lot of densely packed noun phrases as key terms are outlined, defined and explained.

6.7 Putting together the process

Outline	Students study an infographic of a process, listen to a written model and then use notes to write their version.
Level	Intermediate (B1+) and above
Time	45 minutes
Aim	To practise writing a description of a process; to highlight the use of passive verb forms in writing the description.
Preparation	You will need to have ready a description of a process and make available an associated infographic with notes of the process for each student (see *Example*). You could create an infographic and write notes based on authentic material (do an online search for 'technical or mechanical process description') or taken from teaching materials you are using.

Procedure

1   Students study an infographic that outlines a process and discuss what is happening (see the example that shows the creation of a new mobile phone model).

2   Show the process notes for the infographic to students, and then read aloud a description of the process. Students match the different stages of the infographic to the notes. Check answers with the whole class.

3   Show the following linking words and expressions and tell students these were used in the description:
    then, after this, at this stage, the next step, once, as a result

4   In pairs, students then write a description of the process using the infographic and notes, and try to include the linking words and expressions.

5   Students do not look at their first drafts, and you read aloud the description of the process a second time. When you have finished, students can make revisions to their draft.

6   Two sets of pairs compare their drafts and suggest changes.

7   Show the description you read aloud for students to compare to their own versions.

Example

Description of a process
Making a new mobile phone
The first step in the making of a mobile phone usually takes place in a meeting room and not an engineering workshop. Ideas for the look and function of the new phone are discussed by engineering, software and research experts. Their ideas are then sent to a research and development laboratory where a prototype is made. At this stage, an important consideration is the design and overall look of the phone. The prototype is passed around to different experts in the company and these people give their opinion on the prototype. As a result, some changes may be made.

The next step is the installation of software into the handset. Usually, software engineers have pre-decided the type of operating system that is loaded into the phone. After this, the way the software works together with the handset is checked. If everything is working as it should, the new mobile is thoroughly tested. The phone is dropped, bent and placed in water to make sure it can still function afterwards. Once the phone has passed all these tests and it is finally approved, mass production of the phones begins.

Infographic

Process notes

1 test mobile phone – drop, bend, place in water – make sure it still functions afterwards

2 pass prototype around to different experts in company – they give their opinion – may make changes

3 pass tests – approved - begin mass production

4 engineering, software and research experts discuss ideas – look and function of new phone

5 software engineers decide type of software system they load into the phone – check the way software works together with handset

6 send ideas to research and development laboratory – make prototype – design and overall look of phone an important consideration

Key
1–e, 2–c, 3–f, 4–a, 5–d, 6–b

Think further
Elicit or establish from students that passive verb forms are commonly used to describe processes. Also elicit that 'once' is usually followed by the present perfect in this context.

Notes
To give students more support, you could provide a gapped version of the model text with alternate sentences omitted. To add more challenge, you could avoid reading the model text aloud at step 2.

Rationale

This activity is a supportive version of a dictogloss where students have to rework notes into a piece of writing on the basis of what they hear. It's an opportunity to diagnose students' ability to notice and use passive forms in the description of a process.

Reference

Description process based on text from Prizm Institute available at: www.prizminstitute.com/blog/how-are-smartphones-made/ [Accessed December 2022]

6.8 A good source

Outline	Students read and discuss problematic examples of in-text referencing and then write a paraphrase of a source text.
Level	Intermediate (B1+) and above
Time	45 minutes
Aim	To highlight good practice in citing longer quotes from an original source; to provide practice in paraphrasing.
Preparation	You will need to make available to each student a source text and one of three example texts in which it has been referenced and paraphrased (see *Example*).

Procedure

1 Divide the class into three groups. All students have the same original source text, but each group has a different text with a problematic reference.

2 Students read the original source and text. They discuss possible problems with the reference with someone in their group.

3 Students work in threes – one from each group. They explain the problems with the referencing in their text to each other.

4 Check answers with the whole class.

5 Still in their groups of three, students write their own text reference paraphrasing the source. Suggest that they consult a thesaurus to help with some words, for example, https://dictionary. cambridge.org has a thesaurus function, but warn students to check the examples of use to make sure a word is appropriate.

6 Groups exchange and give feedback on each other's text. They could also check it against a model text.

Example

Post World War II economic growth in the USA

> *Original source*
>
> That growth was achieved, in part, by consumer spending, as factories outfitted for wartime production were converted to manufacture consumer goods, from roller skates to colour televisions. The idea of the citizen as a consumer, and of spending as an act of citizenship, dates to the 1920s. But in the 1950s, mass consumption became a matter of civic obligation. By buying 'the dozens of things you never bought or even thought of before,' *Brides* magazine told its readers, 'you are helping to build greater security for the industries of this country.'
>
> (from *These Truths: A History of the United States* by Jill Lepore (2018). New York: W. W. Norton & Company. p.528)

Text A

Lepore (2018) notes that post World War II economic growth in the USA took place because factories that produced supplies for the war switched to producing consumer goods for people to buy. She adds, 'The ideas of the citizen as a consumer, and of spending as an act of citizenship, dates to the 1920s. But in the 1950s, mass consumption became a matter of civic obligation. By buying 'the dozens of things you never bought or even thought of before,' *Brides* magazine told its readers, 'you are helping to build greater security for the industries of this country' (p.528).

Text B

Lepore notes that post World War II economic growth in the USA took place because factories that produced supplies for the war switched to producing consumer goods for people to buy. She adds:

> The ideas of the citizen as a consumer, and of spending as an act of citizenship, dates to the 1920s. But in the 1950s, mass consumption became a matter of civic obligation. By buying 'the dozens of things you never bought or even thought of before,' *Brides* magazine told its readers, 'you are helping to build greater security for the industries of this country'.

Text C

Lepore (2018) notes that post World War II was achieved by consumer spending because factories that had been carrying out wartime production were converted to make consumer goods like roller skates and colour televisions. The idea of a citizen as a consumer was not new – in fact, it dates back to the 1920s. However, in the 1950s mass consumption became a matter of civic duty. Magazines at the time suggested to readers to buy things they had never bought before because this would help provide greater security for industries in the USA.

Key

Text A – has a quote that is too long with no indent and an awkward secondary quote from a popular magazine
Text B – has a long quote that is correctly indented but has no date or page number and includes an awkward secondary quote from a popular magazine
Text C – includes a paraphrase that has wording that is too close to the original

Model text

Lepore (2018) notes that post World War II economic growth in the USA was the result of domestic consumerism. Wartime industry switched to the production of household goods and media organisations encouraged citizens to buy. The idea that consumerism could be a way of demonstrating citizenship was not new, but in the 1950s buying goods almost became a civic duty.

Think further

Establish with students that it is generally better to paraphrase than quote because their essay must be in their own words. Point out that you can quote when you want to critique another writer's point of view or when the original is well written and supports your point of view.

Notes

This activity can be simplified by getting students to focus on just two in-text examples. You could also provide students with some vocabulary to use in their paraphrase in step 5. For stronger students, this activity can be adapted by using a longer quotation that students need to cite in an essay or report they are currently working on.

Rationale

In academic essays and reports, students often quote too much original material and their writing can sometimes seem a little like a string of quotes. While pointing out correct procedure for in-text quotes, this activity aims to reinforce the idea that paraphrasing is often preferable.

6.9 Notes on cause and effect

Outline	Two groups make notes on different cause and effect paragraphs, then students swap notes and write a paragraph based on them, using phrases to describe cause and effect relationships.
Level	Intermediate (B1+) and above
Time	45 minutes
Aim	To practise writing a cause and effect paragraph; to practise structured note taking; to practise using phrases to signal cause and effect relationships.
Preparation	You will need to make available for each student a note taking grid and one of two cause and effect paragraphs on different topics (see *Example*). You can write or find cause and effect paragraphs on different topics and create a different kind of note taking grid depending on what appeals to or works well with your students.

Procedure

1 Divide the class into two groups. Group A reads a cause and effect paragraph on one topic, and Group B reads a paragraph on a different topic.

2 Provide students with note taking grids that include cause–effect graphic note organisers (see the example below).

3 In pairs in each group, students make notes on key points and the cause and effect relationships in their paragraph. Their notes must be clear and legible – other students will need to work with them.

4 A pair from each group now swap their notes. Show students examples of cause and effect language (see below).

5 In their pairs, students write a cause and effect paragraph based on the notes they have received. They use appropriate examples of cause and effect language.

6 Sets of pairs work now read each other's paragraphs and give feedback.

7 Students can read the original paragraphs to compare with their own.

Example
Group A

Sugary drinks

For many people, there is nothing more refreshing than a cool, sweet drink on a hot day. However, these drinks, which include fizzy soft drinks as well as fruit juice and energy drinks, contain large amounts of sugar and are a major source of calories, particularly for children and young adults. Drinking one of these drinks results in a high calorie intake, but it does not make a person feel full. As a result, the person is likely to also have a snack, and this leads to them putting on weight. It is estimated that just one sweet drink a day could cause a two and a half kilogram weight increase in a year. When people are overweight, they run the risk of serious health problems. A range of studies indicate that a rise in diabetes and heart disease are due to high consumption of sugary drinks. As a consequence, there is increased pressure on the health system to manage these medical problems.

Group B

Mobile phone overuse

Most of us find it difficult to leave home without one, and, as a result, we are more and more dependent on our mobile phones. Are we too dependent? Psychologists now identify mobile phone addiction as a serious health issue that can cause problems for our physical and mental well-being. Some people suffer from 'text neck', neck and upper back pain that is caused by looking down at our phone too much. Mobile phones can disturb our sleep patterns. The bright light of a mobile phone screen is often the reason for insomnia, which leads to tiredness during the day and an inability to concentrate on work or study. Furthermore, mobile phone overuse can cause an obsessive-compulsive disorder, which means a person constantly checks their phone and can no longer relate to people around them. This can then result in a serious psychological illness such as severe anxiety or depression.

Note taking grid
Key points

cause   **effect**

cause		effect
	→	
	→	
	→	

effect   **cause**

effect		cause
	←	
	←	
	←	

Language

cause → effect	effect ← cause
a/the reason for	is/are caused by
leads to	is/are due to
cause(s)	a/the result of
result(s) in	is/are a consequence of
	an/the effect of

Think further

Elicit from students typical words for indicating a cause and effect relationship between ideas to establish *because* and *therefore*. Check that students understand that the language they were shown in this activity were verb and noun phrases with the same meanings. Also suggest that students can explore other online templates and experiment with different ways of organising notes.

Notes

To give students more support, you could fill in one or two examples of notes in the notetaking grid. With stronger groups, you could just tell them to note cause–effect and effect–cause relationships in the paragraph and come up with their own grid. Students could then share their ideas with each other.

Rationale

At lower levels, linking words and expressions are a way of showing cause–effect relationships (or reason–result relationships – see Activity 3.5). This activity also encourages students to use a wider range of language. Analysing and taking notes on an example paragraph allows students to see a model before writing their own paragraph. The exchange of notes means students need to think more carefully about the way they make notes, and indirectly, it gets them to consider different ways of structuring notes.

References

Sugary drinks text based on 'Sugary Drinks' from The Nutrition Source website available at: www.hsph.harvard.edu/nutritionsource/healthy-drinks/sugary-drinks/ [Accessed December 2022]
Mobile phone overuse text based on information from PsychGuides.com website available at: www.psychguides.com/behavioral-disorders/cell-phone-addiction/signs-and-symptoms/ [Accessed December 2022]

6.10 The right academic word

Outline	Students replace words and expressions with words from the Academic Word List in example sentences from essays and reports and then write their own sentences.
Level	Upper intermediate (B2) and above
Time	40 minutes
Aim	To develop students' awareness of the Academic Word List as a tool for their writing; to extend students' lexical range.
Preparation	Before the lesson, remind students to bring a digital device to the lesson so they can search the Academic Word List online. You will need to prepare a set of sentences and make them available to each student (see *Example*). You can write the sentences that relate to a topic you have been studying, or that focus on words from the Academic Word List that you think would be most beneficial for your students.

Procedure

1 Students read example sentences from academic essays and reports with a word or phrase that can be replaced with a word from the Academic Word List.

2 Students search for verbs in the Headwords from the Academic Word List (available at: www.wgtn.ac.nz/lals/resources/academicwordlist) that can replace the underlined words and phrases.

3 Check answers with the class.

4 Searching the Sublists of the Academic Word List, students find and choose one different part of speech of the verbs they found in the Headwords list.

5 Students write example sentences including each of the Sublist words. They can either reformulate the original example or they can write an example of their own.

6 In pairs, students compare word choices and sentences.

Example

1 It is important to <u>get an idea of</u> the language ability of all learners before carrying out the research.
2 For the experiment, we decided to <u>have a detailed look at</u> computer code from 27 different programmes.
3 To begin with, we <u>give an explanation of</u> some basic rules to describe the features of a valid example.
4 The land is largely underdeveloped and this <u>tells us</u> the planned expansion of the urban area has not happened.
5 Conflict <u>takes place</u> naturally in human relationships when each person has a different point of view.
6 From the archaeological evidence, it is difficult to <u>come to a decision</u> that there was interaction between different social groups.
7 Staff performance was <u>judged</u> in order to determine future training needs.
8 Contexts where communities become 'families' <u>point to the fact</u> that people can learn through active social participation.

Key
1 assess, 2 analyse, 3 define, 4 indicates, 5 occurs, 6 conclude, 7 evaluated, 8 imply

Think further
Point out that the Academic Word List is a useful resource for checking vocabulary choices students make when they are writing. Establish the strategy of searching for (an)other form(s) of a word from a sublist and making a note of this new vocabulary.

Notes
If you would like to give your learners more support, you could indicate the first letter of the verb that they need to search for. Alternatively, you could select a pool of 20 to 30 words from the Academic Word List for students to select from. For higher-level students, you could increase the level of challenge by not underlining the words and expressions that need to be replaced – students would need to identify them and then search for a more academic replacement.

Rationale
Many learners struggle to adopt an appropriate academic register in their writing. The Academic Word List is a freely-available and extremely useful tool helping students develop their register awareness. At the same time, it can help increase their lexical range.

6.11 Noting the relevance

Outline	In two groups, students assess the quality of different sets of notes about a text, then compare their ideas to create a full set of notes.
Level	Upper intermediate (B2) and above
Time	35 minutes
Aim	To give students practice in identifying and prioritising relevant information from a text; to demonstrate effective notes for paraphrasing.
Preparation	You will need to select a suitable text and prepare two sets of notes containing points of different quality (see *Example*). You could use a text from the course materials you are using. If teaching online, you could consider using breakout rooms for part of this activity.

Procedure

1 Divide the students into Group A and Group B. Students read the same original text material but a different set of notes about the text in preparation for writing a discursive essay.

2 Working in their groups, students decide if each point in their set of notes is:
   a. incorrect (I)
   b. contains language too similar to the text (S)
   c. not relevant for the essay (NR)
   d. correct and relevant (C)
   They also note down any information that they think is missing from their notes.

3. When groups have finished, students work in pairs with someone from the other group. They show their notes, explain their decisions and say what they think is missing. Their partner adds to their own set any notes that are correct and relevant. (Pairs should end up with a complete set of correct and relevant notes.)

4. Check answers with the class.

5. Students work alone and write a summary paragraph using the notes. They can then compare their paragraphs in pairs.

Think further

Establish with students that one of the challenges of making notes is finding alternative words and expressions to those used in the original text. Suggest they use a dictionary and/or thesaurus to help with this, and that it's better to do so when taking notes, rather than when writing the summary.

Notes

If you feel your students need more support, you could tell them the number of points in their notes they need to correct, or include just one point that needs to be identified as inappropriate. With a stronger class, you could provide only four correct points in total in the two sets of notes and get students to make additional notes of what's missing.

Example

It is estimated that more than 65% of the world's population has access to the internet. This makes it the largest 'country' in the world. In the early years of the twenty-first century, the internet was perceived as a highly democratic platform that offered anyone and everyone the opportunity to participate and voice an opinion. However, over time, a range of technology and social media companies have gradually manipulated this democratic ideal by means of powerful algorithms. These companies monitor what we do online attentively. They form an idea of our preferences and direct our attention to products and services that are likely to appeal to us. In effect, they have used the internet to monetize our online activity.

The argument that these companies put forward is that they offer a wide range of free online services. It must be acknowledged that the internet is a vast treasure trove of largely free and easily available information. It also provides a wide range of entertainment options and opportunities to connect with people all over the world. While this access is both useful and appealing, it is also the core problem with the internet. Our online behaviour provides technology and social media companies with enormous amounts of information about us which they sell to advertisers or other organisations that believe they can gain an advantage from the data.

Group A

1 The internet is like a nation that has 65% of everyone in the world.

2 In the early years of the twenty-first century the internet was seen as highly democratic.

3 IT companies have used algorithms to control online democracy.

4 IT companies have a preference for certain products they want to advertise.

5 The internet is a good source of information and allows people to communicate.

6 Video streaming services have made a lot of money.

7 IT companies sell information about us to other companies who want to use it for their own benefit.

Group B

1 The internet is like a very large nation that used to be very democratic.

2 The algorithms IT companies use are very good at finding out what people do online.

3 IT companies employ a lot of programmers to develop algorithms.

4 IT companies say people benefit from the many free services they provide.

5 There is no censorship of information on the internet.

6 The availability of content that isn't really free is a key issue with the internet.

7 IT companies have an enormous amount of information they sell to advertisers or organisations that gain an advantage from the data.

Key
Group A: 1 (C), 2 (S), 3 (C), 4 (I), 5 (C), 6 (NR), 7 (C)
Group B: 1 (C), 2 (C), 3 (NR), 4 (C), 5 (I), 6 (C), 7 (S)

Rationale

Learning how to paraphrase information from a text is a key challenge for students studying EAP. The first step in the process is learning to identify relevant information in the text and then take notes using language that is different from the original. This activity gives practice in determining relevant information while also modelling the kinds of changes in language that can occur when making notes.

6.12 Fixing the draft

Outline	Students draft a paragraph from notes, evaluate a model paragraph that needs improvement, then use their first draft and the corrected model to write a final draft.
Level	Upper intermediate (B2) and above
Time	45–60 minutes
Aim	To provide practice in drafting from notes; to develop awareness of typical weaknesses in first drafts.
Preparation	You will need to make available for each student: a set of notes, and if desired, a model paragraph (see *Example*) that needs improving. You can create a set of essay notes and first draft based on a text students need to work on.

Procedure

1 Students write a paragraph from the notes – (see essay notes below for a business studies essay on the advantages for companies when employees work from home). It may pay to set a time limit and move to the next step even if two or three students haven't quite completed a first draft.

2 Students put their first draft aside and read a paragraph written from the notes (see example *Paragraph for improving*). They identify any issues with the example and compare answers in pairs. Ask them to think about:
referencing, definition of terminology, relevance of/or incomplete information, language.

3 Check answers with the whole class. Students should then not look at the corrected, first draft paragraph, and in pairs, evaluate each other's first drafts written in step 1.

4 Students then write a second draft of their paragraph incorporating what they have learnt from the model and feedback from their partner.

5 They can then check their second draft against a model paragraph.

Example

Essay notes

- before known as 'telecommuting' → more recent term 'working from home' (WFH) (Lee, 2018; Alvarez, 2019; Burns, 2020)

- increase productivity = increase profit

- companies need less office space – lower rents, less office equipment (computers phones) (Vergiani, 2019: p.58)

- employee productivity better – concentrate on task longer period (Burns, 2020: p.163)

- companies now employ people who with commuting problem, e.g. working parents, people with disability, live far away (Alvarez, 2019: p.37)

- less absenteeism (people don't turn up – illness, family event) – employees log on & work with mild illness (Singh, 2019: p.72)

Paragraph for improving

Previously known as 'telecommuting', more recent academic articles that evaluate that kind of work have used the term 'working from home' (WFH) (Lee, 2018; Alvarez, 2019; Burns, 2020). A key question is how much WFH increases an organisation's productivity, and therefore, its profit. One obvious benefit is a reduce in costs associated with office space. Companies need less space, and this means they pay lower rents, and they need less office equipment such as computers and telephones (Vergiani, 2019: p.58). Employees often enjoy having a work laptop at home that they can use in their spare time. Many organisations have noticed that the productivity of employees has increased because they seem to be better at concentration on a task for a longer period of time. Another benefit of WFH is that companies can now employ people who previously have problems commuting to the office, for example, . . . (Alvarez, 2019: p.37). Finally, absenteeism is less of a problem with WFH. While employees can choose not to log in to their work computer, they tend to keep working when they have a mild illness (Singh, 2019: p.72).

Key

(Issues highlighted)

Previously known as 'telecommuting', more recent academic articles that evaluate that kind of work have used the term 'working from home' (WFH) (Lee, 2018; Alvarez, 2019; Burns; 2020). A key question is how much WFH increases an organisation's productivity and therefore its profit. One obvious benefit is a reduce [***language – word form: 'reduction'***] in costs associated with office space. Companies need less space, and this means they pay lower rents, and they need less office equipment such as computers and telephones (Vergiani, 2019: p.58). Employees often enjoy having a work laptop at home that they can use in their spare time [***information in this sentence not relevant to the paragraph***]. Many organisations have noticed that the productivity of employees has increased because they seem to be better at concentration [***language – word form: 'concentrating'***] on a task for a longer period of time. [***missing reference***] Another benefit of WFH is that companies can now employ people who previously have [***language – tense: 'had'/ 'have had'***] problems commuting to the office, for example, . . . [***missing information***] (Alvarez, 2019: p.37). Finally, absenteeism [***term not defined***] is less of a problem with WFH. While employees can choose not to log in to their work computer, they tend to keep working when they have a mild illness (Singh, 2019: p.72).

Model paragraph

Previously known as 'telecommuting', more recent academic articles that evaluate that kind of work have used the term 'working from home' (WFH) (Lee, 2018; Alvarez, 2019; Burns, 2020). A key question is how much WFH increases an organisation's productivity and therefore its profit. One obvious benefit is a reduction in costs associated with office space. Companies need less space, and this means they pay lower rents, and they need less office equipment such as computers and telephones (Vergiani, 2019: p.58). Many organisations have noticed that the productivity of employees has increased because they seem to be better at concentrating on a task for a longer period of time (Burns, 2020: p.163). Another benefit of WFH is that companies can now employ people who previously had problems commuting to the office, for example, working parents, people with disabilities and those who live far away (Alvarez, 2019: p.37). Finally, absenteeism, when employees do not come to work because of illness or family events, is less of a problem with WFH. While employees can choose not to log in to their work computer, they tend to keep working when they have a mild illness (Singh, 2019: p.72).

Think further

Ask students what they focus on when they evaluate their own first drafts. Establish that they need to consider organisation, content, language and academic conventions, e.g. referencing.

Notes

The second draft could be written in pairs. This activity can be adapted so that the model includes issues with a focus on just one feature that students have been struggling with in the course, for example, referencing or relevance of information.

Rationale

Students are often unsure how to effectively evaluate a first draft and their focus tends to be mostly on language accuracy. This activity highlights other issues that should be evaluated. Taking away the model that students have improved prevents them from copying the language of that example and refocuses them on their own writing.

7　Writing for business

Business English is a sub category of English for Specific Purposes (ESP) and focuses on a variety of English used for communication in the business world. This can range from language used to buy and sell goods and services through to language used to socialise with colleagues. While Business English had previously been focused almost entirely on replicating model texts – primarily business letters – the advent of the communicative approach (in the mid-1970s) shifted the emphasis onto spoken language and what are often called 'business communication skills' (Frendo, 2005: p.7). This is evident from a skim read of methodology books and coursebooks that focus on Business English. However, as is the case with general English, digital media, such as email and texting, and their capacity to allow rapid and often instantaneous communication have seen increased interest in written business communication. This can be inferred when comparing two books focusing on Business English. Ellis and Johnson's (1994) book *Teaching Business* makes only passing reference to written texts and writing skills. By contrast, Nickerson and Planken's *Introducing Business English* (2016) devotes four out of 12 chapters to written texts and writing. The business world is a context where speaking and writing often work in tandem. For example, an email about delayed delivery may result in a phone call reply from the recipient of the email.

As with EAP (see Chapter 6), this area of ESP has its own specialist literature. And similarly again, it is not possible here to cover every aspect of written Business English, but the range of activities in this chapter provide an overview of this area of English language learning. Teachers wanting a broader and deeper view of the topic should read subject-specific literature.

Functions, genres and patterns

In a genre study that contrasted a sales letter with a job application letter, Bhatia (1993), as cited by Nickerson and Planken (2016), noted that both texts had the same purpose: they aimed to promote either a product or a person. It could be argued that the function of promotion runs through a lot of business writing. In addition to the two texts that Bhatia focused on, reports and proposals can also include the function of promoting. While reports aim to provide information, they typically end with a summary that directly or indirectly promotes a particular point of view or idea. A business proposal involves more direct promotion. The writer typically has an idea for a new product, service or process that they want to 'sell' to colleagues. All these genres can also include the broader core text functions of description and narration. For example, a proposal will describe the new product or service and perhaps narrate a series of events that has led the writer to come up with the idea for the proposal.

Other written business texts encompass a varied range of functions. Email messages can introduce a new staff member, invite people to meetings or functions, make or confirm arrangements for meetings or events, elicit feedback from colleagues or companies, and complain about products and services. As was the case for many of the texts in Chapter 4, the functional language used in this kind of communication is often very similar to that used in oral communication.

The wide variety of text functions coupled with the range of possible audiences for texts means it is difficult to perceive business writing as a stand-alone genre. However, it is possible to look at broader genre categories such as business emails, business reports or business proposals. These, in turn can be broken down into sub genres. For example, emails can include an email of enquiry, of confirmation, or for making arrangements, etc. (Frendo, 2005).

Bhatia's study of business texts (1993), cited in Nickerson and Planken (2016), investigated three levels of analysis for determining a business text genre. Firstly, the kind of grammar and vocabulary used in the text. Secondly, the use of prefabricated chunks of language, for example, *I look forward to hearing from you*, and finally, it examined the organisation of the texts in terms of 'structural moves' (p.66). This refers to the language and information that business people would expect to find at different stages in a text of that genre. For example, an email of complaint from one company to another would begin by providing key information about the product in question (invoice number, date of dispatch, etc.) followed by a description of the problem that has generated the complaint. This view of genre highlights the way in which these texts are written and understood within a community of users. At the same time, it suggests a link to the broader notion of coherent organisation of texts. Bhatia also noted that the structural moves of business genres can vary from one culture to another. For example, job application letters in the US include more information about the applicant than those in South East Asia do (1993, cited in Nickerson & Planken, 2016: p.68).

Frendo (2005) emphasises the notion of a varied audience in written business communication. Texts may be aimed at both internal and external colleagues as well as customers, who may not have any specialised business knowledge. He goes on to say that writers more often than not assume there will be some kind of response to their written communication as well as the fact they need to maintain an on-going business relationship. This might mean that a letter or email of complaint from one company to another will avoid an angry or demanding tone.

The tone and style of internal written communication is also important. Scott and Tribble (2006) make a distinction between internal and external communication, on one hand, and between a distant and close relationship between writers, on the other. This means texts can be categorised within one of four quadrants that refer to the audience of the text: internal–close, internal–distant, external–close, external–distant. Consequently, writers vary their tone and style in relationship to the quadrant in which their audience lies. For example, if they are writing to someone who is more senior in the management structure of a company (internal–distant), a formal style is more likely. However, if they are writing to someone at the same level (internal–close), a neutral style is more likely to be adopted. Workers also need to ensure they are not overly assertive in email messages they write to colleagues they know well in the interests of maintaining a good working relationship.

The transactional nature of much business writing means general–particular and problem–solution discourse patterning is likely to be predominant in key genres. For example, a report on a business process might begin with a general overview and then describe specific aspects of the process in more detail. A business proposal is often triggered by some kind of problem (a gap in the market or a perception of inadequate service) and begins by outlining what the issue is before going on to propose an idea that acts as the solution to the problem. A claim–counterclaim pattern is less likely to be found frequently in business writing, but it may appear in reports and proposals where alternative options are being considered.

Language

As indicated above in discussion of Bhatia's genre analysis, much written business language is made up of expressions or formulaic chunks of language. This is particularly the case with different email genres. For example, a job application email often begins with *I am writing to enquire . . .* , while a request might finish with *I'd be grateful if you could . . .* , and an invitation would begin *We'd like to invite you to . . .* .

There are no specific grammar features that are typically found in business writing in general. However, it is possible to predict the grammar of some specific genres. For example, a description of a process is likely to include passive constructions while the recommendations of a proposal will incorporate modal structures. Specific instructions to employees are likely to be expressed in imperatives probably listed with bullet points, and reports that include a description of a situation to date are likely to use the present perfect. In business texts with a clear promotion function, a range of adjective phrases with a positive connotation might be used.

Formal style choices that business writers make often centre around the expression of modality, the use of noun forms and ways of expressing tentativeness. For example, in a formal email to a senior manager, a writer might say: *I would welcome the opportunity to discuss the necessity of staff cuts.* This sentence uses *would* to make the suggestion tentative together with the noun phrase *the opportunity*. Also, modality is expressed using another noun phrase, *the necessity,* and the Latinate verb *discuss* is used as opposed to a phrasal verb. Compare this to a neutral way of making the same suggestion to a colleague who works at the same level in the company hierarchy: *Let's talk through having to make staff cuts.* This uses the plural imperative followed by a phrasal verb and the *-ing* form of a modal verb. In general, modal noun phrases (*the necessity*) and modal adjective phrases (*it is essential to*) are used to make a text formal whereas modal verbs (*have to, should*) are used in a neutral style.

Frendo (2005) notes that business writing often includes a lot of specialist terminology or jargon that is relevant to the nature of the business being written about. This can also include abbreviations that are generally understood, for example, ETA (estimated time of arrival), COB (close of business) and RFD (request for discussion). Bargiela-Chiappini et al (2013) discuss a Business English Corpus created by Mike Nelson, which includes examples of both written and spoken language. Overall, Nelson discovered that only a small number of business words appeared amongst the most common words found in a general English corpus. He identified the 50 most frequent keywords in the Business English Corpus (BEC) that he created. The top five were *business, company, market, customer* and *OK*. When a comparison was made between the frequency of Nelson's keywords in the BEC relative to a general English corpus, they were shown to be more frequent. This suggests they are useful lexical items to focus on in a Business English course. In addition, Nelson made a comparison between keywords in specific categories of general English and Business English. For example, when referring to people, general English keywords are *man, mum, wife, dad, baby* while keywords for people in Business English are *customer, contractor, manager, seller, buyer*.

In the classroom

As noted above, people working in a business context often write and speak when communicating with each other. This means the two productive skills are often combined in Business English classroom activities. For example, a simulated meeting or discussion could lead to the writing of a report. Writing activities can be contextualised in broader communicative tasks that could involve all four language skills which, while they may not be exact representations of real-world business activity, should aim to simulate typical business tasks (Evans, 2012, cited in Nickerson & Planken, 2016). This suggests that Business English writing activities will often be interactive and/or collaborative in nature. In order to facilitate the communicative nature of business writing, it helps if students have digital tools that they can use during the course of a lesson.

Many Business English students have their studies funded by the organisation that they work for. This means there is often the expectation of some kind of formal evaluation and assessment of students as evidence of learning. Many institutions offering Business English provide an achievement test that usually includes writing tasks – the Cambridge Linguaskill test also has a Business English option. The evaluation or result of a test or examination is usually provided together with a report on the student's ability in different skills.

References

Bargiela-Chiappini, F., Nickerson, C. & Planken, B. (2013) *Business Discourse 2nd Edition*. Basingstoke and New York, Palgrave Macmillan.

Bhatia, V. K. (1993) *Analysing genre: Language in professional settings*. London, Longman.

Ellis, M. & Johnson, C. (1994) *Teaching Business English*. Oxford, Oxford University Press.

Evans, S. (2012) Designing email tasks for the Business English classroom: Implications from a study of Hong Kong's key industries. *English for Specific Business Purposes*, 32(4), 195-207.

Frendo, E. (2005) *How to Teach Business English*. Harlow, Pearson Education Ltd.

Nickerson, C. & Planken, B. (2016) *Introducing Business English*. Abingdon and New York, Routledge.

Scott, M. & Tribble, C. (2006) *Textual Patterns: Key words and corpus analysis in language education*. Amsterdam, John Benjamins Publishing Company.

7.1 The right request

Outline	Students read three versions of an email request, deciding which has an appropriate tone and then write an email of their own.
Level	Elementary (A2) and above
Time	35 minutes
Aim	To practise writing a request email; to highlight an appropriate tone for written business communication with peers.
Preparation	Make available to each student three different request emails from an employee, two with areas for improvement and one as appropriate model (see *Example*). You could write emails for any kind of business request that you think your students should focus on.

Procedure

1 Students read three different versions of a request email asking for leave, and decide which is the most appropriate. Tell students the email is to a Team Leader the writer gets on with well.

2 Check answers with the class and get students to say why each version is or isn't appropriate.

3 Highlight any useful language features in the text you are using. For the example emails below, highlight the two collocations: *take leave* and *have time/a day off*. Also, the use of the less formal *Hi* – acceptable with a person you report to directly.

4 Working alone, students write a similar email of request on the same topic, but think of different reasons from the example emails for the request.

5 In pairs, students read each other's messages and give feedback on the tone.

Example

Request 1

● ● ●   Reply   Forward

Dear Margie

On Friday 27 April my sister is getting married in Liverpool. I need to go to the wedding, so I need to take some leave. I need two days leave because I need to travel to Liverpool on the Friday.

I need to know as soon as possible so I can book travel.

Yours sincerely
Tom

Request 2

Reply   Forward

Hi Margie

Next month my sister is getting married in Liverpool. The wedding is on Friday 27 April in Liverpool. Could I please take some leave to attend? I need to travel to Liverpool on the Thursday, so could I have two days off?

Can you let me know as soon as possible so I can book travel?

Many thanks
Tom

Request 3

Reply   Forward

Hi Margie

How's it going? Some exciting news: my sister is getting married in Liverpool on 27 April! I can't believe she's found the right man.

Anyway, the whole family is going up to Liverpool for the wedding. It's not going to be a big wedding – just family and a few friends. Of course, I have to be there! So would it be OK for me to take two days of leave? I need a day to travel to Liverpool so that that means I'll need to take off the Thursday and the Friday.

I really hope that's OK with you and can't wait for your reply. I need to buy my train tickets!

Many thanks and all best wishes
Tom

Key
1 there is no request question; the verb 'need' is overused – the email sounds unfriendly
2 appropriate, clear, polite and a friendly tone
3 includes too much unnecessary personal information – seems unprofessional

Think further
Elicit or establish with learners the structure of a request email from the example: describe the situation → make the request → ask for a reply.

Notes
The activity can be simplified by getting students to read just two versions of the same request, for example, the first two request example emails. Being overly direct is more likely to be a problem with lower-level students. For a stronger class, you could give them only an email with too much information (such as the third email example) and ask students to edit it.

Rationale
This activity focuses on a typical example of written communication between peers at a similar level in a company and highlights the importance of an appropriate tone – neither formal nor informal, but clear and friendly. It is useful for students to be aware of this from a low level onwards.

7.2 Accurate cover

Outline	Students correct language problems in a covering letter, then write one of their own and proofread a partner's.
Level	Elementary (A2) and above
Time	30 minutes
Aim	To encourage and practise close proofing of a covering letter.
Preparation	You will need to make available a job application covering letter to each student (see *Example*). This activity can be adapted for any kind of email, but it is important that you double check that mistakes are not highlighted by a word processing programme. At higher levels, you may wish to provide students with a longer text with a wider variety of errors.

Procedure

1 Tell students they are going to read a covering letter for a job application. It contains mistakes that a word processing spell and grammar check do not notice (the example email below contains the following mistakes: spelling, wrong word, wrong form).

2 Students read the email and find mistakes. Set a time limit and see who can find the most mistakes in that time.

3 Check answers with the class.

4 Students now write their own covering letter, but should not have sight of the example email.

5 In pairs, students proofread each other's letters.

6 Allow pairs to ask about language points they are unsure of and/or collect in the covering letters to correct for accuracy.

Example

● ● ●   Reply   Forward

Dear Sir or Madam

I am wiring to enquire about work opportunity in your company. As you can seem from my CV (attach), I have for years' experience as a marketing co-ordination, and I am just complete an MBA.

I look forward to hearing about you.

Yours faithfully

Key

●●●   <u>Reply</u>   <u>Forward</u>

Dear Sir or Madam

I am **writing** ~~wiring~~ to enquire about work **opportunities** ~~opportunity~~ in your company. As you can **see** ~~seem~~ from my CV (**attached** ~~attach~~), I have **four** ~~for~~ years' experience as a marketing **coordinator** ~~co-ordination~~, and I **have** ~~am~~ just **completed** ~~complete~~ an MBA.

I look forward to hearing **from** ~~about~~ you.

Yours faithfully

Think further

Establish with learners that digital tools can't spot all language problems, and they still need to read to check written language. Suggest that they use online dictionaries and online example template letters and emails to help with language they are not sure about.

Notes

If your class needs more support, you can show the covering letter to the whole class and elicit two or three errors to get students started. Then, in step 4, they could continue to read the example letter. With a stronger class, you could show them the letter for a set period of time, for example, 30 seconds, during which time they can't write anything down. Once you stop showing the letter, students write down as many language problems as they remember.

Rationale

While digital tools offer a lot of support for students' writing, some errors can still slip through. In the business world, image and presentation are often very important, and incorrect or sloppy language use can create a negative impression of a prospective employee or of the company the person is representing. This activity reminds students of the need for their own vigilance in combination with digital tools. Taking away the corrected version of the email encourages students to use their own language resources rather than merely copying what they have seen.

7.3 CV workshop

Outline	Students research online examples and templates to help them write a short CV, and then in groups compare and give feedback.
Level	Pre-intermediate (B1) and above
Time	90 minutes (30 minutes if steps 1 and 2 are done as homework – see *Notes*)
Aim	To practise writing a CV; to highlight different CV styles.
Preparation	For this lesson, it's preferable if each student has a digital device and access to the internet. It would pay to do some online research and choose some specific websites to direct students to. There is a lot of choice available, and it helps if students access examples that are relevant to the context in which they are learning and working. In selecting websites, try to ensure students are offered a choice of work-focused CV templates and skills-focused CV templates so you can make this distinction in *Think further*.

Procedure

1   Students go online to find examples and templates of CVs – ask them to choose a short version of a template they want to use. In pairs, they discuss reasons for their choice.

2   Working alone, students write their CV using the template they have chosen to help them. If any students have no or little work experience, suggest they write an imaginary CV – what they hope their CV will look like two or three years into a career in their field.

3   Students work in groups of six to eight. They read each other's CVs and note anything that is unclear or any language errors they detect.

4   In their groups, students give feedback and discuss the different approaches to CVs.

5   Ask the class as a whole which style or approach to CV writing they found most suitable.

6   Students revise their CVs on the basis of group feedback for homework.

Think further

Elicit the two main CV styles: work-focused and skills-focused. Establish that work-focused CVs are more suitable when you have had some work experience while skills-focused CVs are more suitable for those with qualifications and little or no experience.

Notes

For some learner groups, it may be easier to set steps 1 and 2 as a homework activity, particularly if you have a class where there is a mix of students – some of whom have work experience and a CV and others who don't. If you do this, it's a good idea to prepare some example CVs to give to students who might forget the homework task. Be prepared for the fact that students who are working and have CVs may well ask you to review theirs after the lesson for language accuracy.

Rationale

Writing and/or revising a student's CV in English is perhaps the most frequently articulated need of Business English students. They will often request that the teacher give feedback on an individual basis. The workshop approach in this activity aims to deal with the need in a more student-centred way. The activity also makes sure students are aware of the range of online resources they can use to write their CV.

7.4 Introduce yourself

Outline	Students write an introductory email to staff at their new company, then read each other's work.
Level	Pre-intermediate (B1) and above
Time	35 minutes
Aim	To practise writing a less formal introductory email; to highlight different ways of signing off a less formal email message.
Preparation	You will need to prepare and make available to students a set of sentence starters (see *Example*). The sentence starters you use could include more or less information, depending on the needs of your students.

Procedure

1   Students imagine they have just begun a new job at a new company – suggest they think of something not associated with their current job if they have one.

2   Show students some jumbled sentence starters that can form the basis of an introductory email.

3   Working alone, students order and complete the sentence starters to write an email introducing themselves to other staff at their new company.

4   Students post their emails around the room or online. They read other students' emails to find someone who has chosen an imaginary job similar to theirs.

5   Show students an example introductory email so they can compare it with theirs and allow them to ask questions.

6   In pairs, students think of things they could ask the staff they meet in their new company.

Example
Sentence starters

I'm the new . . .
I've worked in [area of work] . . .
Hello . . .
I'm looking forward to . . .
I'd love to . . .   feel free to . . .
My name's . . .
Before I joined [company] I was . . .

Example email

Reply   Forward

● ● ●

Hello everyone

My name is Megan Scott and I'm the new Leader of the Digital Marketing Team. I'm looking forward to meeting you all and working together with you.

I've worked in Digital Marketing for the past nine years. Before I joined Trade On Ltd, I was at Leonards Communications for three years.

I'd love to speak to you all in person, so feel free to book a time for a chat.

Best wishes

Megan

Think further

Highlight to students the way Megan signs off her email in the example. Elicit other ways of signing off the same kind of email, for example, *Kind regards, Thanks, All the best, Best.*

Notes

If your class needs more support, you could elicit some example continuations for the sentence starters you think will be most challenging for your students. With a stronger class, you could just give instructions on what to include but no sentence starters, for example, name, new role, experience, previous job, friendly greeting.

Rationale

This kind of email is routine for people starting work in a new company or moving to a new branch. It's a useful writing activity early in a Business English course. Getting students to choose an imaginary job is a way of avoiding any discomfort for class members who may not be employed. The sentence starters are scrambled so that students have to consider the organisation and coherence of the message. The final step in the activity is a way of linking writing to speaking.

7.5 Complete invitation

Outline	Students identify missing information from a business invitation email, before writing their own and then responding to a partner's invitation.
Level	Pre-intermediate (B1) and above
Time	50 minutes
Aim	To practise writing an invitation to a business event; to highlight the need for detailed information in invitation emails.
Preparation	You will need to make available a business invitation email for each student (see *Example*). You might create an invitation associated with the kind of business event your students are familiar with and perhaps including local details.

Procedure

1 Students read an invitation to an event and decide what information is missing.

2 Check answers with the class.

3 Show students an improved model of the same email.

4 Working alone, students write an email invitation to an event linked to the area of business they are interested in, e.g. for a product launch, a new office or premises, a seminar discussion, a social get together or networking opportunity.

5 In pairs, students exchange their invitations. They then write a reply either accepting or declining the invitation. If there is missing information from their partner's invitation, they should ask about it in their reply.

6 With the whole class, ask if the invitations they received contained all the necessary information.

Example

Email to correct

● ● ●   Reply   Forward

We would like to invite you to the opening of our new CT Fitness downtown gym on Wednesday 19 June. This is an opportunity to find out about the new facilities and the latest in digital workout equipment that make the gym the most up-to-date in town.

For some years now, the old CT Fitness downtown gym in Renton Street was a bit small, particularly at busy times of the day. The new gym in Short Street is almost twice the size.

We will offer snacks and drinks, and our fantastic team of personal trainers will demonstrate one of our great new group fitness workout routines. And it's a chance to have a close look at the new spaces and equipment.

We hope you can join us for a fun evening and this first look at our fabulous new facility. Could you RSVP by email?

Susie Marshall
CT Fitness Marketing

Key

no opening salutation (*Dear . . .*); no address of the new gym; no time of the event; no email address for RSVP; no closing salutation; it would also benefit from more description of the new gym (see model).

Model

Reply   Forward

Dear Luisa

We would like to invite you to the opening of our new CT Fitness downtown gym, 15 Short Street, on Wednesday 19 June at 6pm. This is an opportunity to find out about the new facilities and the latest in digital workout equipment that make the gym the most up-to-date in town.

For some years now, the old CT Fitness downtown gym in Renton Street was a bit small, particularly at busy times of the day. The new gym in Short Street is almost twice the size. The main gym is spacious, and we have extra workout rooms for group classes.

We will offer snacks and drinks at the opening event, and our fantastic team of personal trainers will demonstrate one of our great new group fitness workout routines. It's also a chance to have a close look at the new spaces and equipment.

We hope you can join us for a fun evening and this first look at our fabulous new facility. Could you RSVP by email to susie@CTF.com ?

Yours sincerely
Susie Marshall
CT Fitness Marketing

Think further

Elicit from students what information is included in the model invitation. Establish the following structure: the opening paragraph gives the key information on the event; the second paragraph adds some background information; the third paragraph gives extra detail on the event; the final paragraph includes a request for reply (RSVP).

Notes

If your class needs more support, in steps 1 and 2, you could show the correct model example and ask students to underline key information. To provide more challenge, the incorrect model could be given with the paragraphs jumbled, or as a single block of text for students to decide on paragraph division.

Rationale

Business invitations tend to be more formal than personal ones and are usually associated with some kind of promotion. This activity shows not only the key information that needs to be included in an email invitation but also the way it is organised (an example of structural moves as discussed above). The pair work in step 5 aims to provide the activity with a communicative focus, but it also acts as peer checking of each other's invitations.

7.6 Something to complain about

Outline Students write a business-to-business email to complain about a product or service and then write replies to a complaint.
Level Intermediate (B1+) and above
Time 45 minutes
Aim To practise writing and responding to complaint emails.
Preparation No preparation is necessary. If students write hard copies of their emails, you could provide paper for them to write on.

Procedure

1 Establish with students why one business might complain to another, e.g. goods haven't arrived (or arrived late), goods were damaged in transit, an order was incomplete, incorrect goods were sent, poor quality service was provided, a lack of support for a product.

2 Students work in pairs and write an email of complaint to an imaginary company – they decide on the nature of the complaint. Remind them to include all necessary details and that the complaint is from one business to another – not an individual complaining to a company. Set a time limit.

3 Collect in the complaint emails and redistribute them randomly.

4 In the same pairs, students write an email reply to the complaint they have received. Indicate their reply needs to be polite, but they can choose to:
  a request more detailed information if the complaint letter isn't clear
  b accept the complaint is justified, describe the action they will take and offer some form of compensation
  c accept the customer is dissatisfied, but disagree that there is a problem, or refuse to accept responsibility for the problem

5 Replies are given to the original complainants, and the pair decide if they are satisfied with the outcome or not and why. If they're still dissatisfied, they decide what action they will now take.

6 As a class, ask students whether their complaint was resolved and, if not, what they plan to do. Also check whether the reply they received was appropriately polite.

Think further

Elicit from learners the tense they can use to talk about actions taken (in reply option b above). Establish the present perfect, for example, *I've spoken to the courier company, I've spoken to our warehouse manager, I've checked with our support staff.* Then elicit that the tense changes to simple past with time expressions, for example, *I spoke to the courier company* **yesterday**, *I checked with our support staff* **two days ago**.

Notes

If students need more support, in step 1, you could elicit the structure of a complaint letter: *reason for writing, detail of problem/complaint, result of problem, suggested solution.* To add a challenge for a stronger class, students could write their emails and replies alone. An alternative for steps 4 and 5 would be to set up a telephone role play in which the two companies resolve the issue. To do this, you would need to ensure sets of pairs exchange texts rather than randomly distributing them.

Rationale

While there is some similarity to personal complaint emails, business-to-business complaints tend to be more formal and polite in tone because both parties probably want to maintain a business relationship. The exchange of complaints and replies ensures a sense of audience and a communicative purpose. The three options at step 4 allow for the fact that the letter of complaint may lack necessary information and allows students to give feedback on the email content to the pair that wrote it.

7.7 Note share

Outline	Using notes provided, each half of the class completes a different part of the same email, and then compares and gives feedback on each other's writing.
Level	Intermediate (B1+) and above
Time	40 minutes
Aim	To practise writing from notes; to highlight the use of bullet points to signal action points.
Preparation	You will need to make available the first half of an email and accompanying notes to half of the class and the end of the same email and accompanying notes to the other half of the class (see *Example*). The email in the example is a typical message to all staff, but this activity can be adapted to any kind of email or report that might have been drafted from meeting notes and contains action points.

Procedure

1   Divide the class into two halves. Students A have the first part of an email and Students B the second part of the same email. All students also have some additional notes which they need to use to complete their email.

2   In pairs from the same group (i.e. two Students A together and two Students B together), students read the email and use the notes to write the part of their email that is incomplete.

3   Each Student A pair then works with a Student B pair. They share each other's writing, but do not show the already completed part of the email they have.

4   Students give feedback, suggesting improvements, e.g. noting any information that is missing or incorrect, but they should not give details about the completed part of the email they have.

5   Pairs revise the email on the basis of feedback. They then compare their second draft to the original.

Example
Student A

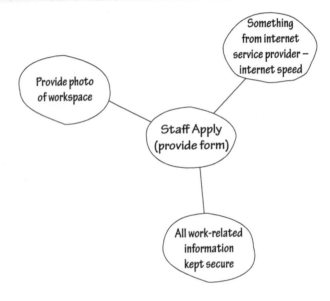

Student B

● ● ●   Reply   Forward

To all staff

[Write this part of the email using the notes.]

If you wish to apply for permission to work from home, please do the following:
- provide a photo of the workspace you will use
- provide a document from your internet service provider that shows your connection speed
- make sure that all work-related information is kept secure

Please complete the attached form with photos and documents to the HR Department.

We hope this now makes working from home clear for everyone.

Best wishes

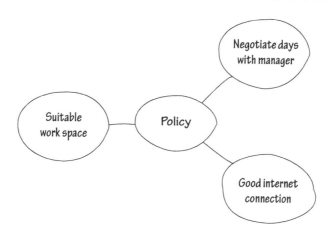

Think further

Ask learners what different points their partners gave them feedback on in step 4. Point out any key relevant features in the email (e.g. the example material uses bullet points to make ideas clear to the reader).

Notes

If you think your class needs more support, you could just use one of the emails that has the first part and elicit or point out key features to students before they begin writing. This means the information gap steps 3 to 5 are no longer possible. With a class that needs more challenge, you could just provide a gloss of the content of the first or second part of the email together with the notes. In this way, students won't see half a model before they begin writing.

Rationale

Writing a text from notes can occur in different business contexts. For example, notes are often taken during meetings and the resulting text is typically either a report or an email communication. It is also typical for the report or email to include action points given in bullet points. Splitting the email into two halves means that students have part of a model to support their writing.

7.8 What the tables tell us

Outline	In groups, half of the class write a summary of data from one table, and the other half a summary of data from a different table. Groups swap tables and summaries and write recommendations in response.
Level	Intermediate (B1+) and above
Time	50 minutes
Aim	To practise writing summaries of data and recommendations.
Preparation	You will need to make available two different tables of data, one for students in each half of the class (see *Example*). The example tables focus on health and safety, and professional development, but you could create tables focused on other aspects of business appropriate for your students.

Procedure

1 Divide the class in half and form groups of three to four students within each half. Groups in one half are given a table of data, and groups in the other half are given a different table of data.

2 Groups write a one-paragraph report that summarises the data and highlights key features. Show students some useful language to help with their summary. Set a time limit for the writing.

3 Groups with different data exchange their tables and summaries. They read the summary and decide on some recommendations to improve the running of the business.

4 In their groups, students write a short paragraph of recommendations. Set a time limit.

5 Groups exchange their recommendations and discuss whether they believe they will be effective.

Example

Useful language
This table shows / illustrates / gives information about . . .
Overall . . .
The most noticeable point is . . . It's important to note that . . .
There seems to have been a problem / issue with . . .
There has/have been more / fewer / less . . . more / less frequently . . .
In light of the evidence / data . . .
It's our recommendation . . . We recommend . . .

Table A

Healthy and Safety Incidents *Greta's Café and Bistro* January to June

Date	Name/job	Injury	Cause	Action	Days lost	Cost
10/1	Sung-Ho Lee / chef	cut to finger	slip with knife	first aid	0	0
23/1	Paul Moulin / dishwasher	ankle sprain	uneven floor in kitchen	doctor / physiotherapist	4	$480.00
6/2	Nora King / chef	burn to left hand	slip – hot saucepan	first aid	1	$224.00
28/2	Paul Moulin / dishwasher	cut hand	broken glass	doctor	3	$360.00
15/3	Harshad Anand / waiter	ankle sprain	uneven floor in kitchen	first aid	0.5	$76.00
8/4	Val Adams / maitre d', waiter	back strain	lifting heavy wine cases	doctor / physiotherapist	3	$552.00
17/4	Rose Swift / waiter	ankle sprain	uneven floor in kitchen	physiotherapist	2	$304.00
23/4	Sung-Ho Lee / chef	cut to finger	slip with knife	first aid	0	0
10/5	Harshad Anand/ waiter	back strain	lifting heavy wine cases	doctor	0	0
13/5	Val Adams / maitre d', waiter	ankle sprain	uneven floor in kitchen	physiotherapist	1	$184.00
24/5	Paul Moulin / dishwasher	cut hand	broken glass	first aid	2	$240.00
14/6	Sung-Ho Lee / chef	cut to finger	slip with knife	first aid	0.5	$112.00

Table B

Professional Development and Training Record for Team 3 at Dunlop and Kirk Accountants Ltd. January to June

Date	Name	Event	Cost	Days released
18/1 – 20/1	Gillian King	Conference on corporate tax - Edinburgh	£1,150	3
2/2	Valeria Monti Ansh Chopra Myra Galanis Matt Bellow	Institute seminar on changes to regulation	0	1
9/2	Myra Galanis	Webinar – tax fraud	0	0.5
9/2 – 10/2	Gillian King	Conference on tax fraud - Brighton	£685.00	2
10/3	Valeria Monti Ansh Chopra	Institute seminar on conducting audits	0	1
13/3 – 14/3	Myra Galanis	Conference on non-profit accounting - Cambridge	£479.00	2
22/3	Ansh Chopra	Conference on information systems - London	£426.00	1
7/4	Ben Hammond	Webinar – client interpersonal skills	0	0.5
14/4 – 15/4	Valeria Monti Gillian King	Conference on women's leadership in accounting - Oxford	£1,460.00	2
3/5	Matt Bellow	Conference on international tax - London	£395.00	1
13/5	Ansh Chopra Matt Bellow	Webinar – Accounting and valuation	£120.00	0.5
7/6	Myra Galanis Valeria Monit	Institute seminar on financial management	0	1

Think further
Ask students whether their summaries needed to refer to all the information in the table. Establish that it is enough to describe an overall trend and then select two or three key features to discuss in the summary.

Notes
With a class that needs a bit more support, the useful language could be made more specific in relation to the data in the table, for example, rather than just *Overall*, you could suggest *Overall, staff have + past participle*. If your class is stronger or perhaps has just recently studied language for describing tables, you could choose not to show the useful language at all.

Rationale

Describing data from infographics is often a key feature of business reports (see also Activity 6.5 for language used to describe graphs). The split writing aims to provide a communicative focus for the activity, and it also gives students practice in writing recommendations – another key feature of business reports.

7.9 Uncluttered slides

Outline	Students brainstorm ideas for presentation slides and then read and collect complete sentences on the same topic. They reduce the sentences down to bullet points for a slide presentation.
Level	Intermediate (B1+) and above
Time	30 minutes
Aim	To practise condensing language appropriate for presentation slides.
Preparation	You will need to prepare a set of sentences and make them available to students. You will also need to create bad examples and good models of slides – ideally these will be shared digitally, but if that's not possible, you can make paper copies (see *Example*).

Procedure

1 Write the topic of a slide presentation on the board. (The topic for the example below is: *The importance of user reviews for small businesses*).

2 Divide students into three groups and assign each group a specific question on the topic. Ask students to brainstorm ideas to address their question. For the example topic, the questions are:
   Group 1 Why are user reviews important?
   Group 2 How do I get started with user reviews?
   Group 3 How do I manage user reviews?

3 Students skim read a series of sentences about the topic of the presentation and select those that are relevant to the specific question their group has been discussing.

4 Give students copies of slides with the three questions on the topic and relevant sentences. Establish that the slides contain too much language and are too detailed.

5 In their groups, students rewrite the slides so that they contain key ideas only in bullet point form. Students can add any ideas they thought of when they brainstormed the topic.

6 Groups check each other's work by swapping slides or you can show each slide and the suggested model examples.

Example
Sentences

1	The key reason why user reviews are important is that there is no doubt that customers read them before they make a decision to purchase a product.
2	The best way to get started with user reviews is by reading the guidelines of other, larger companies that use these reviews.
3	Sometimes customers plan to write a review, but they forget, so it's a good idea to send a follow up email to customers to remind them to give a review.
4	It also helps if you look around, find and buy software that's going to be easy for your customers to use.
5	If you receive a positive review, you should thank that customer to show you appreciate it.
6	Rather than paying attention to marketing messages, customers are more likely to trust the opinion of other customers.
7	You will probably get some negative reviews, but don't remove them because some negative reviews mean all your reviews look real to new customers.
8	Then it helps to talk to your employees and encourage them to ask their customers for user reviews.
9	If a customer sees their review online, they feel good about it, so it's a way of building customer loyalty.
10	It helps if you respond to negative feedback quickly because it shows you care about customers.
11	It's not a good idea to offer money or free products or anything like that to try and get a review from a customer.
12	It's also a way of showing new customers how you respond to customer feedback.

Slides

Why are user reviews important?

The key reason why user reviews are important is that there is no doubt that customers read these reviews before they make a decision to purchase a product. Rather than paying attention to marketing messages, customers are more likely to trust the opinion of other customers. If a customer sees their review online, they feel good about it, so it's a way of building customer loyalty. It's also a way of showing new customers how you respond to customer feedback.

How do I get started with user reviews?

The best way to get started with user reviews is by reading the guidelines of other, larger companies that use these. It also helps if you look around, find and buy software that's going to be easy for your customers to use. Then it helps to talk to your employees and encourage them to ask their customers for user reviews. It's not a good idea to offer money or free products or anything like that to try and get a review from a customer.

How do I manage user reviews?

Sometimes customers plan to write a review, but they forget, so it's a good idea to send a follow up email to customers to remind them to give a review. If you receive a positive review, you should thank that customer to show you appreciate it. You will probably get some negative reviews, but don't remove them because some negative reviews mean all your reviews look real to new customers. It helps if you respond to negative feedback quickly because it shows you care about customers.

Model slides

Why are user reviews important?

- customers read them when they are buying a product
- customers are more likely to trust the opinion of others
- a way of building customer loyalty when they see their review posted
- a way of showing how you respond to customer feedback

How do I get started with user reviews?

- do research – read the guidelines of larger companies
- buy review software that's easy for customers to use
- encourage your employees to ask for reviews.
- never offer money or free products to get a review

How do I manage user reviews?

- send follow up reminder emails to customer to give a review
- thank customers who leave positive reviews
- don't remove negative reviews – they make all the reviews look real
- respond to negative feedback quickly – it shows you care

Think further

Elicit from students other ways they can make their slides effective, for example, by keeping punctuation simple, using bullet points and easy-to-read fonts, having a clear contrast between background and fonts. Suggest that students do some research online for key tips for writing presentation slides.

Notes

If you have a large class, there could be more than one group working on one of the topics. If your class needs more support and you feel they will find the reading and selecting stage of the lesson challenging, you could give them the completed slide as suggested in step 5. If your class is at a higher level, you could read the text of each slide aloud and students make notes to turn into bullet points.

Rationale

Students sometimes struggle to know what information to include on presentation slides and tend to provide too much information. Choices about what to include can depend on conventions and audience expectations in a specific context (there may be certain company conventions, for example), but in general, information should be kept to a minimum. The reading and selecting of relevant specific points mirrors the kind of reading and research that is often needed when creating a slide presentation.

7.10 The right recommendation

Outline	Students use notes and consider the appropriate language to write the recommendation section of a report/proposal; half writing for senior managers, and half writing for their peers.
Level	Upper intermediate (B2) and above
Time	40 minutes
Aim	To practise writing report/proposal recommendations; to highlight the different style of recommendation expressions.
Preparation	You will need to make a set of notes available for each student and some recommendation phrases (see *Example*).

Procedure

1   Give students notes to use for the recommendation section of a report or proposal (the example below is a recommendation to change a company's mode of freight from lorry to rail). Also show some useful phrases for writing recommendations – a mixture of formal and neutral language.

2   Divide the class into two halves. Working alone, Students A write a recommendation for senior management, and Students B write a recommendation for peer employees. They must choose appropriate language with the correct level of formality.

3   In pairs from the same group (i.e. two Students A together and two Students B together), students compare their drafts focusing on the use of expressions and, if necessary, revise their drafts.

4   Then in Student A and B pairs, they compare their drafts focusing on the use of expressions.

5   You can show students example models.

Example
Notes for recommendation

considered all freight options → move towards sending goods by rail – bit more expensive, but road transport costs increase – also the green option

two agreements with lorry companies – first due for renewal next March – the other six months later → give both companies 6 months' notice of move to rail

lorry companies maybe offer discounts → say 'no' – discounts won't last & slows down move to rail

give customers plenty of advance warning – need to make changes to their distribution routes

v. important to announce change – public relations & advertising campaign – way to reach new customers

Recommendation phrases

we think (that)	it is our recommendation	it would make sense to
we should	it'd help to	we believe that
it is essential to/that	we need to	it'd be a very good idea to
it is advisable to/that	we strongly recommend that	we ought to

Models

Recommendation to senior management

Having considered all the freight options, it is our recommendation that we move towards sending all our goods by rail. Although a little more expensive in the short term, we see the cost of road transport increasing. Furthermore, rail freight is the greener option, and this will appeal to our customers.

We have two agreements with lorry companies. The first is due for renewal in March next year and the second six months later. It would make sense to give both companies six months' notice of our intention to change to rail transport. It is likely they will offer generous discounts to try and keep our business. We believe that it is essential that we do not accept these terms because the discount will be short-term, and it slows down the transition to rail freight.

It is advisable that we give our customers plenty of advance warning of the change. They will need to make their own changes to their distribution routes.

Finally, we strongly recommend that the change to rail is announced in a public relations and advertising campaign. This would be a good way to reach new customers.

Recommendation to peer employees

We've looked at all the freight options and we think we should move towards sending all our goods by rail. Although it's a bit more expensive in the short-term, the cost of road transport will increase, and rail freight is the greener option that will appeal to our customers.

We've got two agreements with lorry companies. The first is due for renewal in March next year and the second six months later. It would help to give both companies six months' notice of the change we want to make. They will probably offer us a generous discount to try and keep our business. We think we need to say 'no' to these terms. The discount won't last and it will slow down the change to freight.

We ought to give all our customers plenty of advance warning of the change. They will need to make their own changes to their distribution routes.

Finally, we think it would be a very good idea to announce the change to rail in a public relations and advertising campaign. This could be a good way to reach new customers.

Think further

Establish from students that the audiences in the two reports in the activity were both internal. Elicit that the other main audience category of business writing is external. Establish that external relationships can be with people they don't know or those they do. You could show a diagram with four quadrants: *internal–distant, internal–close, external–distant, external–close* to outline the different relationships.

Notes

You could simplify the activity by giving students the model of the recommendation to peers together with a set of formal recommendation phrases, which they use to make the recommendation more formal (or vice versa with the model of the recommendation to senior management and a set of less formal phrases). For higher-level classes, you can give students the notes without the recommendation phrases, and they have to make their own language choices for the target audience.

Rationale

The recommendation section of an investigative report or proposal is a common feature of business writing. This is a key area where students need to have a good awareness of their audience because the ultimate aim is to persuade a particular course of action (or non-action). To help achieve this aim, it's important to adopt an appropriate style and tone, the focus of this activity.

7.11 PEST workshop

Outline	In groups, students research one aspect of a PEST analysis report and then work in groups to prepare a full report.
Level	Upper intermediate (B2) and above
Time	70 minutes (or see *Notes* for alternative suggestion)
Aim	To practise researching and writing a PEST analysis report.
Preparation	You will need to make a written proposal that can be used for a PEST analysis available for all students (see *Example*). You may wish to use a scenario that is close to students' interests, needs and location.

Procedure

1 Elicit or establish what a PEST analysis is – the political, economic, social and technological factors surrounding a business or a business proposal.

2 Elicit some internet search phrases students could use, for example:
political / economic / social / technological issues in [name of country] or *between [country] and [country]*

3 Give students a brief summary of a business or a business proposal (the example proposal below regards an Australian sportswear company extending their range to leisurewear).

4 Divide the class into four groups. Each group focuses on only one aspect of the PEST analysis (political, economic, social or technological).

5 Students conduct online research into their part of the PEST analysis. They should aim to find two to three factors to consider. Each group discusses and agrees what these key factors are and each student makes a note of them.

6 Put students into a group of four with one student representing each aspect of the PEST analysis.

7 Students read and give feedback on each other's sets of notes and then collaboratively write their complete PEST analysis. Remind students that the analysis needs to be in the form of a report with complete sentences and not just a series or notes or bullet points.

8 Groups swap and read each other's full analysis, making a note of any differences.

Example

GLAZE Clothing are an Australian sports clothing manufacturer based in Melbourne and Adelaide. They currently make high quality sportswear for the domestic market and export to key markets in South Korea, Thailand, Vietnam, New Zealand and Canada.

They use modal fabric – a bio-based synthetic material made from beech trees. It is expensive but has a soft and luxurious feel to it. GLAZE currently imports modal from China and their clothing is manufactured in Australia.

The company plans to begin producing casual leisurewear that features colourful designs by indigenous Australians. GLAZE has done market research on these products, and there is demand in key markets for such a product.

Their manufacturing plants in Australia do not have capacity to produce a new range of clothing, so GLAZE aims to manufacture the leisurewear in Bangladesh. This will also help reduce costs.

Think further

Elicit from students whether they used conditional structures in their PEST analysis. If not, elicit an example on the board, but leave the verbs in their base form, for example, *If GLAZE (manufacture) in Bangladesh, it (increase) their output and (reduce) production costs.* Establish that use of a first conditional is more likely because the proposal suggests the new venture is a definite possibility.

Notes

This activity could be spread across more than one lesson: steps 1 to 3 set up in the first lesson with students conducting the research as homework. Some learner groups may need more support in the form of suggestions on what they should look for when they research the factors for their part of the PEST analysis. Alternatively, you could suggest they research this online and read example PEST analyses. In order to do this activity more quickly in one lesson, you could provide two parts of the PEST analysis of a situation and get students to research and write the remaining two parts (this has the benefit of providing a model). In step 6, students should be reminded of the audience of this report (normally for circulation to senior management) and the need for it to be clearly organised and cohesive.

Rationale

Analytical reports of this nature are a common occurrence in the business world (there are also SWOT – strengths, weaknesses, opportunities, threats – reports). The aim of this activity is to highlight the importance of research and collaboration in the process of producing such a report.

7.12 Natural chunks

Outline	Students replace formal expressions with more neutral language chunks in an email, and then write a similar email to colleagues.
Level	Upper intermediate (B2) and above
Time	40 minutes
Aim	To highlight the use of neutral language chunks in email communication to peers.
Preparation	You will need to prepare and make available to students an email with overly formal expressions (see *Example*). This idea is adaptable for any written communication text by replacing commonly used language chunks with less idiomatic formal expressions followed by a neutral word prompt. There may be a set of language chunks that you have focussed on recently in class that you could usefully revise.

Procedure

1   Give students the email to colleagues that has a neutral style, but with some expressions unnaturally formal (the example email below is asking for feedback and ideas from colleagues).

2   Students replace the phrases in bold with a less formal word chunk of three or more words and including the word in brackets. It may pay to do an open class example to get students started.

3   In pairs, students check answers and then you check with the whole class.

4   Students then write an email to colleagues in a neutral tone. They include at least six language chunks. It can be similar to the example (seeking feedback), or it could be about making arrangements for a meeting, informing colleagues of a change, etc.

5   In pairs, students exchange emails and identify what chunks their partner has used.

Example

● ● ●   Reply   Forward

Hi everyone

If you have been tracking online sales over the past couple of months, I'm sure [1]**it's evident** (see) there has been a 3.5% drop. While this isn't a big worry [2]**at present** (stage), I'd like to get feedback from you all on why sales are down and [3]**simultaneously** (same) get your ideas on any improvements that can be made.

Customer feedback has indicated that [4]**the presence of certain** (number) issues with the checkout process – sometimes the customer address field is empty when they go to pay, and at other times customers don't receive confirmation of payment. I've checked with our IT department, and [5]**the outcome appears to be that** (turns) there may be [6]**a category of** (sort) bug in the coding we need to fix.

But I also wonder if the drop in sales [7]**concerns** (something) the design and overall look of our website. [8]**In direct comparison with** (look) our competitors, our design is a bit outdated and could do with a refresh. [9]**Similarly** (way) our website copy maybe needs a rewrite – it's probably a bit text heavy.

These are just a couple of observations. I'd really like to get your input, so can you send me your thoughts by the end of the week [10]**with the objective to** (order) draw up a list of key issues, then we can have a meeting to [11]**have a wide ranging discussion** (things).

Many thanks
Andy

Key

1 you can see; 2 at this stage; 3 at the same time; 4 there are a number of;
5 it turns out that; 6 some sort of; 7 has something to do with; 8 if you look at;
9 in the same way; 10 in order to; 11 talk things through

Think further

Ask students if they note down expressions like the language chunks. If they do, elicit some examples. If they don't, suggest that they note down language chunks as well as individual words in their vocabulary record.

Notes

If your students need more support, you can put two words in the brackets to help them. If they are a strong class, you could get them to replace the formal expressions without any word prompts.

Rationale

This activity again signals the importance of style in written business communication in line with the kind of colleagues that students are communicating with. In this instance, the focus is on neutral and commonly used language chunks (the language items in the example are selected for their high frequency in the Cambridge Corpus). The activity also aims to signal the value of students noting and learning language in fixed chunks.

8 Teacher development

Some of the ideas and activities in the previous chapters will hopefully have helped you think about new or different ways of implementing methodology associated with writing skills. If you felt that any idea was not entirely suitable with your particular learner group, you may have been able to adapt it in some way. This process of exploring new teaching ideas, adapting them and making them your own all have a central part to play in the development of any teacher.

There are many other ways that you can explore the analysis of written texts and the methodology associated with teaching writing in the classroom. Here is a list of generic teacher development ideas:

- Do background reading on written discourse and writing skills methodology (the references in each chapter in this book are a good place to start).
- Set up discussion groups (perhaps in response to reading you have done) with other teachers at your school or in a local network of teachers.
- Attend professional development workshops or conferences that include sessions on writing.
- Find online webinars that focus on written text and writing skills.
- Carry out peer observation of writing lessons with a colleague – take turns observing each other.
- Team teach a writing lesson with a colleague.

While the activities in Chapters 1–7 are ideas for things you can do to help develop your learners' writing, in this chapter the activities are for you to do, to explore ways you might improve as a teacher of writing. Some of these activities can be done alone, but it is usually more motivating to carry out this kind of development with another colleague or a group of colleagues. Whatever approach or approaches you choose to take, it can be beneficial to keep some kind of log or journal where you reflect on your experiences and insights on a regular basis. In effect, this means you use writing to think *about* writing in more depth.

Each activity is inspired by the focus in each chapter of the book, so, for example, the first activity in this chapter is linked to the theme of writing about people in Chapter 1. The one exception is Activity 8.8 that focuses on the assessment of writing. Some of the activities involve an action–research element while others suggest ways in which you can interact with your students in a more comprehensive way than you might normally do in your day-to-day interaction. The implication here is that colleagues and peers are not the only people who inform our professional development, and our learners, and what they bring to the teaching and learning space, can also be a source of insight.

The way to carry out the activities are only suggestions and the procedure is not set in stone. You should feel free to adapt the ideas in light of your own knowledge and experience, and with regard to the context in which you are working. While there is no necessity to share insights from these activities with a wider audience, this always remains an option. Reporting back on these activities, their outcomes and the insights gained from them, could form the basis of a workshop or seminar delivered to a wider audience. This, in turn, may open up more professional development opportunities.

While writing skills may not have quite the same predominance in ELT methodology or teaching materials as speaking skills do, they are nonetheless an extremely interesting avenue of professional development enquiry. The apparent ubiquity of IT and digital tools has resulted in a proliferation of written texts in our daily lives. It has also made writing more immediate and direct. Students in the twenty-first century need to develop their writing skills in ways that were not imaginable just a few years ago. In short, if you do choose to explore written text and writing skills as part of your professional development, you are guaranteed to find plenty to explore.

8.1 Getting to know your students – speaking or writing?

Outline	The teacher carries out two versions of a 'getting to know you' activity with two different groups at the beginning of a course, one that involves mostly speaking, the other mostly writing and then compares the results.
Time	In class, the speaking is likely to take about 30 minutes, but the writing is more likely to take up to 50 minutes. You will need to spend about an hour reading, analysing and noting results.
Aim	To determine whether speaking or writing activities provide teachers with more or less information about students at the beginning of a course.
Preparation	No preparation is necessary, but it may be useful to create a template for each group in which to record information about each student.

Procedure

1   With the first group (speaking), do a typical 'get to know you' spoken activity at the beginning of the course.
   a.   Show students the following topics:
      job/study, hobbies, family, food, past achievements, future plans/goals
   b.   Put students in small groups and ask them to tell each other about themselves on the topics.
   c.   Monitor and note down interesting information and any language needs you can hear.
   d.   After students finish speaking, ask the whole class what they found out about each other.
   e.   Make notes on interesting pieces of biographical information and language needs for each student.

2   With the second group (writing), get students to write a short biography about themselves on the same topics.
   a.   Put students in small groups and get them to read each other's biographies – they can ask follow up questions.
   b.   Check what they found out about each other and then collect the biographies in.
   c.   Read the biographies and make notes on biographical information and language needs.

3   Compare the two sets of notes and decide which provided you with the most useful information about students and their language ability.

Notes

If you cannot do this with two groups at the same time, the two approaches can be done at different times and then compared. If you are very familiar with the spoken version of this activity, you could just do the version that involves writing and compare that to your previous experiences. While it could be argued that differences between spoken and written language will highlight different needs, the kind of language used in the informal written biography is likely to be similar to that used in speaking. Clearly, the written biographies won't signal any pronunciation needs, but these can potentially be picked up when students ask each other about the information in their written biographies.

Rationale

'Getting to know you' activities are most commonly done as speaking activities as group work or mingles. This has the benefit of being very active and communicative. However, a lot of information about students is conveyed in these speaking activities that teachers may not manage to hear. Nor is it always possible to determine specific student needs. The aim of this particular activity is not to suggest an either/or scenario but to make a comparison and to consider whether writing can play a more prominent and useful role at the beginning of a course.

8.2 Text comparison

Outline	The teacher compares two texts produced by a fluent speaker on the same topic – one written and one spoken. They then do an analysis of the vocabulary and readability of both texts using an online tool.
Time	Work on this activity can be spread out over time, and is likely to be between five and six hours, excluding any teaching.
Aim	To compare the lexical density of a spoken and written text on the same topic; to practise analysing texts using an online tool.
Preparation	You will need to find a suitable written text by a volunteer who you know.

Procedure

1 Find an authentic written text written by a fluent speaker of English you know (if possible, try to find someone who is not an English language teacher so they won't monitor their own language production). The text could be, for example, an email or social media posting and should involve the person telling someone about something that happened to them.

2 Ask the person to retell the story to you orally and record what they say. (You can make it interactive and ask prompt questions if that helps.) Ask permission to do an analysis of the two texts and let them know you will anonymize any personal information, for example, by changing names and places. Transcribe the recording.

3 Do an analysis of the lexical density and word frequency of both texts. You can do this using www. lextutor.ca (if you are unfamiliar with this tool, you can watch a video on how to use it here: www. youtube.com/watch?v=LWQ-YjR9Ipk).

4 Compare the results and reflect on the following:
   • Are the differences significant or not?
   • How do you account for this – the genre, the topic or theme of the texts?
   • Which of the two texts is more readable for learners?
   • Are there any interesting or surprising results in the analysis?

5 Decide whether you could use one or both of these texts with your learners. If so, ask permission from the person who generated the texts to use them in a lesson.

6 Plan and deliver a lesson based around the text(s). Include some analysis of the vocabulary and some kind of productive outcome.

7 Share the results of the analysis and teaching experiment with colleagues.

Notes

If you decide to use one or both of these texts with your students, you may want to change any lexical items that Lextutor predicts as being low frequency and difficult to understand – as suggested in the video that shows you how to use the tool. How much you change will depend on the level of your students.

Rationale

This activity is a way of exploring whether there are significant differences in written and spoken language. The Lextutor analysis may not provide all or complete answers, but it should provide you with some insight and an indication of the readability of these texts. You may consider how you can use such online tools to analyse authentic texts you would like to use with your students.

References

Cobb, T., Compleat Lexical Tutor Available at: www.lextutor.ca [Accessed September 2022]
Macalister, J., Victoria University of Wellington, *Using the Lextutor website* www.youtube.com/
    watch?v=LWQ-YjR9Ipk [Accessed September 2022]

8.3 Opinion wall

Outline	The teacher sets up an opinion wall where students can post and respond to opinions about topics of interest in their daily lives.
Time	Across a course programme
Aim	To provide on-going insight into students' interests, needs and concerns; to map this information on to a life competencies framework.
Preparation	If you are using a physical wall in your classroom, you will need to clear a designated space and provide something students can use to pin their opinions to the wall. If you and your students have access to an LMS, you will need to set up a page or area where students can type in their opinions.

Procedure

1 Early in your course do a lesson that focuses on opinion writing in some way – a blog post, a discursive essay, etc.

2 Tell students you want them to build an opinion wall.

3 At least once a week, students should write their opinion or reaction to something related to the world outside the classroom. It could be a comment on a news event, a reaction to a sports outcome, a music, TV or film review. If you think your students might forget, you can set this as a regular homework activity. Reassure them that the opinion can be just two or three sentences – not a complete essay.

4 The opinions are posted on the wall and classmates are encouraged to respond to each other. It may pay to agree some rules about being polite and respectful in their replies, and perhaps teach some key structures, e.g. *I don't totally agree . . . While I can see that X is true, I think that Y is also . . .*

5 Refrain from adding your own opinions or reactions so that the discussion between students evolves.

6 As the wall develops and grows, use the following questions as a means of analysing the opinions:
   • What topics are popular with your students?
   • What topics/opinions seem to generate most conflict between writers?
   • What themes emerge from the discussions?
   • What do you learn about your students' lives?
   • What do you learn about students' language needs?

7 Consult the *Cambridge Life Competencies Framework* (www.cambridge.org/gb/Cambridge english/better-learning- insights/cambridgelifecompetenciesframework) and focus on the following competency areas:
   • critical thinking
   • communication
   • social responsibilities
   What are student needs in these areas that are evident in the opinion wall? How can you address them?

8   If appropriate, prepare a short talk or presentation for other teachers in your institution about what you have discovered through the opinion wall and give examples.

Notes
If you carry out this activity with another teacher (or group of teachers) who are teaching at a similar level, the opinion wall could be shared by classes and result in inter-class communication. It could also lead to class-to-class speaking activities, for example, a debate on hot topics from the opinion wall.

Rationale
A lot of time is often spent at the beginning of a course getting to know students and finding out what their needs are. While this continues to some degree during the course, it's easy to get caught up with delivering the programme and become very focused just on students' language needs. An opinion wall keeps the door open on students' lives beyond the classroom and can give insight into what interests and/or bothers them. In recent years, there has been a greater emphasis on life skills associated with second language learning as evidenced, for example, by the development of *The Cambridge Life Competency Framework*.

8.4 Materials comparison

Outline	Two teachers work together to evaluate two different writing activities focusing on the same genre.
Time	Across two to three months
Aim	To critically evaluate two writing skills activities in light of students' needs and suggest improvements; to develop teachers' critical evaluation skills.
Preparation	You will need to find two different writing activities from two pieces of published material that focus on the same instrumental genre, for example, an email making a request, or complaint; a recipe or instructions for doing something.

Procedure

1 Work together with a colleague teaching at the same or similar level.

2 Find two writing activities at the same level in the same genre.

3 Compare the strengths and weaknesses of the two approaches. Use the following criteria, bearing in mind your students' needs:
   • suitability and naturalness of the example text in relation to the level
   • relevance of language analysed or focused on
   • relevance of writing skills focused on
   • scaffolded support for learners
   • provision of relevant writing task outcome
   • logical flow of tasks within the activity

4 You both teach a lesson with the material, although you may choose to make some changes based on your analysis in the previous step.

5 Ask your students for their thoughts on the lesson and the material. *How useful did they find it? How easy or difficult was it? What suggestions do they have to improve the material?*

6 With your colleague, compare your insights as well as students' feedback from the two groups. Reflect on what you learnt from this experience using the following questions:
   • What are key areas to address when adapting writing materials? Why?
   • In general, what are students in your context likely to need more/less of? Why?
   • Do published materials mostly serve my students' writing needs? Why / Why not?
   • Do I need to produce more of my own materials? Why / Why not?

7 If appropriate you can share your discoveries with other teaching colleagues by means of a presentation or perhaps a written report.

Notes

This activity is more interesting to do with a colleague, but you can carry it out on your own. In step 3, you may come up with a criterion of your own that is relevant to your particular context, for example, if you focus on a genre that you know will form part of your students' summative assessment, then the degree to which the activity prepares students for this may be a criterion.

Rationale

The activity provides a framework for evaluating published material that aims to practise and develop students' writing skills. The kind of focus provided by the criteria in step 3 may, with time, become automatic when evaluating teaching materials. More broadly, the activity encourages consideration of all teaching materials in a critical light and suggests that teachers look for opportunities to adapt materials to meet students' needs.

8.5 Commonplace book

Outline	The class maintains a digital Commonplace Book of small text excerpts of language they find interesting.
Time	Across a course programme
Aim	To encourage more extensive reading in students; to provide a springboard for students for expressive writing; to encourage whole class collaboration.
Preparation	You will need to set up an online space or document as the Commonplace Book for students to access.

Procedure

1 Set up a Commonplace Book that students can access online.

2 Explain to students what a Commonplace Book is – a place where they can record short excerpts from texts that they find interesting. It could be a few lines from a book or poem, a quote, some song lyrics, a short excerpt from a magazine article, some dialogue from a film or TV programme, something they overhear in their daily life. You could mention that Commonplace Books have been popular with writers, politicians and inventors.

3 Ask students to do the following:
   • post excerpts regularly to the Commonplace Book.
   • state the source of the excerpt and add their name (but they don't need to say why they chose this bit of language)
   • read what their classmates have posted
   • respond directly by messaging rather than writing in the Commonplace Book

4 Monitor the students' use of the Commonplace Book – you may need to remind them frequently at the beginning of the course to post language. Ask students what messages they have received in response to a posting.

5 As the course progresses, look for specific themes that emerge. These could be used for speaking activities in class, for example, three quotes on a similar topic could form the basis of a discussion. Alternatively, you could ask students to respond to two or three posts as a writing task.

6 Towards the end of the course, students could read through the Commonplace Book to find the most interesting / funniest / most surprising examples to discuss in class. You could also get learners to reflect on the value of the Commonplace Book, for example, how they found about interesting ideas, how it helped their language development, how it helped them get to know each other.

7 Make your own reflections on using a Commonplace Book and consider the degree to which students were motivated or not, what it told you about the students, the impact it had on students' reading and writing skills.

8 Share your experience with colleagues.

Notes

Inevitably, some students will like this idea more than others and be more regular contributors. Less motivated students will need more active encouragement, perhaps in a tutorial situation. Remind them that just one line from a song that they like is enough by way of contribution.

Rationale

The American writer Joan Didion said that one of the ways she learnt to write was by copying excerpts of Ernest Hemingway and developing an understanding of the way he crafted a sentence. The aim of this Commonplace Book has less lofty ambitions, but there is doubtless value in getting students to write out interesting examples and models of written language use. Another key idea behind a Commonplace Book is that it can act as a source of inspiration or a springboard for expressive writing. It is also a way to encourage students to read more extensively. Not to be overlooked too is that it's another way for students to interact and get to know each other and foster a positive group dynamic.

8.6 Common needs

Outline	Both the teacher and each student maintain a journal that prioritises the student's academic writing needs. At a midway point in the course, the journals are compared and the teacher and student determine an action plan.
Time	Across a course programme
Aim	To systematically determine and prioritise students' academic writing needs; to balance the teacher's perceptions of student needs with those of the students.
Preparation	No specific preparation is necessary, but it would be a good idea to set up a digital journal of some kind that makes it easier to track individual students' needs.

Procedure

1 This activity can be done with all the students in your class, but it may pay to select a smaller group of volunteers who are willing to participate.

2 Explain to students that you plan to monitor and record their academic writing needs. When you read their work, you will give feedback on all relevant needs. However, you will also make notes on what you see as priorities without indicating this to students. Students should also note what they see as priorities.

3 Show students broad needs categories:
   • interesting and relevant content
   • logical organisation
   • cohesive ties in the text
   • a good range of grammar and vocabulary
   • accurate grammar and vocabulary

4 Keep track of the prioritised needs as students submit any written work. Students should do the same thing, and you both gradually build up a needs journal.

5 At a midway point in the course, hold a tutorial with individual students and compare your needs and priorities. If they are similar, agree on a plan of action. If they are different, you will need first to find areas of compromise. Repeat this process later in the course.

6 Reflect on the way this approach to students' needs changed your perceptions (if at all) when compared to responding to students writing merely on a task-by-task basis. Ask students to do the same and share your reflections.

7 Share your experience and impressions with colleagues.

Notes

If you do this activity with a colleague who is teaching academic writing at a similar level, you can look for typical needs' patterns associated with students at that level. You may find that you begin with a larger group, but only really motivated students will maintain focus. The notes that you make do not need to be very detailed. They should be based on a 'first-impression' rather than a painstakingly detailed analysis.

Rationale

While teachers usually have a general impression of students' needs, they often only note and respond to them on a task-by-task basis. This activity aims to track needs in a more systematic way, building a more complete picture of an individual student's writing strengths and weaknesses. It also aims to break down the barrier between what the teacher perceives as a need and what the student is concerned about – they are often not the same thing.

8.7 Chunk collection

Outline	The teacher uses an online language corpus to check the frequency of language chunks that students have collated in a database, and encourages the use of high frequency examples in their writing.
Time	Across a course programme
Aim	To provide a greater emphasis on language chunks to encourage fluency in your students' writing; to practise using an online language corpus; to discover what language is of interest to your students.
Preparation	You will need to set up a simple database that all students can access and plan a lesson that includes a focus on chunks in written language.

Procedure

1 Do some background reading on language chunks (also known as clusters and lexical phrases), for example, *Lexical Grammar: Activities for teaching chunks and exploring patterns* by Leo Selivan. Alternatively, see Scott Thornbury's (2019) online paper: www.cambridge.org/elt/blog/2019/11/01/chunk-spotting-users-guide/

2 Set up a simple online database where students can record language chunks.

3 In class, do a lesson that highlights language chunks in a written text (for example, Activity 7.12) to ensure students understand the concept.

4 Ask students to make a note of language chunks that they find in texts and record them in the database. Initially, it may be a good idea to spend a small amount of class time doing this to guide students and get the activity going.

5 As the language chunks are posted, check the frequency of each item by doing a corpus search (free English language corpora can be sourced here: www.english-corpora.org). If any examples are random sequences and not frequently occurring chunks, let the student who posted the example know.

6 At some point during the course, show students the ten most common chunks that they have recorded in the database and get them to predict the frequency by ranking them. You could also do a writing activity using the chunks. (See Leo Selivan's book for more teaching ideas using chunks.)

7 Encourage students to continue adding to the database. You could also show them how to do a corpus frequency search for themselves.

8 Towards the end of your course, ask students to reflect on the activity and whether they think they are using chunks more frequently than they used to. Check whether they feel these clusters of language come to mind quickly.

9 Share the outcome with colleagues. You can show the kinds of chunks students collected, the most frequent in the corpus, examples of student writing using chunks and the comments from students' reflection.

Notes
Students are likely to need regular reminders to contribute to the database, and you could do regular checks after reading example texts to see if students can find any language chunks. Whether you can hand over frequency checks to students as suggested in step 6 will depend on the level of your students' motivation.

Rationale

This professional development activity aims to get you, the teacher, and your students more focused on lexical chunks. These are often highlighted as providing more fluency in speaking (Selivan 2018), but they can also provide more fluency in writing. If students are focusing on writing skills for business or a written exam, an ability to call on prefabricated chunks of language quickly is a useful skill. This activity also gives insight on what chunks of language are of interest to students and it provides practice using a language corpus.

References

English-Corpora.org Available at: www.english-corpora.org [Accessed September 2022]
Selivan, L. (2018) *Lexical Grammar: Activities for teaching chunks and exploring patterns.* Cambridge, Cambridge University Press.
Thornbury, S. (2019) *Chunk-spotting: a user's guide.*
Available at: www.cambridge.org/elt/blog/2019/11/01/chunk-spotting-users-guide/ [Accessed 30 March 2022]

8.8 Standardising written assessment criteria or grade norming

Outline The teacher uses two or three samples of writing from a validated exam where there is a grade to standardise their evaluation.

Time Two 60-minute sessions; approximately 30 minutes preparation per session plus the reading of the examiners' comments. Some time will also be required over a longer period to add examples of students' writing into a standardised bank of texts.

Aim To ensure teachers in an institution are maintaining consistency in their evaluation of learners' writing; to create a bank of standardised tasks.

Preparation For the first session, you will need two or three sample answers to a writing task from a validated exam, which include a grade and examiner comments. They could be from an international exam, or they might be from a validating agency within your country.

For the second session, you will need three or four samples of students' work for a writing task that is used for assessment purposes in your school. Make sure all the answers are from students who are at the same level of language competence.

It's helpful if there are a couple of teachers who act as session leaders for this extended activity. They can be responsible for the distribution of writing examples and the collation of feedback.

Procedure

1 *Before the first session*, teachers mark and evaluate the samples of written work from a validated exam (the grade and examiner comments should not be visible at this point) against the institution's written assessment criteria. If your institution does not have written assessment criteria, it would pay to brainstorm some areas to focus on, for example:
   - response to task
   - communicative effectiveness
   - lexical and grammatical range and accuracy
   - organisation and cohesion

   Alternatively, you could use or adapt criteria from a validated formal written examination.

2 In the first session, teachers work in pairs or small groups and compare their evaluations. They make a note of any differences.

3 The session leader can collate the evaluation to the board. This is then compared against the examiners' grade and comments. Teachers note and discuss any differences.

4 *Before the second session*, teachers identify pieces of their students' written work that could be used in a standardisation session. (You should check with students that they agree to having their writing used in this way, and it may be necessary to get them to sign an agreement form. Students should also be allowed to read the collated feedback if they wish.)

5 Teachers mark the samples of work noting strengths and weaknesses without allocating a grade.

6 In the second session, teachers compare their marking in pairs or small groups. They agree on a grade.

7 The strengths and weaknesses of each piece of writing are collated, and the group now agrees on a grade. They also decide what developmental feedback should be given to each student.

Notes

Over a longer period of time, teachers can repeat this process with written work at a complete range of levels. The samples of work and the collated answers can be filed for use by new teachers who join the institution. In effect, the standardisation bank can become a useful teacher development resource for less experienced teachers.

Rationale

While an institution might have well-articulated criteria for assessing students' writing, the actual evaluation can be subjective. Organising regular writing task standardisation sessions is a way of ensuring teachers are making sound and consistent judgments when they evaluate students' writing.

Index

Activity names are in **bold**.